Homilies for Weekdays

Year II

Homilies for Weekdays

Year II

Don Talafous, O.S.B.

LITURGICAL PRESS
Collegeville, Minnesota

www.litpress.org

Cover design by Joachim Rhoades, O.S.B.

Other acknowledgments continue on p. vii.

2	3	4	5	6	7	8	9

Library of Congress Cataloging-in-Publication Data

Talafous, Don, 1926–
    Homilies for weekdays / Don Talafous.
        p.   cm.
    Summary: "Short, sample homilies based on the two-year weekday cycle of the Catholic Lectionary for Mass"—Provided by publisher.
    Includes bibliographical references.
    ISBN-13: 978-0-8146-3032-7 (pbk. : alk. paper)
    ISBN-10: 0-8146-3032-4 (pbk. : alk. paper)
    1. Catholic Church—Sermons.   2. Church year sermons.   3. Catholic Church. Lectionary for Mass (U.S.).   I. Title.

BX1756.T34H66   2005
252'.02—dc22

                                                    2005019726

Contents

Acknowledgments

Acknowledgments

Where noted, Scripture reference is given to the Amplified® Bible, © 1954, 1958, 1962, 1964, 1965, 1987, by The Lockman Foundation. Used by permission.

The quotation from the Sequence of Pentecost is from the *Lectionary for Mass for Use in the Dioceses of the United States of America, second typical edition* © 1998, 1997, 1970, Confraternity of Christian Doctrine, Inc., Washington, D.C. Used with permission. All rights reserved. No portion of this text may be reproduced by any means without permission in writing from the copyright owner. The Pentecost Alleluia verse, found in the same *Lectionary*, is © 1997, 1981, 1968, International Committee on English in the Liturgy, Inc. All rights reserved.

The excerpt from St. Francis, "Canticle of the Sun," is from http://www .franciscan-archive.org/patriarcha/opera/canticle.html and is reprinted with permission of Br. Alexis Bugnolo.

References to Abraham Heschel are from *I Asked for Wonder: A Spiritual Anthology*, ed. Samuel H. Dresna (New York: Crossroad, 1988) and *The Wisdom of Heschel*, selected by Ruth Marcus Goodhill (New York: Farrar, Straus and Giroux, 1975).

Season of Advent

Monday of the First Week of Advent—*Growing to Christ*

Readings: Isa 4:2-6 (Year A); Isa 2:1-5 (Years B, C); Matt 8:5-11
Responsorial Psalm: Ps 122:1-2, 3-4b, 4cd-5, 6-7, 8-9 (*L* 175)—*Lectionary for Mass*
  number

In Advent we are not playacting when we wait for the birth of an important baby. We know that this all-important baby, Jesus, was born about two thousand years ago. And in our baptism he was born in us; he became our Savior. But, aware that we still stymie our transformation by the Messiah (the Christ), we concentrate in Advent on opening ourselves to him and to that presence in us. "[L]et us walk in the light of the LORD!" (Isa 2:5). An immediate and total transformation into the likeness of Christ is, if not unheard of, at least very rare. Through the celebration of Advent we hope and we pray that this Christmas will mark a deeper penetration of our lives by the Lord. Unfortunately, the quiet preparation that is Advent is almost drowned out by the noise of Christmas sales. We ourselves probably feel torn between the two, the calm of Advent and the clang of carols and cash registers. Advent is almost a secret known only to those of us who are able to share daily in its Scriptures and the Eucharist. After all these years of beginning the celebration of Christmas at Halloween, many a Christian may think of Advent only as some Sunday thing. We recall the waiting for the Messiah's arrival as a babe but life in the Messiah is pictured as a banquet for all peoples. Here too we are not simply waiting for dinner, for the banquet; we already share it at this table. May Advent sharpen our appetite for the food of this table and for the presence of the Lord.

Tuesday of the First Week of Advent—*Worldwide harmony*

Readings: Isa 11:1-10; Luke 10:21-24
Resp. Psalm: Ps 72:1-2, 7-8, 12-13, 17 (*L* 176)

Only a prophet could have a dream that sees peace and harmony in all of creation, since such a vision is contrary to the world we see. In the

1

prophet's dream, people are united in harmony with one another and with the animal creation. Now sheep, instead of panicking at the sight of wolves, rest next to them. Cows, instead of worrying they will be eaten by bears, eat with the bears, and together they raise their young. Only a prophet could have such a dream. This dream can make us glad that strife, jealousy, violence, fear, and destruction are not God's intent. God's desire is that there will be no destruction on the holy and divine mountain of the Lord. Isaiah dreams of a time when the knowledge of the Lord will spread over and around the earth just as the oceans do now. But the reality of Isaiah's world cannot offer this hope. Isaiah's people, once a grand and noble nation, have been devastated in wars with their enemies. Only a stump of past glory remains. In that stump, in the people themselves, there is no hope for the future. Isaiah does not resign himself to despair over what he sees. He dreams of what God will do. What we believe is impossible, God makes possible. Just as the oldest of enemies are made into friends, God's kingdom disrupts our old ways and turns despair into hope.

Wednesday of the First Week of Advent—
Food for the whole person

Readings: Isa 25:6-10a; Matt 15:29-37
Resp. Psalm: Ps 23:1-3a, 3b-4, 5, 6 (L 177)

Someone says that if there is anything we like to talk more about than eating, it's not eating, a reference to our concern about weight and dieting. Recognition of this basic interest of ours runs throughout the Scriptures, another indication of how earthy and human is the language of the Bible. Isaiah, speaking of what God has prepared for us, finds the picture of a lavish and happy feast most appropriate. The responsorial psalm too speaks of how God the Good Shepherd refreshes the flock with food. And in the Gospel, Jesus, moved with pity for the crowds following him, feeds them with multiplied loaves of bread. And, of course, we're gathered here to share in the Eucharist at this, the Lord's table. No matter how much or how little we may concern ourselves with the preparation of food, the basic truth is that we need this nourishment. Joining the act of nourishing ourselves with good company and conversation helps assure nourishment of the whole person. At Mass we are nourished by the Word of God and a homily about it and by the food our Lord gives. Through these the follower of Christ is fed and formed in the likeness of Christ. Our faith and Advent both presuppose our nourishment must come from outside ourselves.

It comes, we know, from the Word of God and the sacrament of the Eucharist and that nourishment is not found in the less nourishing snacks our world offers us.

Thursday of the First Week of Advent—
Our rock, and our redeemer

Readings: Isa 26:1-6; Matt 7:21, 24-27
Resp. Psalm: Ps 118:1 and 8-9, 19-21, 25-27a (L 178)

When we are healthy, prosperous, self-confident, even simply young, calling the Lord our rock may seem interesting but hardly relevant. We're more likely to think of ourselves as "Rocky." In such periods it is easy to forget how radical our dependence on God is, even though we may actually pray it in words. To genuinely know what it means to call the Lord our rock often requires the experience of feeling no firm ground beneath us, of having nothing sure to hold on to. Spiritual and emotional experiences that are the equivalent of an earthquake really teach us how fragile and shaky we are. How unstable are the world and the persons and things in which we've put so much trust. The people of the Bible learned early to think of God as their rock, the one who is always there, firm, unshakable, dependable, a sure support. In Isaiah today we hear their faith expressed: "Trust in the LORD forever! / For the LORD is an eternal Rock" (Isa 26:4). By a slight extension, Jesus, in the gospel, says that those who cling to his word and try to put it into practice are building their lives on a rock. Advent calls us once again to learn or relearn that there is no absolute security for us anywhere but in God and God's Word. For those of us who can spend time every day or often at Mass, this is an oasis of quiet in this frenzied season where we can once again learn that God is our rock and our redeemer (see Ps 78:35).

Friday of the First Week of Advent—
My light and my salvation

Readings: Isa 29:17-24; Matt 9:27-31
Resp. Psalm: Ps 27:1, 4, 13-14 (L 179)

The physically blind must learn early what is so difficult for the rest of us to comprehend: we depend on others. Resentment of our dependence on God and others, is that perhaps what "original sin" is all about? Watch the two-year-old learning to walk as he or she pushes away the helping hand. "I want to do it by myself." Blindness is another way of

3

expressing our need for the Savior who is born at Christmas. Knowing and accepting our blindness, that there is much we fail to or refuse to see, about God, ourselves, and others, this is another way of describing the right disposition for Advent. To really understand is a gift from God, a gift that comes from opening ourselves to God's help and touch: "he touched their eyes and said, 'Let it be done for you according to your faith.' And their eyes were opened." The promises in Isaiah come to realization in Jesus: "On that day the deaf shall hear / the words of a book; / And out of gloom and darkness, / the eyes of the blind shall see" (29:18). It would be hard to find a more beautiful and encouraging expression of this in prayer than Psalm 27, used today between the readings. Its words are worth memorizing and using anytime: "The LORD is my light and my salvation; / whom do I fear? / The LORD is my life's refuge; / of whom am I afraid? / . . . / Wait for the LORD, with courage; / be stouthearted, and wait for the LORD!" (vv. 1, 14). "The LORD is my light and my salvation" (v. 1).

Saturday of the First Week of Advent—*Everyone a healer*

Readings: Isa 30:19-21, 23-26; Matt 9:35–10:1, 5a, 6-8
Resp. Psalm: Ps 147:1-2, 3-4, 5-6 (L 180)

When we hear of cures by Jesus or the promise in Isaiah that the Lord will heal the people, we may think too exclusively in terms of evangelistic rallies and Hollywood versions of healing. The healing that is to accompany the Messiah is not reserved for dramatic situations; it can and must begin with us, with pretty ordinary people. "Without cost you have received; without cost you are to give," Jesus says (Matt 10:8). Rather than feel our world lacks the great cures we read of in the Bible, why not do the healing that is in our power? Besides lacking confidence in God, we may lack a justifiable confidence in the gifts we have. Doesn't each of us have something to share with others? What are our gifts? The gift of an encouraging word or pat on the shoulder; the gift of a smile and some friendliness; the gift of consolation for someone going through a sorrow we've felt; the gift of bringing some cheer to an anxious friend; the gift of introducing a bit of humor into someone's life; the gift of hope and the assurance of better times to someone going through a disappointment; the gift of our visit and sensitivity to an invalid or someone hospitalized. All these help heal very real wounds. Who really knows how much good these do beyond medicine? Every time we're at this table, we receive God's gifts. And the presumption is that we will share them with others.

Monday of Second Week of Advent—*Free for what?*

Readings: Isa 35:1-10; Luke 5:17-26
Resp. Psalm: Ps 85:9ab and 10, 11-12, 13-14 (L 181)

A lot of "don't do this and don't do that" forms of Christianity have made many see the following of Christ as the opposite of freedom. And we often think and act as if being able to give in to all our impulses, passions, appetites would be genuine freedom. We think: if we didn't have to control this or that, if we didn't have to do this, we'd be free. Yes, we'd be free to be slobs—selfish and unreliable persons. But true freedom is the unhampered ability to love and serve God and others, to become all that we can be, to realize the full potential of our creation. What prevents that is our selfishness and self-seeking, more simply, sin. Sin paralyzes our ability to love and serve, to be really free. Sin cripples our generous intentions and prevents us from running the way of God's commandments. If God sees our faith, our trust—as Jesus saw the faith of the men in today's Gospel—God can make our passions and powers agile, responsive to the good, no longer stiff and immovable in the face of suffering and need. Lord, make us free, free to serve, to give, to love.

Tuesday of the Second Week of Advent—
Comforted and coming home

Readings: Isa 40:1-11; Matt 18:12-14
Resp. Psalm: Ps 96:1-2, 3 and 10ac, 11-12, 13 (L 182)

Today's reading from Isaiah, chapter 40, begins a large section of Isaiah which is often called the Book of Consolation (or Comfort). The political situation of the Jewish people has changed and the author sees deliverance. Christians have taken this deliverance from exile over the centuries as picturing what Christ will do for all who trust in him. The beautiful words of this part of Isaiah were set to music memorably in Handel's well-known oratorio, *Messiah*. Lines from today's reading in an older translation are familiar to many. "Comfort ye, comfort ye my people" (see v. 1). And "In the desert prepare the way of the Lord!" (v. 3). And "Go up onto a high mountain" (v. 9). No matter how happy our family life, there are enough reminders around us that we are in a kind of exile. We live amid sin, suffering, pain, unspeakable tragedies and disasters, above all with the certainty of death. The joy of our approaching celebration of Christmas is about the comfort we have in Jesus and the salvation he brings to us. Part of that salvation is

God's comfort for the mourning, the sick and oppressed, the poor and exploited, the weary and disappointed. We have received and do receive this comfort at this altar and in prayer and we share it when we pass it on to the afflicted around us, in our neighborhood or family. No matter what our situation, there are many around us with whom we can share the comfort we have received from God. There are the struggling young families, the bedridden, the neglected and the elderly, the lonely, the bereaved and crushed. "Comfort, give comfort to my people, / says your God" (Isa 40:1).

Wednesday of the Second Week of Advent—*Quiet hope*

Readings: Isa 40:25-31; Matt 11:28-30
Resp. Psalm: Ps 103:1-2, 3-4, 8 and 10 (*L* 183)

We speak today of compassion fatigue, meaning that through our media we can be aware almost instantly of floods, starvation, hurricanes, slaughters, any sort of devastation almost anywhere in the world. As a result we become sort of callous to new requests for help. We may experience devotion fatigue too, especially if we faithfully give ourselves to prayer, good works, volunteer efforts, etc. We may feel a bit tired, possibly bored; the temptation may be to self-pity too. We wonder, why do I do all this when there seems so little appreciation at times, when I see no good effects? Add to all of this a touch of the flu, a cold, an aggravating pain in the knee and we may simply be dragging ourselves to Mass, to prayer, to our volunteering. In both readings today we are promised some refreshment, a renewal of strength, flying instead of trudging. We can't suddenly get very fervent and continuous in prayer and expect instant rest and refreshment. Jesus says, "Take my yoke upon you and learn from me, for I am meek and humble of heart; and you will find rest for yourselves. For my yoke is easy, and my burden light" (Matt 12:29-30). The refreshment we need and that Jesus promises is a spin-off of that daily faithfulness that at times seems so dry and unrewarding. It is a deep-down assurance and support from the Lord which will be there if we are patient. There's no promise of a great emotional jolt but of something deeper, the quiet and refreshing hope and assurance of Advent and Christmas.

Thursday of the Second Week of Advent—
Don't just sit there

Readings: Isa 41:13-20; Matt 11:11-15
Resp. Psalm: Ps 145:1 and 9, 10-11, 12-13ab (L 184)

There are some harsh words in today's Gospel. "From the days of John the Baptist until now, the Kingdom of heaven suffers violence, and the violent are taking it by force" (Matt 11:16). A similar saying of Jesus occurs in Luke (16:16). With so little explanation surrounding it, the saying really surprises us. Does it refer to the violence done against people like John the Baptist and eventually against Jesus and his followers? Or is it some sort of obscure invitation to us to get serious about the kingdom in our life? We're more accustomed to words like those in Isaiah which assure us that God will act to save his people; that God will turn around the unfavorable circumstances of the present (see Isa 41:13-20). It may be that this odd saying in the Gospel is one of a few such we find that stress very strongly our part in receiving the kingdom. God's good for us is always a gift but our receptivity or willingness to have it does involve our cooperation. "Violence" in this case would mean our energetic and positive efforts to work with God's grace. Elsewhere Jesus commends the worldly for thinking ahead, taking initiative. We can profitably take today's words as a reminder that we are not simply sponges in relation to God but like Mary are transformed by our receptivity. The reference here may mean: don't just sit there and wait. You can also act, move, do something.

Friday of the Second Week of Advent—
To each his own, to each her own

Readings: Isa 48:17-19; Matt 11:16-19
Resp. Psalm: Ps 1:1-2, 3, 4 and 6 (L 185)

Jesus complains that if people don't want to listen they will find fault with anything a prophet does. John is crazy, they say, and he, Jesus, is a drunkard and a bum. He says they're like petulant little kids (see Matt 11:16-19). Jesus leaves the conclusion pretty wide open with the phrase, "But wisdom is vindicated by her works" (Matt 11:19). After twenty centuries perhaps we can hazard a guess at what the wisdom is. Is it possibly that all of us could learn to be more tolerant of varying approaches to spirituality, to religion, to worship? Some may have a gift for penance, others for celebrating. Some like more formality, others less. As we get older, especially, we learn from our own experience that certain approaches work for us and we may even decide that we want to pray, to worship, in a particular manner and avoid other ways. It's like our decision, despite years of trying, that we simply do not like Brussels sprouts. Our developed tastes in food and our preference for a particular kind of liturgy may be part of the wisdom that age and experience bring, but it may still not be valid for everyone else. Within religion, within the church, given the diversity of human personalities, we could use more tolerance for various methods of operating, for praying, for worshiping. The real wisdom may be to see more room for diversity.

Saturday of the Second Week of Advent—*The force of love*

Readings: Sir 48:1-4, 9-11; Matt 17:9a, 10-13
Resp. Psalm: Ps 80:2ac and 3b, 15-16, 18-19 (*L* 186)

The pre-Christian prophet Elijah had a huge reputation among the Jews, and the expectation had developed that he would precede the Messiah. But Jesus' disciples seem to have missed him; Jesus tells them that Elijah has come in the person of John the Baptist and "they did not recognize him" (Matt 17:11). Jesus supports the identification further by saying that like Elijah, John the Baptist himself suffered. Instead of some triumphant, maybe military figure who "will . . . restore all things" (Matt 17:11), the Elijah Jesus speaks of had to follow the way of suffering and death to accomplish anything. Despite the rejection by Jesus of the way of power, the church and Christians have unfortunately relied on it in disastrous ways at times. Christian emperors have had whole tribes forcibly baptized; fire and sword have been used to teach opponents the truth. In everyday life, on the job, at home, in the school, in the church, we still face the necessity of resisting the use of power in place of persuasion and love. Lord, give us the patience to trust that you and the good will prevail without our might. Help us say no to anger, force, and coercion, and help us to rely instead on love and good example.

Monday of the Third Week of Advent—
I see him, though not now (Num 24:17)

When this day is December 17 or December 18, the appropriate readings for the calendar date take precedence.

Readings: Num 24:2-7, 15-17a; Matt 21:23-27
Resp. Psalm: Ps 25:4-5ab, 6 and 7bc, 8-9 (*L* 187)

"I see him, though not now; / I behold him, though not near" (Num 24:17). These are the kind of words we typically expect from a seer, a prophet. They seem teasing, almost purposely obscure, yet for us Christians, they offer a viewpoint about the Savior, the Lord, which enshrines much of the truth. Every Advent and Christmas celebrates the coming, the presence of the Lord, yet with limitations. "I see him, though not now; / I behold him, though not near" (Num 24:17). If this were not so, there would be no reason for us to celebrate these seasons year after year. There is always space for more of the Lord in our life, our world. Our faith and religious experience may tell us that the Lord is present in our lives. But that same faith tells us that there is still more he can do and be for us. The Lord, even after our best celebration of Advent and Christmas, is not exhausted; there is more of him for us to receive; there is more receptivity to be found on our part. We see the Lord, but not completely; the Lord is near but still a ways off. That is why we can always truthfully pray the prayer of Advent, "Come, Lord Jesus!" (Rev 22:20).

Tuesday of the Third Week of Advent—
The proof of commitment

When this day is December 17 or December 18, the appropriate readings for the calendar date take precedence.

Readings: Zeph 3:1-2, 9-13; Matt 21:28-32
Resp. Psalm: Ps 34:2-3, 6-7, 17-18, 19 and 23 (*L* 188)

To be or not to be—to do or not to do—to commit ourselves or not to commit ourselves—the doubts and questions of a Hamlet are those of all of us to some degree. Today's Gospel continues the theme of commitment. The son who agrees to do the work required by his father, who says "Yes" (Matt 21:30) and then never does it, represents people like the chief priests and scribes among the fellow Israelites of Jesus. These are the officially faithful Jews; they make a public show of being members of the covenant. Yet their lives fall far short. The tax collectors and prostitutes, on the other hand, do not make any such profession but, Jesus says, by their responsiveness to John the Baptist they actually do what God wants. Formally, they may have said no to the covenant, but in practice, by their repentance, they are saying yes. We were made members of the new covenant in our baptism and committed to dying and rising daily with Christ. As we celebrate once again the coming to birth of the Son of God, it is a good time to look at the nature of our yes to God in baptism. Prayer, public profession of faith, regular sharing in the public worship of the church, all these certainly look like a yes to God. How we act towards the poor and unloved in our midst, the suffering and needy, family members and friends who have a special claim on us, this determines whether, after having said yes, we actually go to work in the Lord's vineyard. We who take the time to come regularly to the table of the Lord have a deeper obligation to carry over into daily life the love and fellowship we celebrate here.

Wednesday of the Third Week of Advent—
Let justice descend (Isa 45:8)

When this day is December 17 or December 18, the appropriate readings for the calendar date take precedence.

Readings: Isa 45:6c-8, 18, 21c-25; Luke 7:18b-23
Resp. Psalm: Ps 85:9ab and 10, 11-12, 13-14 (*L* 189)

"And blessed is the one who takes no offense at me" (Luke 7:23). These are the words Jesus sent to John in response to his question. From the context of Luke's Gospel it seems apparent that the Lord is being sensitive to the different style of John's proclamation. Whereas John was scorching in some of his denunciations of the unfaithful, Jesus in this Gospel makes it a regular custom to eat with sinners, those not abiding by the law. The suggestion is that John may be a bit startled by the style of Jesus' ministry. We know some of the early Christians found some of Jesus' teaching very liberal and open; they wondered if they had understood it properly. The temptation for all who think they are making a good effort to follow the Lord is to write off the apparently less faithful, to limit our love and concern to those of our own kind. Jesus' teaching and example, especially in Luke's Gospel, show us one concerned for the poor, the outcast, the powerless and despised. We are never mistaken in doing all we can to show God's loving concern for these. Through our imitation of the Savior's love, the words of Isaiah come true: "Let the earth open and salvation bud forth; / let justice also spring up!" (Isa 45:8).

Thursday of the Third Week of Advent—
Renewing the marriage

When this day is December 17 or December 18, the appropriate readings for the calendar date take precedence.

Readings: Isa 54:1-10; Luke 7:24-30
Resp. Psalm: Ps 30:2 and 4, 5-6, 11-12a and 13b (*L* 190)

Strong and evident in today's reading from Isaiah is the picture of God's relation to humankind as a marriage. God is the husband, the people, the wife. Like many another marriage, it has had its rocky moments but now a reunion is in the offing. The groom says: "In an outburst of wrath, for a moment / I hid my face from you" (Isa 54:8). But that is all over: "My love shall never leave you" (Isa 54:10). All this, of course, is written in very human terms, in our language. It seems to be almost entirely from the Lord's side. As in any marriage, the good and less happy elements of the relationship probably involve responsibility on both sides. If we are married, today's readings can remind us of this old and necessary truth about a happy marriage. For all of us, Advent is a time to work with the Lord to repair our off-and-on relationship, our taking God's loving presence too much for granted. God took the initiative in uniting with human nature in the birth of Jesus. On December 25 we celebrate the anniversary of the wedding—another good time to renew the promises made in baptism.

Friday of the Third Week of Advent—*All are chosen*

When this day is December 17 or December 18, the appropriate readings for the calendar date take precedence.

Readings: Isa 56:1-3a, 6-8; John 5:33-36
Resp. Psalm: Ps 67:2-3, 5, 7-8 (L 191)

Undemocratic, arrogant. These are probably the terms that come to mind today when people hear a term like "chosen people" (see 1 Pet 2:9). If God considers one people or a certain group "chosen" and not the rest, it sounds to our contemporaries like a form of divine prejudice. But properly understood the term is much more generous and has a more profound meaning. In today's first reading from Isaiah we hear of foreigners (non-Jews) becoming members of God's people, the chosen people, and of the Temple becoming a place of prayer for "*all peoples*" (Isa 56:7; emphasis mine). In a way, that God would choose a particular people to be the vehicle for his message and love is much like God becoming human in Jesus Christ rather than in "Luke Dolan" or "Peggy Lopez." In the practical order God has to begin somewhere. The Word that comes to us from God in Jesus Christ is of God's loving embrace of all human beings. Being chosen, being the recipient and object of God's love, carries with it a huge and demanding dignity. Like John in today's Gospel we are each meant to be "a burning and shining lamp" (John 5:35) before the world we live in. As we approach Christmas and evidence our belief in the one who is to come we are

11

reminded that our lives should witness to him. They should be incomprehensible apart from our belief in Christ.

December 17—*That family background*

Readings: Gen 49:2, 8-10; Matt 1:1-17
Resp. Psalm: Ps 72:1-2, 3-4ab, 7-8, 17 (L 193)

In our personal reading of Scripture we are likely to skip over genealogies and assume there is nothing interesting in them. Matthew's genealogy tells a different story. In this list of names, God's grace is at work in ways we might not expect. The patriarchs are the first group of people in the genealogy. Not everyone in that list is noble or saintly. Jacob, for instance, stole his father's blessing. Israel's kings make up the second group. The kings reflect the best and the worst of Israel. Among those listed are idolaters, murderers, and adulterers like King David. Unknown people make up the third group. Yet God is at work in people others might consider forgettable. Finally, the women in this genealogy have marital histories that include scandal or scorn. Jesus has an interesting family tree. If it were ours, we would not want it published. In this family tree we see how God's grace is at work through saint and sinner. It invites us to see how God's grace works through sinners and the unknown around us, and even through us, in unexpected ways.

December 18—*Home from exile*

Readings: Jer 23:5-8; Matt 1:18-25
Resp. Psalm: Ps 72:1-2, 12-13, 18-19 (L 194)

Even people who like traveling often say, "How good it is to come back home." This is much more the case, of course, for those who have been driven out of their homes or forcibly deported. We, in our times, should certainly be familiar with the sight of wandering, homeless refugees. In the first reading the prophet Jeremiah promises that God will give the Israelites a new king, a good king, unlike the previous ones who have been responsible for the people's hardships, especially exile. The new king will bring the house of Israel back from all the lands to which they were banished. "They shall again live on their own land." Advent aims, among other things, to help us come back home from our exile, our state of being away from God, of being lost in a world of consumerism, competition, self-seeking. No matter how well life goes or how well we become adjusted to it, our life here is in some sense an exile from our true and lasting home. We are in exile as long as we attempt to organize our life around something other and invariably less than the Lord Jesus Christ. Advent, by pointing us day after day to the coming of Jesus, tries to focus us also on our true home. That home, of course, is life in eternity with God but also a life here and now where God and God's values predominate and permeate all our life. Without that orientation, our life here is simply like living in a tacky and run-down motel.

December 19—*Fathers and sons*

Readings: Judg 13:2-7, 24-25a; Luke 1:5-25
Resp. Psalm: Ps 71:3-4a, 5-6ab, 16-17 (L 195)

Echoing and repeating what we heard recently about Elijah, the angel tells Zechariah that his son John will be an instrument in turning the "hearts of fathers" to their children (Luke 1:17). We certainly may take this as a reference to more general reconciliation, that between generations and races, between neighbors, between rich and poor. But there is reason to think very particularly of reconciliation between fathers and children because that relationship is so often deficient in our society and it is of such importance to faith. Those who lack a relationship to a loving father often find it difficult, if not impossible, to see God as a loving father. An absent or emotionally distant father often makes trust in God problematic. People with such an experience of father often don't expect God the Father to be any better. The lack of a loving father in the lives of many leaves them without any natural foundation for trusting in a loving God the Father. They may have known a loving mother and can relate to someone close to God who is like that loving mother. What the solutions are to this problem of cold and absent fathers is a bigger subject than probably should be tackled in a short homily. At least all of us can do our part to encourage in boys and men the loving and caring qualities that model the God proclaimed by and in Jesus. We can also model in our own behavior the faithfulness and commitment that make for a stable, dependable father.

December 20—*On the wings of prayer*

Readings: Isa 7:10-14; Luke 1:26-38
Resp. Psalm: Ps 24:1-2, 3-4ab, 5-6 (L 196)

We all know relatives or friends in difficult circumstances: struggling with cancer, separated from loved ones, depressed or discouraged, saddened by death or other losses. What can we say or do, if anything? Believers, one would expect, end up saying, whatever else they say by way of consolation: "I'll pray for you; I'll remember you at Mass." To those without faith, of course, that expression can mean about as much as "we'll have to do lunch sometime" on the lips of an old acquaintance you run into on the street. But our promise of prayer is based on what the angel says to Mary: "Nothing is impossible with God." Speaking to Ahaz also, God makes the same statement: ask anything, deep as the nether world or high as the sky. Mary models the kind of faith that makes "I'll pray for you" mean something. In one of his sonnets the poet Gerard Manley Hopkins speaks of his and our concern for friends who for various reasons are no longer within the reach of any good we can do. Where we can't go, he says, Christ follows and cares; in his words, Christ is "their ransom, their rescue, and first, fast, last friend." One of the lessons of Advent is persistence in prayer. Because we believe nothing is impossible for God, we trust that God can care for others and do for them good way beyond our small conceiving.

December 21—*Another focus*

Readings: Song 2:8-14 or Zeph 3:14-18a; Luke 1:39-45
Resp. Psalm: Ps 33:2-3, 11-12, 20-21 (L 197)

Most of us have realized at one time or another, no matter how fleet-ingly, that the solution to many of our personal problems may be found in just forgetting ourselves. More positively, in concentrating our attention and energy on someone else, some good cause. We easily fail to notice that the first verse of today's Gospel ("Mary set out in those days and traveled to the hill country in haste" to see Elizabeth) follows immediately on Mary's words of acceptance to the Angel after the annunciation of the birth of Jesus to her. Certainly Mary could have been so excited to tell her cousin that she undertook the arduous trip. But a bit later we're told that she stayed with Elizabeth about three months. That suggests that it was not only the desire to share the good news but also a concern to be with her pregnant cousin, to help her. It shows an absence of self-preoccupation, a willingness to forget herself and concern herself with another. Isn't such selflessness the kernel of our following of the crucified Lord? Too often it's not only the mate-rialistic and grasping who are self-centered but even those who aim to follow the Lord. Too much preoccupation with our self, even with our spiritual growth, with our prayer life, with degrees of development, all this can be a kind of self-centeredness, a kind of spirituality that is more about "me" than about God. Advent points us to the one who is to come and away from self. Mary's example points us in the direction of the service and comfort of others —away from self.

December 22—*The place of praise*
Readings: 1 Sam 1:24-28; Luke 1:46-56
Resp. Psalm: 1 Sam 2:1, 4-5, 6-7, 8abcd (*L* 198)

Two figures dominate these last days of Advent, Mary and John the Baptist. While both seem almost more than human because of the importance with which they're clothed in Scripture, they are human enough to be helpful to us. Today it's Mary. We have the song which she pours out after Elizabeth declares her blessed. It's called the Magnificat from the opening word in the old Latin text. That word is related to our common English word *magnify* which means, of course, to make larger. Mary doesn't really make God larger in her song but cries out how great God is: "My soul proclaims the greatness of the Lord; / my spirit rejoices in God my savior." The whole poem, while it is aware of what God has done for Mary, primarily dwells on the greatness of God, the great things God has done. Three emotions or strongly felt reactions dominate: praise, thanksgiving, and joy. There is an acknowledgement of what God has done for her: God has looked on her lowliness, made her blessed for all ages, done great things for her. But certainly there is none of the modern self-promotion: I'm number one, for instance. Mary's spirit as it comes through this song is what is helpful, instructive for us. By example it calls us to thank God for all his actions, God's goodness to us; it calls us to praise and recall all the great things God has done in our own lives; it gives us the go-ahead to be joyful, exultant. Many of our Christmas carols which we've been hearing for weeks echo these feelings of thankfulness, praise, and joy for what God does in sending Jesus into human flesh and life. Clearly, the spirit of Scripture in regard to the birth of Jesus is thankful and joyous, full of praise, not simply intent on what it will mean for me.

December 23—*We've never done it that way*
Readings: Mal 3:1-4, 23-24; Luke 1:57-66
Resp. Psalm: Ps 25:4-5ab, 8-9, 10 and 14 (*L* 199)

People's names are important in the biblical story. Names do not merely identify a person in a crowd. Biblical names tell you something about who that person is. The name Isaac means "he laughs"; his name echoes the laughter of Abraham and Sarah when they're told that the aged Sarah will have a child. The name Israel means "one who strives with God"; it is given to Jacob after his late-night wrestling match with the Lord. Jesus gives Simon a new name; he names him Peter, which means "rock," a name as solid as the foundation of his confession of Jesus as the Messiah. Today Zechariah wants to name his child John. The trouble is that Zechariah ignores a custom of naming a child after the father or grandfather. Zechariah was being obedient to the angel's message. However, the family responds in a way that any one of us might, "We've never done it that way before." The name John points to the new thing that God is doing. John's name means, "The Lord shows favor." As Zechariah sings in his canticle, a new day dawns. The Lord shows favor to all people. John will declare a new day dawning in Jesus Christ. "We've never done it that way before" is precisely the point. As we move into the future trusting in God, we'll see things in our lives that were never done before.

December 24, Mass in the Morning—*A time for caroling*

Readings: 2 Sam 7:1-5, 8b-12, 14a, 16; Luke 1:67-79
Resp. Psalm: Ps 89:2-3, 4-5, 27 and 29 (L 200)

The Gospel of Luke starts out a bit like a Broadway musical. The chief characters break into song at big moments to clarify what is happening in the story. In the early chapters of Luke's Gospel Mary visits Elizabeth and then sings her Magnificat. Jesus is born, and the angels in heaven break out into song. When Jesus is presented in the Temple, the old man Simeon sings his farewell song. Now today, after the birth of John the Baptist, his father Zechariah takes up a song of his own. As Zechariah sings we begin to hear the themes that really matter. Though the song is sung after the birth of John the Baptist, very little of this song tells the story of John. Only two lines sing of John's ministry as a messenger and prophet. The rest of the song sings the melody of God's mercy and salvation. This sort of song that sings about God's salvation and not about John himself is right in harmony with John's life as a prophet. John the Baptist is always pointing to Jesus, always singing about the one who reveals God's kingdom. We are about to follow the pattern of Luke's Gospel and the pattern of Broadway musicals. We can only talk about the peace which dawns in Jesus Christ for so long before we ourselves have to break out into song. The birth of Jesus Christ is at hand. It is time to sing those carols.

Season of Christmas

December 26, Saint Stephen, First Martyr—
An echo of the Cross

Readings: Acts 6:8-10; 7:54-59; Matt 10:17-22
Resp. Psalm: Ps 31:3cd-4, 6 and 8b, 16bc and 17 (L 696)

The story of Stephen is a bit like the harsh winds of winter with which we in the Northern Hemisphere are familiar at this time of year. The carols, the poinsettias, the sweets and dinners of Christmas justifiably reinforce the coziness of celebrating the birth of a little baby. It takes a pretty hardened heart or insensitive person to be able to resist the attraction of a baby. And part of the reality of the Incarnation is that the Lord of all took on the form of such an infant. The feast of Stephen, by retelling the story of his martyrdom and in putting before us Christ's own predictions of such martyrdom, balances the warmth and coziness of the baby with the cold fact of rejection. That too is part of what it means for the Son of God to enter into human life. Rejection and martyrdom are definitely cold blasts. They give us a chill. His hearers rushed at Stephen as one man, dragged him out of the city, "and began to stone him" (Acts 7:58, NAB; see v. 57). And the Lord says, "Beware . . . . You will be hated by all because of my name" (Matt 10:17, 22). This child whom we celebrate at Christmas will arouse opposition and ultimately face death, as do his followers like Stephen. We can't identify our belief in Christ with a lovable, non-threatening message with which no one can disagree. Living out our faith can and will entail conflict and opposition. May his promises and presence strengthen us now and always.

December 27, Saint John, Apostle and Evangelist—
Witnessing

Readings: 1 John 1:1-4; John 20:1a and 2-8
Resp. Psalm: Ps 97:1-2, 5-6, 11-12 (L 697)

These days immediately after Christmas seem to be all about testimony, witness to the meaning of what happened at Christmas. The

Word of Life who was with the Father has become visible so that in the fellowship of Father, Son, and Holy Spirit we may share eternal life and have our joy complete (see 1 John 1:4). We all have some part in witnessing to this newborn child. If we've been given promises of eternal life and complete joy, there must be some echo of that in our lives, words, and actions. In some way or other in the course of our lives we all have opportunities to see, hear, and touch this Word, Jesus. In our offense at aggressive and demeaning evangelism we have possibly muted and hidden our witness all too well. Our gathering for Mass is, of course, itself a witness but it shouldn't absolve us from all other forms of testimony. For instance, to tell the anxious, the sick, the suffering, the unemployed, and the mourning around us that we remember them in prayer can itself be a refreshing witness in the face of a contemporary culture which usually just wishes others "good luck." As we let the significance of the birth of Jesus sink in we will think of other forms of witness. What we have seen and heard, that we now proclaim (see 1 John 1:1-2).

December 28, The Holy Innocents, Martyrs—
The way of fragility and innocence

Readings: 1 John 1:5-2:2; Matt 2:13-18
Resp. Psalm: Ps 124:2-3, 4-5, 7cd-8 (*L* 698)

The events we have witnessed in our own day and still encounter on television make such things as the slaughter of little children all too believable. Our times have seen tyrants slaughtering children, governments exterminating Jews, one ethnic group "cleansing" its land of another. The powerful and corrupt often see the powerless and innocent, such as children, as threats. Possibly they know that their corruption ultimately can be no match for the genuine power of the lowly and innocent. Jesus exerted his power to save us by allowing himself to become totally powerless on the cross. In his temptations he rejected the way of power and domination, the way of success at any price (see Matt 4:1-11 and parallels). Could today's feast be another way of reminding us of the power of innocence? Whenever we resist the way of falsehood and greed, of disrespect for others, whenever we choose honesty and patience over manipulation and abuse of others, we are opting for innocence, trusting that God will support the good. In sharing the bread and wine of Christ's offering at this altar we are again committing ourselves to his way, the way of lowliness and innocence.

December 29, The Fifth Day in the Octave of Christmas—
Human dignity

Readings: 1 John 2:3-11; Luke 2:22-35
Resp. Psalm: Ps 96:1-2a, 2b-3, 5b-6 (*L* 202)

A divine dignity and destiny for human beings—that is a major theme this Christmas season in the writings attributed to John. The Son of God, he tells us, took on human flesh in order to fill us with divine life and eventually in the resurrection bring us to eternal life with God. A day or two ago we heard how this way of thinking elevates and dignifies all human life. Today we hear more: that those who believe in Jesus know him, abide in him, and are in the light. But in today's selection from the First Letter of John the emphasis is on our seeing this same dignity in our fellow human being. The dignity of sharing God's life and light can only survive, John says, if we see that same dignity in others. Without love for our sisters and brothers, the writer says, our claim to this dignity is a lie. To say we know God and not keep the commandments is to lie; to claim to be in the light while hating others means we are really still in darkness. The test of our dignity as sharers in God's life, the test of the genuineness of our fellowship at this altar, the test of our claim to be Christians is how we treat others. To see the glory shining around others because of God's grace requires treating them with respect, being concerned about their needs and pains, sensitive to their hurts and sorrows. Despite temptations in that direction the Christian cannot dismiss another human being as of no worth. Christians cannot simply take for granted the slaughter of other human beings in fratricidal war or the suffering of others living in subhuman conditions. "[T]he way we may know that we are in union with [Jesus the Word]: whoever claims to abide in him ought to live {just} as he lived" (1 John 2:5-6, NAB).

December 30, The Sixth Day in the Octave of Christmas—
God's world or another

Readings: 1 John 2:12-17; Luke 2:36-40
Resp. Psalm: Ps 96:7-8a, 8b-9, 10 (*L* 203)

The First Letter of John which we hear almost daily for about two weeks presents some stark oppositions, between light and darkness, for instance, and between good and evil. These seem so obvious, but the truth is more complicated. Today we hear, "Do not love the world or the things of the world. / If anyone loves the world, the love of

19

the Father is not in him. / For all that is in the world, / . . . / is not from the Father . . . " (1 John 2:15-16). If we took that apart from other more positive evaluations of the world we'd have a hard time even stepping outside the church after this Mass. The opening chapter of the Bible in Genesis tells us that all God made is good. Elsewhere John's Gospel tells us in a most famous passage that "God so loved the world that he gave his only Son, so that everyone who believes in him might not perish but might have eternal life" (3:16). And the following verse says the Son came "that the world might be saved through him" (v. 17). "[T]he world" (1 John 2:15, for example) in John's Letter means more like what we call worldliness, an attitude which prizes the superficial sheen of material playthings and the empty promises of the baubles which amuse us for a short time and never satisfy. But the world God made is a world where people rejoice over the birth of a child, where people have hope and trust like Anna, where a child can grow like Jesus in size and strength, where scientists can devise cures for diseases, where good people can alleviate poverty. This is the world that God loved so much that he sent Jesus to help us through its imperfections and rescue us from its sin and evil. This is the world we can love and serve by living as adopted daughters and sons of God.

December 31, The Seventh Day in the Octave Christmas—
The Lord next door

Readings: 1 John 2:18-21; John 1:1-18
Resp. Psalm: Ps 96:1-2, 11-12, 13 (L 204)

"[T]he Word became flesh / and made his dwelling among us" (John 1:14). The latter part of that sentence may be translated as "he pitched his tent among us." The Son of God took on our life and moved into the apartment next door. Two implications stand out in this, in the Incarnation. One, God has taken on human form, human life, to share all of it with us: suffering, joy, rejection, camaraderie, meals, friends, enemies, work, and death. This is a consoling truth. And, two, God is living next door. This is a more prickly truth. God is living in that fellow who keeps us awake with his music, in that woman who always has a new complaint, in that con man on the job, in that lonely old woman whom no one visits, in that ruthless climber at the office, in the child with leukemia, in . . . There are others more frightening we could include. In the days of Christmas we have time during which we can reflect on its meaning. But if we've been around for a decade or two, we know that we are never finished with reflecting on this—or with acting on it. How do we keep before ourselves in life's difficulties the fact that the Lord is with us in all of that? How do we consistently and continually see the Lord in the suffering, the difficult, the frightening, the needy, people around us? Like the commandment to love, this task is endless (see Mark 12:30:31, for example). The end of another year urges us to evaluate our successes and failures in this matter in the months just past. The endlessness of the task tells us that we still need, will always need, God's grace to forgive our failures and strengthen our resolve. "From his fullness we have all received" (John 1:16).

January 2—*Let God and others do the promoting*

Readings: 1 John 2:22-28; John 1:19-28
Resp. Psalm: Ps 98:1, 2-3ab, 3cd-4 (*L* 205)

In answer to the question put to him, "Who are you?" (John 1:19), John the Baptist passes by an opportunity for self-promotion. He doesn't even claim to be a prophet, only one who is not worthy to unfasten the sandal strap of the one he announces (see John 1:21, 27). In proclaiming or acknowledging Jesus, "the Son" of the first reading (1 John 2:22-23), he "has the Father as well" (1 John 2:23). Though John the Baptizer does not use the terminology (John the Evangelist does), he undoubtedly knew that to be able to claim the Father was identity enough. In professional and academic life, in presenting ourselves for employment, many of us must do what amounts to self-promotion. We get our resume together and list our experience and achievements. It is unavoidable. However, in our personal relations, among our family, our friends, and neighbors, John's model should prevail, some of his self-effacement. In that milieu we shouldn't have to continually be asserting our worth; we should be able to trust those who know us to value us correctly. The ancient Chinese sage, Confucius, was strong on this. In fact he would have extended humility and self-effacement even into the marketplace and public life. Over and over he stresses that the ideal person is always more concerned to *do* the things that merit recognition than to have recognition. Jesus said that there was no human born of greater dignity than John (see Matt 11:11), yet this John is content to simply point out the greatness of the Lord. Obviously there are some lessons here.

January 3—*The difficulty of waking up*

Readings: 1 John 2:29–3:6; John 1:29-34
Resp. Psalm: Ps 98:1, 3cd-4, 5-6 (*L* 206)

"I did not know him" (John 1:31, 33). If John the Baptist, the forerunner of Christ, can confess his inability to see the Christ in Jesus, then at least we have some exalted company in our own inability to see God's action in our lives. The first reading speaks of the same problem: "The reason the world does not know us is that it did not know him" (1 John 3:1). Much of our lives is spent waking up to realizations, learning after the event what its significance was, seeing the value of a moment only when it is past, recognizing the blessing of a human life only when it is over. Again, what all this suggests is that we need more of that wakefulness, alertness, attention to what is before us of which we've heard so often in Christ's teaching. Think of the many examples there are in our lives of our non-recognition of something or someone very important, of someone or something that was actually a grace. And we kicked against it or experienced only irritation. Maybe it was that downsizing in our company that really freed us from work we never liked; perhaps it was that person who never met us except to arouse us to argument; perhaps it was the person who falsely accused us of harassment. So many people, unintentionally or seemingly with hostile intentions, can bring us God's grace.

January 4—*Not perfect but loving*

Readings: 1 John 3:7-10; John 1:35-42
Resp. Psalm: Ps 98:1, 7-8, 9 (*L* 207)

There's a famous line in the Sermon on the Mount which is often translated as "be perfect . . . as your heavenly Father is perfect" (Matt 5:48). Over the centuries, it has served to justify tendencies to meticulous scrupulosity, as if it were demanding that we somehow imitate God's way of doing everything without any mistakes. In its context, Jesus' words follow others about how God's love is like the rain; it falls on the good and the bad. "[B]e perfect . . ." therefore refers to our imitating God's love which is indiscriminate like the sun and the rain. The "perfection" referred to is a very demanding love, not a meticulous observance of laws. If we take the last two lines of our first reading today as parallel, repeating each other's meaning in slightly different words, we have the same message. Line number one: "no one who fails to act in righteousness belongs to God" (1 John 3:10). Line number two: "nor anyone who does not love his brother" (1 John 3:10). NRSV for both lines: "all who do not do what is right are not from God, nor are those who do not love their brothers or sisters." Holiness, then, seems essentially to be love of others, desiring their good. That's where the emphasis is in the New Testament: holiness or perfection is identified with love, with an active concern for others. Let us not put it on the same level as observing traffic laws or regulations about snow or trash removal.

January 5—*Solidarity with the poor*

Readings: 1 John 3:11-21; John 1:43-51
Resp. Psalm: Ps 100:1b-2, 3, 4, 5 (L 208)

"We know that we have passed from death to life" if we love (1 John 3:14)—there he is, old "one note John." The letters of John seem to have nothing else more important to say. "If someone who has worldly means / sees a brother in need and refuses him compassion, / how can the love of God remain in him?" (1 John 3:17). While this is a tough enough question to ask ourselves individually—and John has put it to us repeatedly—it's still a more difficult one when we put it in global terms. How can many of us live amid surplus and waste, while our brothers and sisters in so many parts of the world lack basic health care, food, clothing, and shelter? Though the question is not capable of a simple answer, it should influence our civic responsibility and what we expect of our politicians. If nothing else, John's insistence on love that shows itself in action should be the backdrop for all our thoughts about public and national policy, and our decisions about voting. "If someone who has worldly means / sees a brother in need and refuses him compassion, / how can the love of God remain in him?" (1 John 3:17).

January 6—*The Lord works through human beings*

The following are used when Epiphany is celebrated on Sunday, January 7 or Sunday, January 8.

Readings: 1 John 5:5-13; Mark 1:7-11 or Luke 3:23-38 or Luke 3:23, 31-34, 36, 38
Resp. Psalm: Ps 147:12-13, 14-15, 19-20 (L 209)

As we have noticed elsewhere, the language of the First Letter of John raises questions for us moderns by its vehemence and exclusiveness. John makes a simple and absolute identification of belief in Jesus with possession of eternal life. We would probably think of some qualifications. For instance, what about the case of someone who was forceful in expressing belief in the Lord but was nevertheless pretty harsh and unjust to employees? In a short few words at daily Mass we can only emphasize the positive points made for us here: believing in Jesus, the Son of God, gives us eternal life and victory over the evils of the world around us. We can't deny that "the light of the world" (John 8:12; cf. 1:9) comes into a world full of pain, hatred, terror, war, and disease. Without the light of Christ's life and word, one would easily be tempted to despair. History should have taught us by now that human beings by their own ingenuity are not going to rid the world of these evils. Our help must come from the Lord (see Psalm 121:2). And, as always, the Lord works through human minds, hearts, and hands. Trusting in God's power and help in overcoming the horrors of human life does not mean sitting on our hands and waiting for God to intervene. What is needed are human beings and even nations more open to the support of grace in building a more humane and just world, in making, for instance, a more effective and well-supported United Nations.

January 7—*God never nods; God always listens*

The following are used when Epiphany is celebrated on Sunday, January 8.

Readings: 1 John 5:14-21; John 2:1-11
Resp. Psalm: Ps 149:1-2, 3-4, 5 and 6a and 9b (L 210)

"We have this confidence in God, / that if we ask anything according to his will, he hears us" (1 John 5:14). So we hear in the reading from the First Letter of John. And, by way of illustration in the famous, beautiful, and strange Gospel reading about the wedding feast at Cana, Mary does just that. Implicitly she asks her son to do something about the lack of wine at the celebration. "They have no wine" (John 2:3). To many earnest people such a request must sound a bit frivolous, if not borderline immoral. Why ask for more wine when it may likely lead to just more uncontrolled revelry and attendant abuses? But if we allow for a bit more exaggeration and poetic license, the whole story taken in conjunction with the reading from First John can be a way of telling us that nothing is too minor or earthly or inconsequential to put before God in prayer. Rather than spending a lot of time to figure out whether our petitions are of the right caliber or level of importance, possibly we would do better to get into a habit of asking God about everything that is of any importance in our life. Anything we think may be of some good is certainly worth setting before God. Let God sort out whether or not it's worthy of God's action. "We have this confidence in God, / that if we ask anything according to his will, he hears us" (1 John 5:14).

The following days are celebrated between Epiphany and the Baptism of the Lord. The number of these days varies from year to year.

Monday after Epiphany or January 7—
The witness of hope

Readings: 1 John 3:22–4:6; Matt 4:12-17, 23-25
Resp. Psalm: Ps 2:7bc-8, 10-12a (L 212)

"[F]or the one who is in you / is greater than the one who is in the world" (1 John 4:4). The one who is in us is the great light mentioned in the quotation from Isaiah in the Gospel, the one who is shown curing disease and pain. Despite the horrors that surround us in our world, horrors of war and persecution, famine and drought, abuse and neglect, poverty and oppression, the Christian, by definition, has to maintain a trust that the one who is us, in me, in you, is greater than the evil that seems to have the upper hand. Already we're at a slight remove from the joy and excitement of Christmas but the conviction that the Lord whose birth we celebrate conquers evil, pain, and sin. This conviction must be kept alive in us and be operative through our faith and hope. The early Christians, we read, were recognizable because of their mutual love. That should still be true. But, alongside that, we should expect that Christians today would be recognizable by their undaunted hope and trust. Surely we're tempted to join the gloom and pessimism of the "realists" around us. But we honor the Savior who has come into the world and enhances life around us by the hope and joy that accompany our belief in the Lord. The joy and exultation of the season's carols are true to the meaning of the birth of Christ and should echo unashamedly in our lives.

Tuesday after Epiphany or January 8—
What we can, with what we have

Readings: 1 John 4:7-10; Mark 6:34-44
Resp. Psalm: Ps 72:1-2, 3-4, 7-8 (L 213)

As so often in Mark's Gospel so too in today's Gospel reading, the disciples come off as ungenerous and uncomprehending. The text reads: "By now it was already late and his disciples approached him" (Mark

6:35). Basically what they suggest is a way of getting the crowds off their backs. After noting the hour and the out-of-the-way place, they are afraid of getting stuck with these people and their needs. Wouldn't it be a good idea, they say, if we sent them off to the neighboring villages so that they could get what they need? It sounds like: shouldn't we palm them off on someone else? We can't take care of them. If they stay here, they'll be a burden to us. It will take the disciples—as it does us—some time to catch the spirit of the Lord. Their understanding of what is said in the first reading from First John is still pretty minimal. Jesus says rather bluntly to them: "Give them some food yourselves" (Mark 6:37). They protest that they can hardly afford that. Jesus says that they will make do with what they have, the few loaves and fishes. Over and over again, the great saints and people of genuine trust have shown that trying to do the best with the little we have often brings about unexpected, good results. Rather than complain about our lack of means we are expected to do generously what we can, with what we have. Working in and for the Lord we can expect more to happen than we can rationally foresee.

Wednesday after Epiphany or January 9—
Changing our plans

Readings: 1 John 4:11-18; Mark 6:45-52
Resp. Psalm: Ps 72:1-2, 10, 12-13 (L 214)

Let's take the most puzzling line in today's readings: "He [Jesus] meant to pass by them" (Mark 6:48). This is the famous story where Jesus walks on the water to the disciples whose boat is being tossed about in a storm. They seem equally terrified of the storm and of the ghostly appearance of Jesus. The phrase about Jesus meaning to pass them by suggests that stilling the storm and comforting the disciples was not his original intention. Scholars are at a loss to explain the phrase. It would make some sense to our own following of Jesus if we understood it somewhat like this: Jesus, after praying in solitude, leaves his spot to go somewhere; we don't know where. He means to pass by the disciples rather than stop where they were. But, seeing their distress and terror, he stops, changes his plans, calms both the storm and their fright. Isn't that how much of the good we do happens also? We have our plans, intentions, duties to fulfill, and it just happens that on the way to them we run into someone who needs help, encouragement, even something as simple as a friendly word or smile. We stop to do this. Even though we originally had other plans, what we end up doing is often something of real value and help to another. "[I]f God so loved us, / we also must love one another" (1 John 4:11).

Thursday after Epiphany or January 10—
We did not begin it

Readings: 1 John 4:19–5:4; Luke 4:14-22
Resp. Psalm: Ps 72:1-2, 14 and 15bc, 17 (*L* 215)

To believe that God has "first loved us" (1 John 4:19), while comforting, is often very difficult. It goes directly against our tendency to credit ourselves, our good will, our take-charge attitude. Our tendency is to think that we discovered God, that we decided to love God. So much of Scripture is counter to this attitude, this manner. And that is why concerning the first reading at least—and often for a long time we find Scripture—to be so ornery, even so absurd. God "first loved us" (1 John 4:19). How? When? To believe that God has loved us is to adopt a certain attitude toward existence, toward life, the world. It means recognizing that we are surrounded by so much unasked for, unmerited goodness, so many signs of God's love. As long as our attitude is that nothing in creation can really be adequate for us, nothing is ever enough for us, we will not be able to accept that we are the recipients. To sense that we are surrounded by good things, by love, by so much we do not deserve, this is itself a gift from God. But we can leave ourselves more and more open to it. We need to be amazed daily at the good we are capable of doing but more even at the good others do, the beauty that shines around us in people, places, and events. Gratitude is not only the response to God's love, but also the means by which we recognize that love. We are thankful because God loves us, but we are also thankful because—possibly long before we recognize that God loves us—we have noted how much undeserved good surrounds us. When we sit back and let ourselves, with a smile, fondly recall how happy someone makes us, how kind and thoughtful someone has been, we are implicitly acknowledging that God loved us first.

Friday after Epiphany or January 11—*Teaching silence*

Readings: 1 John 5:5-13; Luke 5:12-16
Resp. Psalm: Ps 147:12-13, 14-15, 19-20 (*L* 216)

"God gave us eternal life, / and this life is in his Son. / Whoever possesses the Son has life" (1 John 5:11-12). This is the life we have in Christ, by our adoption in baptism. There doesn't seem any way of knowing this life or really believing in it apart from some reflection, some prayer, some quiet. It doesn't impose itself on us with bells, sounds, thunder, or even necessarily, feelings. It requires that we allow ourselves to be acted upon, to be influenced by grace. If we can allow ourselves at least a few minutes every day, after communion or after Mass or after rising or before retiring, to be quiet—"Be still, and know that I am God!" (Ps 46:10; NRSV)—in time we can learn that we live deep down on another level than that of the world of the senses. So often in our day we define life by the amount of bustle and noise involved, by the fact that we never have to be alone or physically inactive. This is so superficial and limiting. Parents easily buy into this with the idea that they must keep their children occupied every moment of the day with soccer, swimming, dance, Boy/Girl Scouts. Why not show them the example of someone sitting quietly reading a book or listening to music or simply doing nothing but praying interiorly or listening to God? Children could learn from adults not only how to be active and involved but how to listen, how to be quiet, how to rest, how to shut out noise and be open to the Spirit, to the eternal life already within us by our baptism.

Saturday after Epiphany or January 11—*Letting go*

Readings: 1 John 5:14-21; John 3:22-30
Resp. Psalm: Ps 149:1-2, 3-4, 5-6a and 9b (L 217)

Parents inevitably allow their children independence and let them go (see, for example, Gen 2:24). Age or other factors can make it necessary for us to let go of a much-loved position or work. A pastor may have to surrender the care of a cherished congregation into the hands of another. Almost any such experience, no matter how well we recognize its necessity, can be wrenching, painful, like the loss of a part of ourselves. That letting go, that surrender, is probably inevitable in some area of our life. Can we prepare for it? Possibly, when we remind ourselves not to clutch the good and rewarding that come our way with too much possessiveness. The Gospels don't talk a lot about this; there aren't discourses on this letting go. But, as so often, the Gospel pictures it in a genuine, concrete situation. John is told in the Gospel today that this other man about whom he has been testifying is now attracting crowds to himself. First, John seems to say that the way Jesus attracts crowds is a gift from God. Second, John repeats what he said earlier, that Jesus is the Messiah and he, John, only the one who comes before. Finally, most generously he says that this is his place in the scheme of things. He is simply the best man, not the groom. The groom's happiness is his joy. "He must increase; I must decrease" (John 3:30). Lord, teach us, help us, to see our work, our position, in the greater scheme of your world; let us not think of ourselves as the end and purpose of creation. Help us find our joy in pointing to you, in having your will and desires take over in our heart.

Season of Lent

Ash Wednesday—*Mortality and renewal*

Readings: Joel 2:12-18; 2 Cor 5:20–6:2; Matt 6:1-6, 16-18
Resp. Psalm: Ps 51:3-4, 5-6ab, 12-13, 14 and 17 (*L* 219)

None of us can put into totally satisfactory language the meaning of what we do today, this Ash Wednesday. The use of ashes on this day is a custom at least nine hundred years old. Unlike words which have settled meanings in the dictionary, such symbols as ashes suggest various meanings to different people. By supplying two formulas for the giving of the ashes today the church recognizes that no one phrase says it all. "Remember that you are dust and unto dust you shall return" (The Sacramentay; see Gen 1:15) says much; "Turn away from sin and be faithful to the [G]ospel" (The Sacramentary; see Mark 1:15) says something else. Both are helpful. As the years go by and we and our world change, we can think of the ashes in any number of ways. They suggest death, penance, the frailty of all worldly things, and much else. The readings attempt to focus our hearts on some aspect of all this. The reading from the prophet Joel stresses well that this is the beginning of a solemn and very important period for the whole community of believers. This season of Lent, the springtime of the Spirit, calls us to renewal, to new life, to a restoration of our baptismal state. In Second Corinthians we hear that Jesus became sin itself so that "we might become the righteousness of God" (5:21). With great trust in God and joy at this opportunity, strengthened by the support of other believers, we pray God to renew the life of Christ in us. Second Corinthians says: "we appeal to you not to receive the grace of God in vain" (6:1). "Even now, says the LORD, / return to me with your whole heart" (Joel 2:12).

Thursday after Ash Wednesday—*More life is the goal*

Readings: Deut 30:15-20; Luke 9:22-25
Resp. Psalm: Ps 1:1-2, 3, 4 and 6 (*L* 220)

Christian life is truly a matter of choosing life, of valuing life at its best and deepest. Lent is our journey to Easter, to resurrection, to new life. Lent is like a short version of our life as it moves to the eternal Easter of heaven. Human life, even if ours seems rosy, comfortable, cloudless, includes much suffering for many people. The neighboring couple is recovering from the suicide of their teenage son; that single woman is regaining her hair after losing it to chemotherapy; whole nations are in dire need of food and water; the poor are jailed or killed for asking for a better distribution of resources. No matter how smoothly our life may go, human life is not all prosperity, love, and health but includes estrangement, hatred, poverty, illness, pain, hard work, disappoint-ment, misunderstanding, grief, betrayal, loss. Choosing life means, in some way, doing what we can in our own spot to improve and en-hance the life of the suffering. Possibly any self-denial we do can be turned into a financial benefit for some needy cause. Possibly, our main activity, apart from prayer, during this season can be volunteering our skill and time for some good cause. Even accepting the Cross in our own lives is to work for life. If you lose your life for my sake, Jesus tells us, you will find it; you will discover its true meaning and value. All God ultimately wills, it seems, despite the hard ways that may lead to it, is life, more abundant life for the world, for ourselves.

Friday after Ash Wednesday—*Genuine fasting*

Readings: Isa 58:1-9a; Matt 9:14-15
Resp. Psalm: Ps 51:3-4, 5-6ab, 18-19 (*L* 221)

While the Gospel provides a sort of justification for fasting (the groom, Christ, has been "taken away" [Matt 9:15]), Isaiah makes clear that fasting is a luxury item compared to the change in our behavior to-wards others that God demands. The prophet speaks harshly to all our stratagems for avoiding the real task by concentrating on things like fasting, abstinence from this or that, bodily self-denial, more prayers, etc. It is so much easier, isn't it, to add a few more prayers or devo-tions during Lent, deny ourselves chocolate or a beer, than to face the suffering and need around us? Shouldn't Lent mean that we dedicate ourselves to the service of others or revitalize that service? Look at the list the prophet gives: "releasing those bound unjustly," "Setting free the oppressed," "Sharing your bread with the hungry, / sheltering the oppressed and the homeless; / Clothing the naked" (Isa 58:6-7). It's a lot like what Christ tells us in Matthew 25 about the basis for our final judgment. When we do these things, we do them for the Lord. We can all ask ourselves the appropriate questions. What about that elderly relative we haven't seen or called in months? How is that poor woman getting along who used to work for us? Should we perhaps get involved with the local food shelf or the homeless shelter? Maybe a daily effort to be more pleasant to that difficult person at the office or shop would be a good Lenten decision. To help the infirm neighbor with his/her shopping might be an excellent idea. We can all find the right action. "This," God says, "is the fasting that I wish" (Isa 58:6).

Saturday after Ash Wednesday—*Self knowledge*

Readings: Isa 58:9b-14; Luke 5:27-32
Resp. Psalm: Ps 86:1-2, 3-4, 5-6 (*L* 222)

As happens so often in Luke's Gospel, Jesus eats with sinners, people known for not observing the Law of Judaism. He does it because they are the ones who need him, who feel their failure and know their sin. Almost any one of us needs to be shaken out of our self-satisfaction into renewed awareness of our need for the Savior. That again is the purpose of such seasons as Lent. We may get so used to ourselves, our way of living, our faults even, that we tend to take the whole package as given, nonnegotiable. But Scripture has hope about our future, more vision of possibilities. If we listen to it carefully and take it to heart, it has the capability of sharpening our self-knowledge, our sensitivity. Each of us could profitably translate the words of Isaiah and examine our consciences in these early days of Lent. He says: remove oppression from your midst (should we think of the underpaid, immigrant farm workers, minorities?); get rid of false and injurious talk about others; share with the hungry; help the afflicted; don't seek your own interests. Asking these questions of ourselves will leave little room for self-satisfaction.

Monday of the First Week of Lent—*Self-forgetting*

Readings: Lev 19:1-2, 11-18; Matt 25:31-46
Resp. Psalm: Ps 19:8, 9, 10, 15 (*L* 224)

When we note the emphasis in the weekday readings for Lent on interior dispositions and significant works, it's hard to imagine how Lent

could ever be reduced to "giving up desserts." We do, of course, have
to be specific in order to get anywhere, but still it looks pretty trivial.
Today's readings are good examples of a stress on essentials. The book
of Leviticus which we often remember for its minute regulations about
eating, dress, and ritual here underlines freedom from grudges, hatred,
and desires for revenge. And in the Gospel, the Jesus whom we meet
at this altar tells us that we meet and serve him when we minister to
the sick, hungry, naked, homeless, and imprisoned. Our Lenten resolu-
tion can be as specific as a determination to visit Sarah Lorenzo who is
home and weak from chemotherapy or to stop by and say a hopeful
word to the Wilson boy who is having a hard time. Here is a way, the
way of living the Christian life, which is totally accessible to every one
of us no matter where we are: no monastery or church or special time
or unusual talent is required. We serve and meet Christ by the good
we do to these suffering people all around us every day, whether in
a school, an office, a refugee camp, or a comfortable condominium.
And there's a happy by-product of all this; it helps us forget ourselves
and to share in the self-emptying of Christ (see Phil 2) which we com-
memorate at this altar.

Tuesday of the First Week of Lent—*Sincere prayer*

Readings: Isa 55:10-11; Matt 6:7-15
Resp. Psalm: Ps 34:4-5, 6-7, 16-17, 18-19 (L 225)

Isaiah tells us that God's word is like the moisture that falls from the
heavens and makes all growth and fertility possible. It must come into
human life and be effective. Perhaps, we could apply this to our ap-
propriation of the Our Father as our prayer. Its setting in Matthew's
Gospel shows us what will make this prayer effective. In Matthew's
arrangement of Christ's teaching and deeds, the Lord's Prayer is
framed (as in today's reading) by (1) a warning against just babbling
on, multiplying words when we pray (see 6:7) and (2) an underlining
of part of that prayer which requires that we forgive as God forgives
us (see 6:12). In other words, prayer should be short and sincere rather
than elaborate and wordy. We need spend no time worrying about the
language or grammar of our prayer; what is essential is sincerity and
directness. The other point emphasizes that prayer be accompanied
by demanding standards for ourselves. We cannot truly pray to God
for forgiveness or a closer union while at the same time holding a
grudge against a neighbor, trying to get even, being unwilling to forgive. Prayer cannot be genuine if isolated from our communion with

the other members of the body of Christ. Our praying of the Our Father and our prayer in general will be fruitful when it is not separated from a generous life. What goes on at the table of the Lord and what happens at home or on the job are meant to be one.

Wednesday of the First Week of Lent—
God's grace, our works

Readings: Jonah 3:1-10; Luke 11:29-32
Resp. Psalm: Ps 51:3-4, 12-13, 18-19 (L 226)

With its urgency and continual push for us to do something, Lent seems almost at odds with the New Testament's insistence that all good comes from God and depends on God's grace. But there is in Scripture and in Christ's teaching a delicate balance between the recognition that the initiative is God's alongside (1 John 4:10, for example) continual exhortations to repentance and action. Jonah's successful preaching tells us that we can and must do something in that direction. In much of the Scripture for Lent we are rather forcefully and continually asked to do something and to avoid something else. The New Testament teaching that we are saved by God's grace and that all the good we do comes from grace (see Eph 2, for example) is no excuse—let alone an invitation—for slackness. When St. Paul tells us that we are not saved by our works (see Gal 2:15-21), he does not mean that they are unnecessary. Rather, he is simply pointing out that we don't do them for the sake of impressing God in exchange for eternal life. Our good works follow from our thankfulness for God's grace and as our just return. Grace, if it is truly operative in our lives, will make the works of love and compassion all the more urgent. We have heard and read the words of one much greater than Jonah; how do we respond?

Thursday of the First Week of Lent—*Prayer is the source*

Readings: Esther C:12, 14-16, 23-25; Matt 7:7-12
Resp. Psalm: Ps 138:1-2ab, 2cde-3, 7c-8 (L 227)

Both readings today join in highlighting once again another essential element of Lent, prayer. If our prayer is primarily a matter of rote recitation, hardly ever in our own words, worse yet, something of a chore to get done with, then Lent could well be spent in bettering this. Even given another half-hour for this homily, the preacher would not be able to prove to any of us the intrinsic value of prayer for a disciple of Christ. In many ways, that has to be learned by doing. A continual deepening of our prayer life, a more constant dependence on it for our life in Christ, this is at the heart of Christian life. Once it becomes, you could almost say, as natural and continual as our breathing, it affects all we do and makes possible a Christian response to all that happens. A good example of this is a man in his late fifties, unemployed for several years as the result of the omnipresent downsizing. Now, near sixty, he has found a position in another part of the country. His wife will finish out her semester teaching and join him at the end of spring. They have lived for thirty-seven years in one city and the youngest child is finishing college. But, almost like Abraham, give or take a few decades, they are leaving friends and neighbors for a new life. Jake and Marge are people of faith and prayer. They aren't paralyzed, as understandably they could be, by this prospect, but they look on it courageously as a new beginning. Jake, who has lived a life of prayer for years, says that his prayer which helps him do this has "become more and more simply: 'let me do what you want me to do, God, and help me to bring others to you.'" Fortified with this the two of them are inspiring their friends and family. Genuine prayer fuels them. What we do here in church can be the beginning for all of us of a true life of prayer.

Friday of the First Week of Lent—*With God's help*

Readings: Ezek 18:21-28; Matt 5:20-26
Resp. Psalm: Ps 130:1-2, 3-4, 5-7a, 7bc-8 (L 228)

As in a number of places, the demands of the Sermon on the Mount from which our Gospel is taken seem to be way beyond most of us. How can we possibly be free from all vengeful, unkind, lustful thoughts? (see also Matt 5:28). Involuntarily, at least (if not more purposefully), such thoughts float through our minds and hearts, maybe daily. They constitute one big cross in our interior life. On the one hand, we are responsible, as Ezekiel emphasizes, we can choose good or bad; on the other, we don't seem able to do all that is asked. We don't always make the right choices. And the words of Jesus in today's Gospel are pretty dire in their warnings about the consequences of our failures. We can sympathize with the disciples' reaction to Jesus' teaching about how dangerous wealth is. They said, if that's the case, "Who then can be saved?" (Matt 19:25). If our minds and hearts must be as free as Jesus demands of thoughts of vengeance, resentment, judgment, lust, and ill will, who can be saved? Jesus told the disciples that "for God all things are possible" (Matt 19:26). There must lie our hope, too. The solution to our inability to live up to the high ideals of the Sermon on the Mount lies in trust in God's forgiveness and saving help. As the responsorial psalm prays, "If you, O Lord, mark iniquities, / Lord, who can stand? / But with you is forgiveness" (Ps 130:3-4).

Saturday of the First Week of Lent—*Getting it*

Readings: Deut 26:16-19; Matt 5:43-48
Resp. Psalm: Ps 119:1-2, 4-5, 7-8 (*L* 229)

We hear so often and rightly the Lord's command to "Love one another" (John 13:34) that it may wash over us like water off a duck's back. But, as we know in other matters, frequent enough repetition sometimes leads to the point where we finally "get" something. A man who has spent a couple of decades in the army, going from post to post, says that Sunday Mass has been one of the constants of his life and that finally, he says, "I'm getting it." He means he's seeing how his life with all its changes and challenges fits into what we call the Paschal Mystery, into the dying and rising of the Lord. The day-by-day experience of life accompanied by a sharing in the self-giving of Christ eventually tells us what it's all about. The same goes for the variations on the theme of love of God and neighbor (see Matt 22:37-39). Today we hear: "But I say to you, love your enemies, / and pray for those who persecute you, / that you may be children of your heavenly Father" (Matt 5:44-45). Jesus goes on to say that God's love is like the rain and the sun which make no discrimination about who receives them. We must be perfect or complete in the same way, having a love that goes both to those we are attracted to and to our enemies. A combination of hearing such words along with reflection, effort, frequent presence at the sacrifice of Christ, and God's grace can help us, we pray, to eventually "get it," that is, this essential command to love.

Monday of the Second Week of Lent—*Creatureliness*

Readings: Dan 9:4b-10; Luke 6:36-38
Resp. Psalm: Ps 79:8, 9, 11 and 13 (*L* 230)

We live in an era when it's usual to excuse ourselves especially—and others less frequently—by referring to our upbringing, genes, or environment. The words of the prayer we heard in the first reading from Daniel may seem excessive to us. All that stuff about "We have sinned, been wicked and done evil" (9:5) and "we rebelled against you / and paid no heed to your command" (9:9-10). Sure, we say, we've sinned;

let's admit it and get it over with. But behind the intensity of this prayer may lie a profound recognition that we are God's creatures, that we owe life and everything to God. We come from God, are nothing apart from God, yet we so often act and speak as if we and God were on the same level. Perhaps a revival of our sense of creatureliness is necessary for a more lively religion. With that would come an acknowledgment that nothing is genuinely owed to us but that, on the contrary, we owe everything to God's goodness (see 1 Cor 4:7). How such an attitude would affect daily life! Instead of grumbling about our bad deal or feeling sorry for ourselves, we'd be more inclined to look for what we might do in thanksgiving. Along with such a recognition would go more willingness to understand and forgive others as we expect to be forgiven (see Matt 6:12).

Tuesday of the Second Week of Lent—*The greatest among us*

Readings: Isa 1:10, 16-20; Matt 23:1-12
Resp. Psalm: Ps 50:8-9, 16bc-17, 21 and 23 (L 231)

We've heard it often but that doesn't lessen the fact that the teaching of Jesus is so contrary to our world's standards. To be able to hear his hard sayings and truly to be shocked by them would be an accomplishment for most of us. Listen again: "The greatest among you must be your servant" (Matt 23:11) and "Whoever exalts himself will be humbled; / but whoever humbles himself will be exalted" (Matt 23:12). All this is so opposed to the self-promotion that is a regular feature of life today. It may have started or been given an impetus by Muhammed Ali, but it's fairly commonplace for us to proclaim that we are, if not the greatest, at least way up there. An approach in line with Christ's words would be to let our goodness, closeness to God, humility shine out and exert their attractiveness. It's probably a legitimate complaint that so much of our life is commercialized. We advertise ourselves to get a promotion, to get a job. We must prepare self-adulatory resumes. "The best can opener on the market" is one thing and forgivable but "I am the best" is of another order. Perhaps we have no choice but to go along with some of the self-promotion in our occupational world, but we should not take it too seriously. In our life in Christ, the pattern is still that of Christ himself, put before us daily at this Eucharist: "The greatest among you must be your servant" (Matt 23:11). "Whoever humbles himself shall be exalted" (Matt 23:12).

Wednesday of the Second Week of Lent—*At the side of Jesus*

Readings: Jer 18:18-20; Matt 20:17-28
Resp. Psalm: Ps 31:5-6, 14, 15-16 (*L* 232)

"Command," the mother of the sons of Zebedee asks Jesus, "that these two sons of mine sit, / one at your right hand and the other at your left, in your kingdom." Apart from her mistaken idea that the kingdom of Jesus would be like Caesar's or Napoleon's, the remarks of the concerned mother probably reflect the ambitions of her two sons as well as her own (cf. Mark 10:35-45). When Jesus says in response, "You do not know what you are asking" (Matt 20:22), he may be thinking of the two who will be at his right and left. At the crucifixion in Matthew's Gospel we read, "Two revolutionaries were crucified with him, one on his right and the other on his left" (27:38). This is the way one gets to be so close to Jesus, at his right hand and at his left—by sharing in his crucifixion. "Can you drink of the chalice that I am going to drink?" (Matt 20:22), he asks the sons of Zebedee. With an almost adolescent nonchalance and unaware of what they are committing themselves to, they reply, "We can" (20:22). We've all probably had the same experience of promising something or taking on something, while not truly realizing all it may mean. We have to grow into what we have promised. Can we really know what the marriage vows will mean in the years to come? Or religious vows? Jesus says to the disciples and to us, "My cup you will indeed drink" (20:23; NAB). The cup is a share in his suffering and death, in a way unique to each of us and which is unavoidably part of living a good life. Here at this altar where we eat the bread and drink the cup of the Lord, we commit ourselves to sharing in his passion and death (see 1 Cor 17-34). Lord, you promise your cup to us and give it to us here; help us also to drink it as you did, in loving service to God and neighbor (see Matt 22:37-39).

Thursday of the Second Week of Lent—
Solidarity with Lazarus

Readings: Jer 17:5-10; Luke 16:19-31
Resp. Psalm: Ps 1:1-2, 3, 4 and 6 (*L* 233)

Pope John Paul II said that "the Lazarus of the twentieth century stands at our doors" (Yankee Stadium, October 2, 1979). Many of them. Compared to the seemingly endless expanse of the universe, we on this planet really are one large neighborhood. The skeletal figures of the starving we see on our televisions are rarely more than a few hours from us in terms of modern transportation. Like the rich man in today's parable, of course, we can pretend not to see them, but they are outside our doors nevertheless. With the number of international agencies that seek to alleviate this poverty and famine, there are means available to all of us to do something about these problems. Many have come to revitalize the idea of fasting by seeing it as (1) a way of experiencing our solidarity with the starving and (2) a way of setting aside money to give to some charitable group. Fasting in the older meaning of disciplining ourselves or subduing the body often seems to stop with the self. But this more utilitarian version of fasting may do something for our self-control while adding our little bit to the alleviation of the lot of the poor of the world. It helps assure that we do not forget the lot of so many of our fellow human beings. It brings into daily life the solidarity with others which we celebrate in our communion here.

Friday of the Second Week of Lent—
Dying and rising in our lives

Readings: Gen 37:3-4; 12-13a, 17b-28a; Matt 21:33-43, 45-46
Resp. Psalm: Ps 105:16-17, 18-19, 20-21 (L 234)

The effective teaching techniques of the Lord show up in this parable about the tenants of the vineyard. After telling the story, a clear picture of what will happen to himself, Jesus says to his hearers, the chief priests and elders, "'What will the owner of the vineyard do to those tenants when he comes?' / They answered him, / 'He will put those wretched men to a wretched death / and lease his vineyard to other tenants / who will give him the produce at the proper times'" (Matt 21:40-41). His hearers in answering his question pronounce their own fate. We all value much more the conclusions we ourselves have come to than those someone else tries to teach us. We've probably all had the experience of learning, in some sense, material in a classroom or a textbook, even passing tests on it or writing about it, only to learn many years later through experience what the material really meant. This is true, above all, of the Paschal Mystery which we celebrate all year round—but especially at Mass and in this Lenten Easter season. Even our attempts during Lent to teach ourselves the value of self-denial or self-giving cannot match the learning that takes place almost while we aren't looking. We learn how suffering and difficulty lead to new life and resurrection only through the hard lessons of daily life. The loss of a family member to death or mental illness often teaches the lesson. Losing our job and going through the attendant discouragement and accepting the help of others too can teach us the same. All we hear about the cross and resurrection of the Lord and their point in our lives becomes ours through experience. Lord, help us through our presence at this re-presentation of your passion and resurrection to see and love the same in our lives.

Saturday of the Second Week of Lent—*God's reckless love*

Readings: Mic 7:14-15, 18-20; Luke 15:1-3, 11-32
Resp. Psalm: Ps 103:1-2, 3-4, 9-10, 11-12 (L 235)

Many have commented on how unsuitable is the usual title for today's Gospel, "The Parable of the Prodigal Son." He may be prodigal, that is recklessly wasteful, but the point of the story is surely how prodigal, extravagantly generous, the father is. It might encourage reflection to know that a commentator in the *International Bible Commentary* (Collegeville: Liturgical Press, 1998) names this story "The Parable of the Two Lost Sons." The younger son is lost and eventually realizes it; the Gospel says he came to his senses or he came to himself. He is lost and knows it. The older son whom we might call the good one "unfortunately knows it," that is, knows that he is good, and therefore can be called lost. His self-righteousness keeps him from being receptive to the Father's love. We don't know what he eventually did; the story is incomplete. The same commentator says: "But as with all of our lives each of us must decide what the ending to our incompleteness will be!"

Monday of the Third Week of Lent—*A wet spring*

Readings: 2 Kgs 5:1-15ab; Luke 4:24-30
Resp. Psalm: Ps 42:2, 3; 43:3, 4 (L 237)

Running through Lent as through any promising springtime are the waters of brooks and rivers. They all remind us of our baptism and renewing that baptism come Easter. The story of the cure of Naaman the Syrian in the Jordan underlines the simplicity of baptism, of using ordinary water as the means of our rebirth as children of God and members of the Body of Christ. For most of us, our journey in Christ to the Father, sometimes through hell and high water, began when people who loved us much as God does brought us to the font for the sacrament. Through our observance of Lent we express our desire for the renewed cleansing that comes through repeating our promises to live for God and abjure the devil. We all know that desire and longing can be simply ineffectual feelings but, on the other hand, they are necessary goads to us as we continue this Lent with hope of a new and better life in Christ. As we hear in the responsorial psalm, "As the hind longs for the running waters, / so my soul longs for you, O God." (Ps 42:2) And "Athirst is my soul for the living God" (antiphon; see Ps 42:3). Today's liturgy renews our determination as we near the middle of Lent that this truly be the springtime of our life in Christ. The Easter renewal of our baptismal promises is to be the full blossoming of our spring.

Tuesday of the Third Week of Lent—*Sin on a national scale*

Readings: Dan 3:25, 34-43; Matt 18:21-35
Resp. Psalm: Ps 25:4-5ab, 6 and 7bc, 8-9 (L 238)

The texts of Lent certainly heighten our personal or individual sense of sin. Today Azariah confesses the sins of his nation. Nations do perpetrate sin. In nations with representative government the sins of a nation are to some degree the fault of all of us. Like individuals, no nation is without sin. Possibly it would be good for most of us First World people to ask ourselves some questions about our national sins. Don't we seem to be too content, unquestioning in thinking our country as always and necessarily "number one"? Does patriotism require blindness to our faults and failures? For instance, it is commonplace for Americans, at least, to speak as if we were the world's greatest benefactor when, in fact, we seem to be way down the list from much smaller nations that proportionately do much more in the way of foreign aid. We might ask ourselves about our military and political activities abroad, in other countries. There are questions to ask about our use or abuse of the world's goods, of the environment, etc. There is our waste and casual use of so many of the world's resources. How long can we go on doing this in the face of so many nations that struggle for what we would throw away? The Gospel today is about the merciless man whose own debt was canceled but who refused to forgive those of his debtors. As we think today a bit about sin on the national level, this Gospel suggests what Pope John Paul II called for—and still many others have been urging: that the rich countries cancel the debts owed them by the undeveloped, poor countries. The disparity in standards of living on our small globe must shock us all and give us pause. What is to be done? What can you or I do? Most probably we cannot answer all this perfectly here and now, but enough of us should be thinking about it to perhaps in some way affect national policy and practice.

Wednesday of the Third Week of Lent—*Willing to listen*
Readings: Deut 4:1, 5-9; Matt 5:17-19
Resp. Psalm: Ps 147:12-13, 15-16, 19-20 (*L* 239)

The Rule of St. Benedict, written as a guide for life in a religious community, opens with these words: "Listen carefully, my son, to the master's instructions, and attend to them with the ear of your heart . . . The labor of obedience will bring you back to him from whom you had drifted through the sloth of disobedience" (RB 1980 [Collegeville: Liturgical Press, 1981]). Irrational examples of obedience have led many of us to think of it as some sort of giving up of intelligence and freedom, some kind of groveling before another. Both Scripture readings today raise the question of obedience for us moderns who so rarely hear the word used seriously. Our only use of it may be in regard to training dogs. Moses promises the Israelites in Deuteronomy that if they obey "carefully" (Deut 4:6) all that he commands them in God's name they will draw close to God and be blessed. And the words of Jesus about minute obedience to every bit of the law and the prophets have caused discussion and perplexity over the centuries. "[W]hoever obeys and teaches these commandments / will be called greatest in the Kingdom of heaven" (Matt 5:19). Some help comes to us from looking at the origin of the word obedience. Our English word is from a Latin word meaning to listen. Obedience today must refer to a willingness to listen to each other, to what God says to us through them and their needs, to listen to what our circumstances or environment are asking of us. Married people with children especially show us, if we're unsure, what obedience means. Their lives are determined, often with great benefit to their character, by every cry and movement of the little people.

Thursday of the Third Week of Lent—*Faithfulness*
Readings: Jer 7:23-28; Luke 11:14-23
Resp. Psalm: Ps 95:1-2, 6-7, 8-9 (*L* 240)

"Faithfulness has disappeared; / the word itself is banished from their speech" (Jer 7:28). One is struck again and again at how contemporary the words of even an ancient book like that of the prophet Jeremiah seem. Divorce rates and a reluctance to make any marital commitment point out how difficult faithfulness is for today's generation. Commentators in our own time, speaking of marriage or any kind of lasting commitment, wring their hands at the lack of lasting commitment, the inability, apparently, of many to promise faithfulness to anything beyond the next ten minutes. "I took the morning off from work to be at the house and the repairman didn't come." Commitment is not up there with fulfillment in today's vocabulary. Religious orders find that men and women either cannot make the commitment at all or are only ready for it when they're in their thirties. During Lent we are preparing ourselves once again to profess our faithfulness to our baptism, to our adoption as sons and daughters of God (in other words, our commitment as Christians). On Easter we will renew our baptismal promises. Perhaps there is hope for commitment in the fact that the younger generation today often does come to it, only later than earlier generations. And even those who don't think it is for them are often impressed by the commitment of a long and happily married couple or by the regular care a family gives to a handicapped child. A love of faithfulness is a treasure.

Friday of the Third Week of Lent—*More than words*

Readings: Hos 14:2-10; Mark 12:28-34
Resp. Psalm: Ps 81:6c-8a, 8bc-9, 10-11ab, 14 and 17 (L 241)

It's a slight phrase and certainly not the heart of today's readings but it may be a handy springboard. "Take with you words, / and return to the LORD" (Hos 14:3). This we hear in Hosea. Words are the stuff, of course, of homilies. And we use them a lot in prayer too, though prayer, of course, can be simply a matter of desires and groaning. We all know something of both the power and the frailty of words. We need words but they have their limitations. When it comes to a strong passion like love—or any profound experience—words often just don't do it. Dance and art and music have to do it. We cannot, for instance, put the Eucharist into words. We try, sure, but whatever we say will always leave out something else. If we stress that the Mass is a sacrifice, we risk forgetting that it is a meal. Words at one time can express our thanksgiving; at another time, our repentance. They are meant by their nature to say something particular or specific. To express ideas and feelings about something profound and large, we need symbols, art, music. Too many words, especially in our life in Christ, can make for a religion which is all in the head. Aware of this, the church breaks up reading and words in the liturgy with music. That's one reason so much of the Mass itself is in the gestures of offering and of a meal. How do you express, for instance, all that a meal can mean? Our Lord's repeated insistence on love as the evidence of union with God shows too how much more our faith is than words (see Mark 12:29-31). It has to be action, deeds, like the ones we have put before us at every Mass.

Saturday of the Third Week of Lent—*Dependence*

Readings: Hos 6:1-6; Luke 18:9-14
Resp. Psalm: Ps 51:3-4, 18-19, 20-21ab (*L* 242)

With all due respect to the philosophers, it seems true that dependence on God cannot be learned from a book or taught in a classroom. Experience must teach us. Certainly, becoming a parent for the first time teaches many a young couple some insight into dependence, the recognition that we come from God and depend on God every instant of our life. Rougher experiences also may teach it: recovering from alcoholism or beginning anew after sinking to the depths in our moral life. Good health, a balanced personality, and a pretty happy life may make it difficult to appreciate our dependence on God; they lull us into a false sense of self-sufficiency. The publican knows his weakness and dependence on God. Lack of experience or lack of sufficiently high ideals for ourselves may fool us into thinking everything's just rosy. Experience and true self-knowledge can bring us to acknowledge lovingly and freely that we need God, that we need forgiveness, that we need help. Such an attitude prepares us to get the most out of our assistance at the Lord's table, at the Lord's sacrifice.

Monday of the Fourth Week of Lent—*Faith works wonders*

Readings: Isa 65:17-21; John 4:43-54
Resp. Psalm: Ps 30:2 and 4, 5-6, 11-12a and 13b (*L* 244)

In these last weeks of Lent, Isaiah presents a vision of what the world of the resurrection will be like: there will be a new earth and a new heaven where there will be no more mourning or weeping, only gladness and happiness (see 65:17-19). The suffering, pain, discomfort, and drudgery that we almost become resigned to is not meant to be. In today's Gospel, the cure Jesus works of the son of a royal official is a sign that this kingdom of joy and peace has arrived. All who put their trust in the word of the Messiah open themselves to the life of the resurrection. It's important to note that the official believed the word of Jesus apart from any signs or miracles, and he then went on to find his faith justified in the cure of his son at that very moment. This is consistent with the famous words of Jesus to Thomas about how "Blessed are those who have not seen and have believed" (John 20:29). Trust in Jesus and in his word brings its own verification in the good that happens within us as a result. There are undoubtedly two approaches to this in Scripture: in many places we do read of the indignation of Jesus, for instance, at those who have seen what he did and still do not believe (see, for example, Matt 11:21-24). Yet here the urging is rather to believe in his Word and to then experience the miracles, the wonders. Faith will enable us to see wonders even if faith is not the results of wonders.

Tuesday of the Fourth Week of Lent—
Renewing our life in Christ

Readings: Ezek 47:1-9, 12; John 5:1-16
Resp. Psalm: Ps 46:2-3, 5-6, 8-9 (L 245)

Water, water is everywhere in today's readings. Undoubtedly we're meant to think of baptism and of Lent as our preparation for renewing our baptismal promises at Easter. Fitting in with the momentum of the season as we move toward Holy Week is also, of course, the narrative about the Sabbath dispute. The claims of Jesus to be able to cure on the Sabbath (see also John 7:19-24) and thus "making himself equal to God" (John 5:18), these explain the animosity of some of his fellow Jews. That eventually leads to Jesus' passion and death. The water motif is certainly dominant in that odd episode from Ezekiel. Whatever else we make of it, we see here the life-giving qualities of water enumerated: water makes possible the growth of the trees which produce our food and often our medicine. Baptism gives life to spirits dead through sin and gives us the medicine of immortality. The man who had been sick for thirty-eight years waits to be let down into the curing waters of the pool. Jesus, the source of all that curative power, heals him. We have been plunged into the water of baptism and are on the way to our full cure, shown in the resurrection of Jesus. Concentration on practices of Lent must not make us lose sight of Lent's meaning. All we do this season is designed to enliven a more generous faithfulness to our baptism—and so open us to healing.

Wednesday of the Fourth Week of Lent—
To cherish and nourish life

Readings: Isa 49:8-15; John 5:17-30
Resp. Psalm: Ps 145:8-9, 13cd-14, 17-18 (L 246)

Implicit in almost every word of Scripture is the value of life, appreciation for a gift which can be so easily and tragically crushed. All that God wishes to do for us humans comes under the heading of enhanced life. The message of hope that we read so often in Isaiah always points to a better life, one free from disease and death. In the Gospel all that Jesus does is focused on life: he cures and tells us he has come to give us life, even eternal life (see John 5:24). Those who petition him know this; they say such things as, "come . . . before my child dies" (John 4:49). And they hear from Jesus, "your [child] will live" (John 4:50). Much of our society's dedication, no matter how distorted at times, to health and fitness comes from the same concern. You can debate about how much should be spent to enhance human life but behind it all is still the strong drive to live. We Christians share our society's passion for life but are more realistic in realizing that life has to mean more than these eighty or ninety years. Because these few decades can hardly be described as fulfilling for many, the eternal dimension of life is all the more important. We share our world's love for life and know through faith that God is the source and best support of that love. That beautiful comparison of God's love for us to the tender care of a mother for her child—that is more testimony to how central life is (see Ps 131:2). Whether we care for children or not, we have daily opportunities to share God's care for all life.

Thursday of the Fourth Week of Lent—
Witnessing to our faith

Readings: Exod 32:7-14; John 5:31-47
Resp. Psalm: Ps 106:19-20, 21-22, 23 (L 247)

We're justified in thinking many of the speeches and/or soliloquies in John's Gospel are a bit rambling. You would have a hard time outlining them as you may have been taught in school with Roman numerals, followed by A, B, C, etc. The thinking and language in John is often described as circular but the themes are obvious. Today we hear a lot about witness or testifying. There is certainly enough here to remind us that we do—or don't—by our lives and words gives testimony, that is, shows others what we believe, what we hope. Too often we Catholics have left any public witnessing to either our own clergy and religious, to a few lay activists, or to some other more militant Christian group. The style and the volume of our witness are up to us and depend, of course, somewhat on our background and temperament. But there should be some evidence in what we say and how we act for our faith in Jesus Christ. For instance, in the case of a coworker or family member whose language consistently lowers the tone of life around us, can we not, without counterproductive nagging, at least express disapproval or suggest something else? Or, with the sad, discouraged, hopeless people we meet, can't we offer some hope flowing from our faith? Certainly we could get some guff for this; so what's new? The Gospel is largely about how Jesus' acts and claims got him in trouble. We are his followers.

Friday of the Fourth Week of Lent—
Jesus, the teacher, and more

Readings: Wis 2:1a, 12-22; John 7:1-2, 10, 25-30
Resp. Psalm: Ps 34:17-18, 19-20, 21 and 23 (L 248)

"You know me and also know where I am from" (John 7:28). A constant theme in John's Gospel is that though his hearers claim to know Jesus' origins (Galilee), they do not really know where he is from—from God. Our faith in Jesus means that we see more in him than a man from Galilee, more than simply a good man or a persuasive teacher. We follow him as one who is from God and who leads us to God. This is what distinguishes Jesus from other authorities, gurus, popular evangelists, great teachers; it distinguishes him from Jerry Falwell, Oprah, and the Dalai Lama. The one whom we follow and who is put to death for his claims not only teaches the way to God but is "the way" (John 14:6), makes possible our movement to God. There are other ways of saying it too: Jesus lives in and makes us one with God through his own union with God, or we live in Jesus and are carried by his power and life to God (see John 17). In the sacraments we are lifted up to God and united to God. The great paradox of Holy Week recalls that human beings put to death the one who is the source of life, above all of the life that unites us forever to God (see Heb 5:9). Jesus is "the way and the truth and the life" (John 14:6).

Saturday of the Fourth Week of Lent—
The passion of many good people

Readings: Jer 11:18-20; John 7:40-53
Resp. Psalm: Ps 7:2-3, 9bc-10, 11-12 (L 249)

While we are already at this point in Lent recalling the events of the passion, death, and resurrection of the Savior, it is important not to separate this recalling from the lives and sufferings of every other human being, ourselves included. The lives of the prophets—like Jeremiah whom we hear in the first reading and the life of the Great Prophet, Jesus—are marked by what is undoubtedly one of the greatest pains a human being can endure. To be misunderstood, considered a deceiver, to be the object of the plotting and schemes of your fellow human beings, to be mistrusted and treated as a danger to the world, this is a kind of ostracism that crushes anyone. Nicodemus tries to suggest to the Pharisees that it might be good to hear what this man Jesus has to say and to get the facts before condemning him, but they only taunt him in return. For most of us misunderstanding and misrepresentation by others will not be a matter that threatens our physical life but the anguish it causes brings an unsurpassed interior pain. It can hurt our reputation; it can cause pain and despair that no one can share. The good word from Jeremiah is in his prayer: "But, you, O Lord of hosts, O just Judge, / searcher of mind and heart" (Jer 11:20). Whatever our private pains and hurts, they are known to God and through them we share in the Cross of Christ. By our solidarity with him in the sacrifice put before us at the altar and by our trust in him we are assured of final vindication. With Jeremiah and the Lord we say, "to you I have entrusted my cause!" (Jer 11:20).

Monday of the Fifth Week of Lent —
You are the object of God's love

Readings: Dan 13:1-9, 15-17, 19-30, 33-62 or Dan 13:41c-62; John 8:1-11 (Years A and B) or John 8:12-20 (Year C)
Resp. Psalm: Ps 23:1-3a, 3b-4, 5, 6 (L 251)

Though the first story of Susanna and her false accusers is quite lengthy, it is one of those memorable stories that lingers in our minds and suggests almost endless reflection. Both stories today picture a disregard for the woman in the case; in the Gospel story the Pharisees don't care about the woman or her injured husband but only about getting at Jesus. In the story from the book of Daniel the woman again is to be sacrificed to the lust and hypocrisy of the two elders. Popular culture today likes to credit our age with every bit of advancement for the oppressed, the poor, the marginal, for women. Such a sweeping claim, of course, needs qualification. The Gospel shows the genuine consideration and respect of Jesus for women. The passage about the woman taken in adultery has a mysterious history, and most scholars do not think it was originally part of John's Gospel where it now stands. It certainly reads in many ways like one of the stories in Luke, who so loves to emphasize the role of women. After the scribes and Pharisees have used the woman in an effort to get at Jesus, it is he who addresses her as a person, "Woman, are they? / Has no one condemned you?" (John 8:10). This reminder to treat every human being as another "you" (see Mark 12:31 and parallels) might be enough to take away from today's readings. Christ died for every "you."

Tuesday of the Fifth Week of Lent—*To expect all from Jesus*

Readings: Num 21:4-9; John 8:21-30
Resp. Psalm: Ps 102:2-3, 16-18, 19-21 (L 252)

"[I]f you do not believe that I AM . . ." (John 8:24)—this expression which Jesus uses strikes our ears as bad English or at least incomprehensible. But with that line the Jesus of John's Gospel offers his antagonists some hope after their very sharp exchanges. We expect when a person ends a sentence with "I am" to hear a bit more about who he or she is. For example, it might have gone, "Unless you come to believe that I am the Messiah or that I am the Savior." "I AM" is used here almost like a title. Jesus is the "I AM." In the Jewish Scriptures the expression was used of YHWH to insist that YHWH was unique, the only God of the Israelites. Jesus uses it in these discourses in John to point to the fact that God is uniquely present in him. Jesus is asked, "Who are you?" (John 8:25). And Jesus says by this expression that he is, as we would say, "the only Son of God" (from the Gloria), God's revelation to the world. The discussion in today's reading tells us to reflect too on who and what we see in Jesus. He must be more than any other teacher or guru or god. To him, in prayer and at this altar, we go for help and consolation in difficult straits, in crushing disappointments, in mortal illness, and in the death of loved ones. "[T]here is no other name under heaven given among mortals by which we must be saved" (Acts 4:12; NRSV).

Wednesday of the Fifth Week of Lent—
With us in the midst of the flames

Readings: Dan 3:14-20, 91-92, 95; John 8:31-42
Resp. Psalm: Dan 3:52, 53, 54, 55, 56 (*L* 253)

The story of the three young men in the fiery furnace without a doubt leaves an indelible impression on our imaginations. The whole story, though abbreviated here, would repay reading in its entirety. It is full of poetic repetition that makes you want to join in the next chorus. Inevitably, the exotic names given the three young men, "Shadrach, Meshach, and Abednego" (Dan 3:14), led to their use in a song. (It's really odd that they haven't caught on more for triplets!) Good writers and speakers capture our attention by the kind of vivid concreteness that we find in this story. Nebuchadnezzar's report of what he saw in the furnace is unforgettable: "Did we not cast three men bound into the fire?" (Dan 3:91). "I see four men, unfettered and unhurt, / walking in the fire, and the fourth looks like a son of God" (Dan 3:92). What a picture for us of our God and Christ who walks with us in every peril, worry and terror, who walks with us even in "the valley of the shadow of death" (Ps 23:4; KJV). The angel sent from God to save Shadrach, Meshach, and Abednego pictures for us the Savior of the world who delivers us all from the terrors of death. We can make ours the words of the hymn that Shadrach, Meshach, and Abednego sing after their deliverance: ". . . bless the Lord; / praise and exalt him above all forever. / For he has delivered us from the nether world, / and saved us from the power of death; / He has freed us from the raging flame / and delivered us from the fire" (Dan 3:88).

Thursday of the Fifth Week of Lent—*Another season of hope*

Readings: Gen 17:3-9; John 8:51-59
Resp. Psalm: Ps 105:4-5, 6-7, 8-9 (*L* 254)

"Are you greater than our father Abraham, who died?" (John 8:53). John's point, of course, is that yes, truly, Christ is greater than their father Abraham. This Gospel is full of such ironic statements. In chapter 4 the Samaritan woman had asked Jesus, "Are you greater than our father Jacob?" (4:12). And, of course, he is greater than Jacob too. Jesus underlines the point, "Abraham your father rejoiced to see my day" (8:56). In Christ and specifically in his resurrection all the promises made to Abraham around two thousand years earlier are fulfilled. Any other fulfillment before this was only provisional: the chosen people received the Promised Land, they were fed in an emergency with manna, and they were delivered from physical slavery. Yet all that pales alongside of the assurance from Jesus that if they are true to his word, they will never see death, that a new world has begun. The discussion here points to the resurrection, to Easter, when every promise ever made to Abraham or the Israelites earlier is surpassed, when God announces through the Son that death has been overcome too. All of Lent and all of life come to a conclusion that could never have been really expected by people like ourselves, used to experiencing sickness, suffering, and death. Like all the seasons of our liturgy, Lent too is a season of hope.

Friday of the Fifth Week of Lent—*Always with us*

Readings: Jer 20:10-13; John 10:31-42
Resp. Psalm: Ps 18:2-3a, 3bc-4, 5-6, 7 (L 255)

These hot arguments between Jesus and his countrymen, called "the Jews" in John (for example, 10:31), may reflect discussions in the early church between these Jews and other Jews who had accepted Jesus as the Messiah. Nevertheless the liturgy puts them before us day after day at this point in Lent to make clear to us the hostility toward Jesus which will lead to his suffering and death. The reading from Jeremiah too points to the events of Holy Week by offering the example of how the prophet was persecuted as a picture of what happens to Jesus. "Denounce!" "Perhaps he will be trapped; then we can prevail, / and take our vengeance on him" (20:10). At the very least the torments that prophets and Christ himself suffer should reassure us who meet much smaller obstacles that this is par for the course. Belief in Jesus, holding on to the Savior is never without its difficulties. For us it may involve many lesser irritations and struggles, everything from boredom and lassitude to differences with others and unsuccessful struggles against the same old faults. Jeremiah again is a model for us. In the midst of his persecutions, he says, "But the LORD is with me, like a mighty champion" (20:11). Every time we share in the body and blood of the Lord and in his sacrifice we are reminded that we have a mighty champion with us, within us, in fact. True, he calls on us to share his Cross, but he stays with us through whatever happens.

51

Saturday of the Fifth Week of Lent—
Happiness is a by-product

Readings: Ezek 37:21-28; John 11:45-56
Resp. Psalm: Jer 31:10, 11-12abcd, 13 (*L* 256)

Despite what it is meant to guarantee, the expression "the pursuit of happiness" from the Declaration of Independence is really misleading. Someone (Eric Gill) has said, speaking of artistic creation, that if you seek truth and goodness in what you make or do, beauty will follow as the result of that pursuit. Similarly, in human life, in our life as Christians, happiness is the by-product of the search for goodness and love, i.e., for the Lord. To seek happiness itself as a goal simply encourages the pursuit of our own and most likely, instant gratification, something far removed from happiness. The verse after today's Gospel offers a pregnant parenthesis (the Gospel having told us that people were looking for Jesus): "For the chief priests and the Pharisees had given orders that if anyone knew where he was, he should inform them, so that they might arrest him" (11:57). The author of this Gospel is very fond of such irony: they were seeking him to arrest him; on the other hand, according to John, everyone should be seeking Jesus because life and salvation are not found anywhere else. If anyone knows where Jesus is to be found they should report it. Of course they should! No one can find genuine happiness unless he or she first finds Jesus. Happiness and joy come, the Christian knows, from finding Jesus in faith and knowing life in him. It follows from that. We who know that Jesus is to be found in the community of believers, in the Scriptures, and in the sacraments will tell others so that they may find life and happiness. Happiness is the by-product of finding Jesus.

Monday of Holy Week—*To kill the "author of life"* (Acts 3:15)

Readings: Isa 42:1-7; John 12:1-11
Resp. Psalm: Ps 27:1, 2, 3, 13-14 (*L* 257)

Irony, the dictionary says, is, "The use of words to convey the opposite of their literal meaning" (*The American Heritage Dictionary of the English Language* [1970]). Again, we hear it in John's Gospel. And it's not rare in ordinary life; we all use it at times. We say to friends when tempting them to the raspberry white chocolate cheesecake, "Sure, no calories in that." Not only words but events in John are presented with irony. In today's reading, Christ has given Lazarus back his life, raised him from the dead, and his opponents want to end Jesus' life. They want to kill the one who gives and restores life! What irony! His enemies may not have seen it that way, but John does, and he expects that we, his readers, too will see what irony there is in their plotting against Christ. It says something about the perversity of human nature that we are all capable of doing the opposite of what we claim to believe and missing the inconsistency. Unfortunately with age and experience we let devious patterns of thought develop and shut ourselves off from seeing things as they are or accepting anything new. Prayer for an open heart and mind, for more of the child's simplicity and wonder is always in order (see Matt 18:2-3). It would help us to see that at times our actions and words are so opposed to what we claim to hold dear. If our actions, words, beliefs, and ideals were all to be truly united and consistent, we would avoid the kind of irony present in today's Gospel reading. We could leave it for more innocent matters, like the calories in cheesecake.

Tuesday of Holy Week—*Peter and/or Judas*

Readings: Isa 49:1-6; John 13:21-33, 36-38
Resp. Psalm: Ps 71:1-2, 3-4a, 5ab-6ab, 15 and 17 (L 258)

Judas and Peter are an age-old pair in the New Testament. They offer contrast and similarity, each a mirror of tendencies and movements within ourselves. Both play a part in the way Jesus fulfills Isaiah's picture of the Suffering Servant of YHWH. The Suffering Servant in Isaiah is one who saves others by his self-sacrifice. Both Peter and Judas contribute to the burdens of the Servant, Jesus. And both show us different degrees of disloyalty and differing responses to their own failures. The complexity, the twists and turns of our human nature, are most evident when we see them on display in the actions and words of other real people like Peter and Judas. If we don't go the whole way with Judas in betraying the Master, at least with Peter we have moments of great inadequacy when faced with the demands of discipleship. So often like Peter we cannot now follow the Lord; we aren't prepared, generous enough. But, as Jesus says to Peter, "you will follow later" (John 13:36). Discipleship has its ups and downs, its steps forward and steps backward. Our Lent has been an effort to prepare us to renew our baptismal commitment to the Lord, to make it less fickle, more steady. Like Peter we promise to lay down our lives for Jesus and then go completely counter to that generosity on another day. Lord, as we share your meal again, help us to greater faithfulness to you, to a life more consistent with what we do here.

Wednesday of Holy Week—*Our plans and God's plans*

Readings: Isa 50:4-9a; Matt 26:14-25
Resp. Psalm: Ps 69:8-10, 21-22, 31 and 33-34 (*L* 259)

No matter what differing perspectives the evangelists bring to it, the paschal mystery is an extraordinarily familiar example of how human passion and action intertwine with God's desire to save us from sin and death. Matthew says that Judas, after being paid the thirty pieces of silver for the betrayal, "looked for an opportunity to hand him over" (26:16). Literally he was looking for a "good moment." Similarly, the Lord says, "My appointed time draws near" (26:18). The time of the betrayer and the time of the Savior meet to bring about the redemption of the world. The corruption of Judas by his desire for wealth (see John 12:6) and possibly other factors in his character lead him to facilitate the arrest of Jesus by the authorities. At the same time, the paradox of God's willingness to be emptied of power and surrendered to the powers of evil is realized with the help of Judas. "God writes straight with crooked lines" has never seemed more evident. Similarly, in incomprehensible ways, our most devious plans as they meet God's presence in the world come to the most unexpected results. Our intentions and activity are never the whole story no matter how much we fool ourselves into thinking so. God acts in all this too. The believer welcomes this and opens to it by prayer. "Prayer is an invitation to God to intervene in our lives, to let His will prevail in our affairs; it is the opening of a window to Him in our will" (Abraham Heschel).

Season of Easter

Monday of the Octave of Easter—
"You will show me the path to life" (Ps 16:11)

Readings: Acts 2:14, 22-33; Matt 28:8-15
Resp. Psalm: Ps 16:1-2a and 5, 7-8, 9-10, 11 (L 261)

If only all those who make daily Mass a practice during Lent could be persuaded to include the Easter week! The readings for this great week are full of the freshness of that great morning when the Lord rose. With only the texts of Lent and without these texts we miss so much of that toward which Lent was tending. In the risen Lord we see what God intends for all of creation, a new life that conquers the evil, sin, brutality, and suffering that mar the present. "God raised [Jesus] up, releasing him from the throes of death, / because it was impossible for him to be held by it" (Acts 2:24). So we hear from Peter. Our confidence that God is working even now in our messed up world and in us, despite resistance and lethargy, finds beautiful expression in the psalm Peter quotes. Good words to take with us today and to make our theme: ". . . my heart has been glad and my tongue has exulted; / my flesh, too, will dwell in hope, / because you will not abandon my soul to the nether world / . . . . / You have made known to me the paths of life; / you will fill me with joy in your presence" (Acts 2:26-28; see Pss 16 and 18).

Tuesday of the Octave of Easter—*God knows us by name*

Readings: Acts 2:36-41; John 20:11-18
Resp. Psalm: Ps 33:4-5, 18-19, 20 and 22 (L 262)

Freud and friends have said endlessly that a religion like Christianity especially is all wish fulfillment, that believers simply take their dreams for reality. They wish to believe in a God who knows them by name and loves them; they wish to believe that the pains of this life will be offset by the joy of new life after death. It might be good to point out here that the difficulty Mary and the others have in recognizing Jesus tells us that they were as surprised as anyone could be by this turn of events. The resurrection was not wished into being by their imagination. Today's Gospel account is full of freshness and surprise. After Mary has mistaken Jesus for the gardener he calls her by her name, "Mary!" (John 20:16). We all know from experience how surprised and happy others are when we remember their names after meeting. You call out, "Jack," and the light in the face tells you how much it means. God, despite Freud and friends, knows each of us by name, as persons. A life of prayer and faith enables us to truly respond to God with similar intimacy, to call God our Father and Christ our Brother. So often it's God who knows our name and calls us by name while we feel awkward in addressing God because of lack of daily experience. The risen Christ walks among us; the more we speak to him, the more we become, in the best sense of the word, familiar with him.

Wednesday of the Octave of Easter—*The Lord stays with us*

Readings: Acts 3:1-10; Luke 24:13-35
Resp. Psalm: Ps 105:1-2, 3-4, 6-7, 8-9 (L 263)

The Lord's resurrection, like other wonderful events, is many sided in its splendor and meaning. And when it is described in the memorable language of Luke this is all the more true. Take the words of the disciples to Jesus: "Stay with us, / for it is nearly evening" (Luke 24:29). While the rising of the Lord is the occasion for incomprehensible joy, it also underlines what his death had told them: he is no longer with them as he had been. But the story beautifully shows us that though risen he is still with us; he definitely has decided to "stay with us." He can be met, served, and loved in the stranger we meet along the way, in the friends yet to be made on our journey through life. Risen, he is more easily available everywhere, no longer simply in Palestine or the first century. He is present in all those we serve and honor in this life. And, further, he stays with us in the breaking of the bread, in the Eucharist, both in the word we hear and the bread and wine we eat. And beyond that he is with us in the community and priest we meet at this table. We can go further and remind ourselves that celebrating his presence with ordinary bread and wine at a table also tells us his risen presence is now all around us. We need not look for visions in the sky but can find him in the ordinariness of life, in both its sorrows and joys, its magnificence and its lowliness. The crises of life especially urge us to call out: "Stay with us." Our celebration of Easter at the very least tells us that risen, the Lord is always with us, always present, in crises and in joy.

Thursday of the Octave of Easter—*Not a ghost*

Readings: Acts 3:11-26; Luke 24:35-48
Resp. Psalm: Ps 8:2ab and 5, 6-7, 8-9 (*L* 264)

Yesterday's passage from Luke, which precedes today's, illuminated the presence of the risen Lord in word, sacrament, and other people. And all that was done through the medium of an unforgettable and evocative story. We have more of the same today, a story again filled with concrete detail, telling us much more than a theological treatise on the risen Lord would ever say. The detail and specifics today stress the reality of his risen presence, one might say the physicality of his body. "But they were startled and terrified / and thought that they were seeing a ghost" (Luke 24:37). To counter this notion and still their fear, Jesus tells them to touch his body. When they remain "still incredulous for joy and were amazed" (24:41), he asks for and eats some fish with them. Despite all the attempts to make something so outside ordinary experience as the resurrection acceptable to human reason, the Gospel writers keep insisting that what they are witnessing is not simply a psychological state. Human life, with its miseries and atrocious tragedies and unimaginable pains, is to be transformed, re-created. And there is continuity with the person we are now: the risen Lord is able to be seen and touched, able to share table fellowship with his friends. Not only is the body not a negligible part of human existence, it is intrinsic to our existence. Even transformed as in the firstborn from the dead, Jesus, our life is in some unheard-of way still bodily. "Touch me and see, because a ghost does not have flesh and bones / as you can see I have" (24:39).

Friday of the Octave of Easter—*Morning has dawned*

Readings: Acts 4:1-12; John 21:1-14
Resp. Psalm: Ps 118:1-2 and 4, 22-24, 25-27a (*L* 265)

We know, of course, that there are those among us for whom the very mention of "morning" produces anxiety or some sort of pain. Yet, morning seems most appropriate for resurrection appearances of Jesus. Morning is the beginning of a new day; the resurrection marks the beginning of the new age, the new life given to those who believe in Christ. A new day has dawned for human beings. "[T]hat night they caught nothing. / When it was already dawn, Jesus was standing on the shore" (John 21:3-4). There is no indication of the time of the year but if Jesus and the disciples are going to have breakfast on the shore it must be a somewhat temperate time. A morning by the lake can be so still and fresh, a time appropriate to a new beginning. With the guidance of Jesus even the disciples' fishing is turned around and they make a huge catch. In chapter 15 of this Gospel, Jesus had said, "without me you can do nothing" (v. 5). The risen Christ, no longer limited by his previous existence to Palestine in the first century, lives in the members of his Body as their strength and hope. Everyone who has shared fresh fish cooked by the lakeside understands the mystique of such a meal. And the words and gestures here remind us of the Eucharist and other meals with Jesus. The Lord "took the bread and gave it to them, / and in like manner the fish" (21:13). Present for all time in our midst through the bread and wine of the Eucharist, the Lord invites us all, on this new day, this new morning, to peace and fellowship: Come and eat your meal! (see 21:12).

Saturday of the Octave of Easter—
Coming to believe in the resurrection

Readings: Acts 4:13-21; Mark 16:9-15
Resp. Psalm: Ps 118:1 and 14-15ab, 16-18, 19-21 (L 266)

Mark's summary of appearances of the risen Christ and in fact all the accounts we've been hearing tell us that our faith in the resurrection is not based on the testimony of a bunch of gullible people. Just two lines in Mark tell us what we have in more detail in the other Gospels. Jesus' followers refused to believe Mary Magdalene's account, and as for the disciples "walking . . . to the country," "they did not believe them either" (16:12-13). The disciples, after the death of Jesus, Mark tells us, were "mourning and weeping" (16:10). They didn't dream up the resurrection as a psychological solution to their distress and sorrow. It was something forced on them by reality and repeated testimony. All the evidence in the Gospels of how slow and uncomprehending the disciples were about who Jesus was during his lifetime and how unwilling they were to believe that he had risen, all this should be a great encouragement to us who may be assailed by doubts and problems about our faith. Some, at least, of our prayer during this Eastertide should be for a firmer, more genuine faith in the risen Lord and all that means for human misery and death. The joy that echoes in the church's prayers and liturgy, in the music of this season, can be truly ours if we'd reflect more on these texts that show us the resistance of the disciples to believing in the resurrection. Eventually, many of them came to die for their belief. May they pray for us that we share in that same faith.

Monday of the Second Week of Easter—*Open to the Spirit*

Readings: Acts 4:23–31; John 3:1–8
Resp. Psalm: Ps 2:1–3, 4–7a, 7b–9 (*L* 267)

Appropriately during this Easter season today's Gospel speaks of that rebirth or birth from above which is our baptism. Nicodemus recognizes that Jesus has come from God and Jesus says to him: "no one can see the kingdom of God without being born from above" (John 3:3; NAB). The "from above" can also be rendered "again" (note in NAB). There is an element in our salvation which is not in our control; the Spirit must bring us to new birth. On Easter Saturday or Easter Sunday we renewed our baptismal promises, ended our Lent with a new birth. While rebirth is a gift of the Spirit, our response, our decision, is the other side of it. There should be signs in our life of a renewed life in us. Things should be different, better. If there is a tendency to let it all slip, we can call on the Holy Spirit prayerfully to ignite and power our willingness to be raised up with Christ to a new life. We died with Christ in baptism in order to walk with him in newness of life (see Col 2:12). Holy Spirit, let us not too easily accept a return to our old way of living; help us to be open to new things in our life and to expect much from you.

Tuesday of the Second Week of Easter—
A community of believers

Readings: Acts 4:32–37; John 3:7b–15
Resp. Psalm: Ps 93:1ab, 1cd–2, 5 (*L* 268)

The lofty language of Christ's discourses in John's Gospel is consoling. Today's Gospel concludes telling us that all who have put their trust in the one who was lifted up on the cross and raised from the dead will have eternal life in Christ. The reading from the Acts of the Apostles is likewise on an ideal plane but suggests to us how in practice this eternal life we have will show itself here and now. Acts describes the daily life of the early Christians—presumably in the glow of the resurrection. Theirs was a profound unity, a sharing of all they had and a concern that no one in their midst should live in deprivation. We know from elsewhere in Acts and our knowledge of ourselves and human nature that such a perfect society was almost too good to be true. Rougher critics among us will go further and dismiss it as "communist." No matter what we call it, such a society where people live in unity and share the goods of the earth would be like a paradise compared to our world. At present our world is divided into the small number who have wealth and consume most of the world's resources and, on the other hand, masses of others who lack the basics for human dignity. Even apart from the concern we all should have as voters that our world and society be just to all, in our more local setting there are immediate things to be done. Parishes, if they are to approach the beautiful ideal pictured in Acts, can do much to show concrete concern for the neglected, the poor, the elderly, the homeless and abandoned in their midst. And they do it with the generous help of their members.

Wednesday of the Second Week of Easter—
To tell of God's love

Readings: Acts 5:17-26; John 3:16-21
Resp. Psalm: Ps 34:2-3, 4-5, 6-7, 8-9 (L 269)

Probably no biblical words have been painted on rocks or printed on bumper stickers more often than the ones we hear in today's Gospel: "God so loved the world that he gave his only-begotten Son, / so that everyone who believes in him might not perish / but might have eternal life." Some just say: John 3:16. And if we're going to paint the words of Jesus on rocks what more appropriate or essential ones could we find? "God so loved this world . . ." The apostles are persecuted and made to suffer for this message throughout the Acts of the Apostles. We hear today that an angel released them from prison so they could resume their preaching "about this life" (Acts 5:20). The new life we Christians have and which we celebrate throughout this Easter season is a life filled with the assurance that God loves us and that in us God will conquer all the forces of sin and death that otherwise make this world such a hostile place. Crime, gangs, violence, injustice, abuse have all been targeted by the risen Christ. In view of, on the one hand, the shortness of life and, on the other, the joyousness of the message, you would expect that we would be doing more to preach this message: "God so loved the world . . ." Lives of trust and joy, of generosity and confidence, preach the message most effectively. But there's room for us to say a word or two also about the message, about God's love in situations of despair, hardship, crushing grief. That kind of preaching cannot be left only to priests, on the one hand, or to extremists and those who use the Gospel to threaten nonbelievers. Those who are confident in the love we celebrate at the altar and hear in the Scriptures will want to share it.

Thursday of the Second Week of Easter—
We all preach the Good News

Readings: Acts 5:27-33; John 3:31-36
Resp. Psalm: Ps 34:2 and 9, 17-18, 19-20 (*L* 270)

We must be struck by what we hear day after day in the Acts of the Apostles about the persecution of the apostles and their unflagging determination to preach about this man Jesus and the extraordinary things that have happened to him and through him. After being imprisoned or chastised for their preaching and released we find them right back in the marketplace preaching again. After being threatened by the authorities, we hear them in today's reading: "We must obey God rather than men" (5:29). And they resume their preaching. As all of us who have sat through or given uninspiring or somehow substandard sermons know, preaching in the strict sense of the word requires work, preparation, and enthusiasm—all aided by God's grace. But in the broader sense of the word, we all can and must imitate the apostles in their conviction that they had to speak out about what they believed. How do we do it? Not necessarily in words. We can profitably think of the appropriate ways in our life: by consoling others, by simply helping with difficult matters, by our presence to the hurting, by bringing cheer or hope to others, and the list goes on. Genuine belief in the risen Lord spills over into life and action, shows itself in hope and perseverance (see Jas 2:18-20). That is preaching for most of us.

Friday of the Second Week of Easter—
Help from other world religions

Readings: Acts 5:34-42; John 6:1-15
Resp. Psalm: Ps 27:1, 4, 13-14 (*L* 271)

Because of a fuller knowledge of the rest of the world since the time of the apostles and because of better communications, we know much more than the New Testament people did of various saviors and religious teachers. We know of religious teachers worldwide who, unlike those mentioned in the first reading, have survived and flourished for many centuries in various parts of the world. Think of the Buddha and Mohammed. Faith that Jesus is the Son of God, the Savior of the world, faces bigger challenges in our world. The Sanhedrin member argues that if a religious leader was from God the teaching or following would survive. At the Second Vatican Council, the church recognized that God's truth has come through these other religions to human beings. Catholics, it said, do not reject any of this. The word catholic, which means universal or all-embracing, reminds us that our faith in Jesus Christ as the Son of God and savior of the world does not require a hostile attitude toward other religions. In fact, our faith urges us to look for elements of the truth in them. A slightly different emphasis than we are used to can be fruitful for our life in Christ; an insight from another religion can deepen our own.

Saturday of the Second Week of Easter—*We all serve*
Readings: Acts 6:1-7; John 6:16-21
Resp. Psalm: Ps 33:1-2, 4-5, 18-19 (L 272)

The text from Acts about the appointment of seven men as deacons has lessons for us today. For one thing, it tells us how early the need arose for some organization among the early Christians. Second, it points to the central position of service in Christian life. Almost any good purpose human beings are ever involved in requires some organization in order to get us to focus energies, to achieve our purpose. Even religious groups in Christianity that grew up in opposition to organization have ended up organizing themselves. All of us are probably right in worrying about organization because there is the undeniable tendency of institutions to become more concerned about their own survival than about their original purpose. We help avoid that ourselves if we are personally committed to the ideal of service, if we realize that there should be many of us lined up to be of service to the poor, the sick, the uninformed, the oppressed. Another word for service is ministry. More and more, in recent decades, we have been recalled to the idea that all of us have some service, some ministry to perform in the Christian community. Where is my place? That's a question we should be sure to answer and soon.

Monday of the Third Week of Easter—*Why we come to God*
Readings: Acts 6:8-15; John 6:22-29
Resp. Psalm: Ps 119:23-24, 26-27, 29-30 (L 273)

The exchange between Jesus and the crowd in today's Gospel should raise questions for all of us about what we expect from God, from Christ, from religion or from faith. "Amen, amen" he says to them, "you are looking for me not because you saw signs but because you ate the loaves and were filled" (John 6:26). Following Jesus around because he is sort of a traveling and low-cost bakery is a pretty crass example of looking to faith for cut-rate products. We human beings with our tendency to make everything revolve around ourselves are prone to look for self-satisfaction in everything, including religion. One hears occasionally of preachers who actually promise material success or well-being for faith. It doesn't have to be that crass to reflect our self-seeking. We can come to religion for peace of mind and a general tranquility. We can look to religion for miracles that will save ordinary human effort and skill. We can come to religion to have our merely human values, for instance, as middle-class people, confirmed. We can come to religion to avoid facing the real problems in our own lives or our world. Certainly religion can produce a profound peace and courage in the face of life's storms and pains. But this is a by-product of centering our lives on God, of giving our faith and trust to God (see Isa 8:17; Heb 2:13). Many can do that and still suffer terribly. God and our faith in God do not take us out of this world but help take us through it (see John 17:15). As someone has put it, we must seek the God of miracles and consolation, not the miracles and consolation of God.

Tuesday of the Third Week of Easter—*Food for the spirit*

Readings: Acts 7:51–8:1a; John 6:30-35
Resp. Psalm: Ps 31:3cd-4, 6 and 7b and 8a, 17 and 21ab (L 274)

"[W]hoever comes to me will never hunger, / and whoever believes in me will never thirst" (John 6:35). Obviously Jesus is not talking about our daily ration of corn flakes, meat and potatoes, coffee and milk. He is speaking of how satisfying is his teaching, the wisdom he brings to humankind. After telling the crowd about the true bread from heaven given by his Father and getting the crowd to want it— "give us this bread always" (6:34), he clinches the discussion by telling them, "I am the bread of life" (6:35). He makes a claim which will seem repugnant to some of our contemporaries. They reject the notion that anyone, God included, can answer any of the big questions definitively. But, part of the satisfaction that God gives us in the Word made flesh (1:14) is assurance about some very big matters. For instance, Jesus teaches that love is indisputably to be preferred to hate; forgiveness is always better than vengeance (see the Sermon on the Mount, for example); God's love for us is eternal and will take us into an eternal life with God (see John 17). Sure, Jesus is not giving answers to questions about the constitution of matter, the size of the universe, or the best way to dispose of atomic waste. Nor is he telling us how to solve the housing crunch in San Francisco or deal with an autistic child. But he does tell us that in him and not in some merely human guru or technique we find rest for our restless hearts, assurance for our fears, hope for the future.

Wednesday of the Third Week of Easter—
Obsessed with the resurrection

Readings: Acts 8:1b-8; John 6:35-40
Resp. Psalm: Ps 66:1-3a, 4-5, 6-7a (L 275)

A Latin American bishop, living close to persecution and martyrdom because of his advocacy for the poor, says that living this way means he values the Cross but always as linked to the Resurrection. "I don't just insist on the Resurrection. I'm obsessed by the Resurrection," he says. In today's reading from Acts the persecution of the apostles seems only to trigger more vigorous preaching. They too must have been obsessed by the Resurrection. The resurrection of the Lord is shorthand for all that faith expects. By it we mean that we trust God will have the last word, will bless the good, second all our positive efforts, turn around the defeats and suffering that mar human life. The Resurrection should be more like an obsession in our lives too, something which propels us onward, encourages us, keeps us hopeful amid discouraging realities. Could it possibly keep us generally happy and pleasant too? It certainly justifies such dispositions. Jesus says, "For this is the will of my Father, / that everyone who sees the Son and believes in him / may have eternal life, / and I shall raise him on the last day" (John 6:40).

Thursday of the Third Week—
"[He] continued on his way rejoicing" (Acts 8:39)

Readings: Acts 8:26-40; John 6:44-51
Resp. Psalm: Ps 66:8-9, 16-17, 20 (L 276)

The early Christian writer Irenaeus says that God could not leave to decay in the earth the body of one nourished in life by the body and blood of the Lord. Our sharing in the sacrament of the Eucharist is our assurance, here and now, of eternal life with God. This view is similar to what Jesus says in this discourse on "the bread of life": "whoever believes has eternal life" (John 6:48, 47; NAB). Eternal life has begun already; it is in us by virtue of faith and, Irenaeus specifies, by reason of our union with the Eucharist. After the Ethiopian eunuch receives the good news about Jesus and is baptized, he "continued on his way rejoicing" (Acts 8:39). Our faith in the Lord, his assurances of what faith does and what the Eucharist does, all this should in the nor-mal course of events make us rejoice. The philosopher Nietzsche, so savagely critical of Christianity, wrote that Christians would have to show a lot more joy to convince him. It seems only appropriate that Christians should add to the overall joy and hope of the world around them. We should expect—and pray for—some joy to follow from our faith and be apparent in our daily life.

Friday of the Third Week of Easter—
Recognizing the Body of Christ

Readings: Acts 9:1-20; John 6:52-59
Resp. Psalm: Ps 117:1bc, 2 (L 277)

"Saul, Saul, why are you persecuting me?" (Acts 9:4). This truly world-shaking phrase is dropped in here so casually and then not developed. "I am Jesus, whom you are persecuting" (Acts 9:5). Perhaps it was taken for granted by the readers, but twenty centuries later it remains a truth we do not sufficiently recognize. For Christians it makes even more pointed the solidarity of the human race which we have from our common origin; it tells us that persecuted Christians in any part of the world, the homeless waifs of our big cities, and the victims of poverty are part of the one body which we all are. More close to home, the poor and neglected widow from the parish, the disabled in the group home, and the sharp-tongued neighbor are members of the same body. There is really only one Body of Christ: the risen Christ, we baptized believers, and the eucharistic Body and Blood of Christ are all one. The reverence we show to the bread and wine at Mass must be matched by similar reverence and love for our neighbors. The Body of Christ is more present than we perhaps imagine; we may limit the presence too much to the altar or tabernacle. Saul's own identification with Christ becomes real when it is said that he must suffer for the name (see Acts 9:16). What we receive here strengthens us for the same struggle, a struggle that ends in joy.

Saturday of the Third Week of Easter—*Both/and*

Readings: Acts 9:31-42; John 6:60-69
Resp. Psalm: Ps 116:12-13, 14-15, 16-17 (L 278)

A television journalist reported some time ago that there were people in medicine today who believed one could depend on both Prozac and prayer. This was presented as some sort of amazing new discovery. For most Christians it's old hat; we've always been able to turn to God and to medicine for help in illness. For Christians it is not an either/or matter: either medicine or divine help. This says something too about the aids we may use in our life as the followers of Jesus. After this strong teaching on the "bread of life" (John 6:48), the writer reports that some left Jesus' company. Jesus asks the twelve if they are going to leave him too. Peter speaks for them and us: "Master, to whom shall we go? / You have the words of eternal life" (6:68). We hear in Peter's words the Christian belief that the words of Jesus have the priority for us; by them we judge all other wisdom. Our faith does not require that we reject all other insight and helps to a good life but that we give the central place to the prayerful study and absorption of the Word of God. Just as we may use Prozac and prayer, chemotherapy and sacraments for our health, we may use psychology and psychiatry, yoga and Zen meditation, science and art—along with Scripture and prayer for our spiritual growth. Jesus has the words of eternal life but they echo in many other places on this planet. He and his words can work with and through all the other good thoughts and practices of human beings.

Monday of the Fourth Week of Easter—
To welcome those who are different

Readings: Acts 11:1-18; John 10:11-18 (Year A); John 10:1-10 (Years B and C)
Resp. Psalm: Ps 42:2-3; 43:3, 4 (L 279)

The critics of Christianity like to paint it and its followers as narrow and self-satisfied. It has to be admitted that Christians over the centuries have given enough excuse for this. Even today one hears television evangelists who urge their listeners to pat themselves on the back for being Christians while at the same time damning Hindus as dirty idol worshipers. Easter is, however, not about the happy lot of a small group of human beings but about the extraordinary destiny of the human race: life with God and victory over death. In today's first reading, Peter faces the narrow and stiff-necked who would begrudge the good news of Christ to non-Jews. Finally, they are convinced that God's love extends beyond their narrow boundaries "and they glorified God, saying, / 'God has then granted life-giving repentance to the Gentiles too'" (Acts 11:18). Jesus too expects his followers to be open to this broadening of the preaching of the Good News: "I have other sheep that do not belong to this fold. / These also I must lead, and they will hear my voice, / and there will be one flock, one shepherd" (John 10:16). Possibly in our day and in our parish this means that we be more accepting of recent immigrants in our parish or people of different ethnic background than ours. In us they can see the Gospel of Christ as welcoming.

Tuesday of the Fourth Week of Easter—*Open to the new*

Readings: Acts 11:19-26; John 10:22-30
Resp. Psalm: Ps 87:1b-3, 4-5, 6-7 (L 280)

Someone has written that miracles do not so much produce faith, as it is faith that produces miracles. In these daily selections from Christ's dialogue with his contemporaries, Jesus seems to appeal to both sides of this issue. At times he urges the miracles and works he has done as reason for believing in him. At other times he insists that some initial faith (or good will) is necessary before one can recognize who he is. This initial faith is a requirement that preserves our freedom. Signs and miracles do not of themselves suffice to force any one of us to believe in Jesus as the Messiah. On our part there must be good will, a receptivity to something, "Someone" beyond ourselves, beyond our powers. The antagonists of Jesus that figure so prominently in this Gospel are really simply people who are not open, who are smug and unwilling to hear any challenge to the way "we have always done it." Wherever we read or hear "Jews" here we can substitute ourselves in our resistance to challenge, in our unwillingness to expect anything new from God. The Gospel of John is not anti-Semitic but anti-smug. Lord, keep us from self-satisfaction and unwillingness to see the unusual ways in which you may appear to us.

Wednesday of the Fourth Week of Easter—
We are our own judges

Readings: Acts 12:24–13:5a; John 12:44-50
Resp. Psalm: Ps 67:2-3, 5, 6 and 8 (L 281)

In the discourse on the bread of life Jesus tells his hearers that those who eat his bread and drink his blood already have eternal life; that life has begun (see John 6). We hear again today from Jesus the same insistence that what we call the last things have already begun in the present. He says: "Whoever rejects me and does not accept my words / has something to judge him: the word that I spoke" (John 12:48). Judgment, contrary to what the artists are almost forced to suggest to us, is not so much a matter of human beings appearing before a judge in a courtroom and having their behavior reviewed. Judgment takes place now whenever we place our actions alongside our conscience, a conscience instructed by the Word of God. No one can replace this internal judge, our own conscience, for any of us. Popes, bishops, priests, moral theologians, all are guides; none can replace the conscience, no matter how much we may feel the need for their help or seek it. The American bishops have written, for instance, that they and we belong to "a spiritual tradition which accepts enlightened conscience, even when honestly mistaken, as the immediate arbiter of moral decisions" (*Human Life in Our Day*, ¶147 [1968]). In other words, no person, no guide outside ourselves, can replace our personal responsibility for what we judge good or bad.

Thursday of the Fourth Week of Easter—*We need silence*

Readings: Acts 13:13-25; John 13:16-20
Resp. Psalm: Ps 89:2-3, 21-22, 25 and 27 (L 282)

If we could only catch more of the excitement of the disciples of the risen Christ who felt compelled to tell the whole world that God had raised this man from the dead and made him everyone's Savior. The driving force behind all this missionary work about which we hear in Acts is the resurrection of Jesus. The world the disciples found themselves in was one of both despair and longing, despair over the emptiness of life and longing for meaning and hope. At times it seems like our world is also one of despair over the emptiness of life but in other ways unlike the ancient world. With the help of technology and the huge industry concerned with our entertainment, we modern people are able to avoid the despair by filling life and time with enough artificial excitement and noise. We only get to the longing, or sharpen our longing for Christ and what he can do, if there is some silence in our life, some willingness to face up to our own interior life. While we all may need recreation and even entertainment—they are different—still we shouldn't be afraid to allow silence in our lives. Silence can help us realize the inadequacy of the noise and excitement, can help us realize that the needs of our heart are deeper and larger than these worldly satisfactions. Even if we aren't caught up in the superficialities of daily life, silence can sharpen our need for Christ, our willingness to allow his activity in us. Silence and reflection throughout our life open us to the power and presence of the risen Christ whom we meet here especially.

Friday of the Fourth Week of Easter—
Let me hide myself in you (cf. Ps 17:8)

Readings: Acts 13:26-33; John 14:1-6
Resp. Psalm: Ps 2:6-7, 8-9, 10-11ab (L 283)

Chapter fourteen of John's Gospel contains Jesus' message of comfort and consolation to his disciples who are distressed at his words about "going away" (8:21; 14:28) from them. He has to tell them that his going will be a greater blessing yet for them. They will come to a closer union and intimacy with him than they have now. May not all the talk about places, rooms, mansions, be a concession to our materialistic thought when we know the real "place" of our consolation is Jesus himself? The fullness of eternal life and the revelation of God's love are all found in Jesus, in his person, not in some place. It's not where shall we go but "to whom shall we go" (6:68). And the answer is Jesus; the "dwelling places" or "mansions" (KJV) or "rooms" (NIV) are all found in him (John 14:2). After he departs this world he returns to make himself present through the Holy Spirit. His risen presence with us is more intimate and close than his physical presence in a room with us could ever be. Before his death Jesus lived among a small number of Palestinian people; after the Spirit is sent, he lives everywhere and within all who believe in him. The old hymn ("Rock of Ages," Augustus Montague Toplady, 1775) has a line "Let me hide myself in thee." This very personal devotion catches the truth that the person of Jesus is the center and that our life as Christians is lived in him. In him God is revealed to us and in him we give God perfect praise and worship.

Saturday of the Fourth Week of Easter—
God present in Jesus

Readings: Acts 13:44-52; John 14:7-14
Resp. Psalm: Ps 98:1, 2-3ab, 3cd-4 (L 284)

There are theological and practical implications in Jesus' strong statement to Philip, "Whoever has seen me has seen the Father" (John 14:9). Jesus and the Father are one in a way which must have been very difficult for his early followers to understand. More immediately we might think what it means to us for Jesus to make that claim. What have we seen Jesus doing in the Gospels? His actions should tell us much about God. In contradiction to philosophical notions of God as above and beyond our world and life, Jesus has shown us a caring and involved God. The God we see in Jesus was willing to depend on his creatures in his infancy, for instance, and after his crucifixion. He was able to identify with the sufferings and hardships of these same human creatures. We see this in his healings, in some cases attended by signs of his strong emotion; we see it in his stilling the storm (see Mark 4:35-41, for example). We see his compassion and love in his tears for Lazarus (see John 11:1-44). On the way to the cross and on the cross he demonstrates a concern for other suffering people (see Luke 23). He even shares on the cross in our sense of abandonment (see Mark 15:34). Above all on the cross (Luke 23:43) but on many other occasions too, he shows the willingness of God to forgive. Any brief recall of the Gospel stories would bring to mind many other examples of the caring and concerned God pictured in Jesus. To see the Father in Jesus is to see a God compassionate to the point of tears.

Monday of the Fifth Week of Easter—*A way of living*

Readings: Acts 14:5-18; John 14:21-26
Resp. Psalm: Ps 115:1-2, 3-4, 15-16 (L 285)

"The Advocate, the Holy Spirit / whom the Father will send in my name— / he will teach you everything / and remind you of all that I told you" (John 14:26). Earlier in the same Gospel reading we heard, "whoever loves me will be loved by my Father, / and I will love him and reveal myself to him" (14:21). These are thoughts found elsewhere in John's writings. The idea here is that the true disciple, in union with Christ and through him with the Father, has this "Advocate" (or "Comforter"—KJV) within and does not need to rely so much on external authorities. We understand this best as referring to the profound and deeply seated assurance and confidence a Christian can have from union with Christ. The idea is not that we will receive special revelations about the end of the world or the beginning of a war or about someone's cancer. As the text says, rather, Christ will reveal himself to us. Our knowledge of Christ, gained from sermons, reading, reflection, etc. will become something we experience, something that accompanies us all the time. Our knowledge of Christ will be like that of someone in love who knows in a way he or she cannot possibly communicate fully to others that he or she is loved. As always, what God wants to reveal to us is not so much a set of truths as conviction about this way of living.

Tuesday of the Fifth Week of Easter—*Encouragement*

Readings: Acts 14:19-28; John 14:27-31a
Resp. Psalm: Ps 145:10-11, 12-13ab, 21 (L 286)

Encouragement. Who does not need it? Further, is there anyone among us who does not give it? We may not always—thank goodness—consciously think of what we do and say as being encouragement, but much of it is. Our friendliness, good cheer, interest in others, a pat on the arm, willingness to help them with their burdens and even lesser needs—all this constitutes a kind of encouragement to others. Much of our ability to survive depends on encouragement. It tells us that what we are doing is worthwhile, helpful, good. The Acts of the Apostles and the letters of Paul all attest to concerted efforts to encourage those who had received the Good News. In today's reading, Paul and Barnabas illustrate a pattern of encouragement. Retracing their steps to where they had been received, "They strengthened the spirits of the disciples / and exhorted them to persevere in the faith" (14:22). They tell their own story and encourage the fledgling disciples in the face of hardships with the account of all they had been through. If they can still hope and preach the Good News, why not you? Giving encouragement could well be a matter of recalling the Gospel, the message of Christ, for our friends and those we want to help. On the other hand, it may not always be so overt. We can encourage by simply affirming the good others are doing, backing their efforts and good will, letting our own faith and trust shine through in a good spirit and hopefulness.

Wednesday of the Fifth Week of Easter—*Vine and branches*

Readings: Acts 15:1-6; John 15:1-8
Resp. Psalm: Ps 122:1-2, 3-4ab, 4cd-5 (L 287)

God's chosen people are frequently called God's vineyard in Scripture (Isa 5, for example). Like sheep and shepherd, vines and vineyards are unfamiliar sights to many an urban dweller, yet with the help of television stories and wine-tasting visits to wineries nearly all of us have some idea of what is meant. Going from calling the people God's vineyard to what Jesus says in today's Gospel seems to indicate an even closer unity of God and people. We hear, "I am the true vine, and my Father is the vine grower" (John 15:2). "I am the vine, you are the branches. / Whoever remains in me and I in him will bear much fruit, / because without me you can do nothing" (15:5). Elsewhere in the New Testament we hear that we live "in Christ" (2 Cor 5:17) and he in us (see John 17:23), that we are made partakers of the divine life (see 2 Pet 1:4), that God "dwells in" us (Rom 8:9; cf. Acts 17:28). In Christ we share one life in God, despite our failings in love, despite our dry and empty feelings at times, despite disease wearing away our

71

bodies. In our union with Christ lies all our hope for strength to do better, the strength to love more generously, the power to forgive and understand. Perhaps we need to call on that life within us more often and with more firm conviction that God's power and love are so available. Each time we share at this altar that life in us is nourished and we are given the opportunity to thank God for it and to draw upon it for strength, courage, and generosity.

Thursday of the Fifth Week of Easter—
The nitty-gritty of love

Readings: Acts 15:7-21; John 15:9-11
Resp. Psalm: Ps 96:1-2a, 2b-3, 10 (*L* 288)

Yesterday we heard and reflected on the beautiful words, "I am the vine, you are the branches. / Whoever remains in me and I in him will bear much fruit" (John 15:5). Today Jesus specifies further what we will produce, "Remain in my love. / If you keep my commandments, you will remain in my love" (John 15:9-10). Love and the results of love are the evidence of our union with the Lord, of our sharing the life of the "true vine" (John 15:1), Jesus. And obeying the commandments of Jesus is evidence of the genuineness of our love. Despite the lofty tone of much of this discourse in John's Gospel, love here is never simply some airy idea, some warm feeling, some ineffectual wish. Love means seeing the opportunities to help others (with getting around, shopping for groceries, paying their bills), being sensitive to their desire for quiet or to the slow pace illness may be causing them. Love means seeing another's need for companionship or for some solitude. Beyond all this Jesus then tells us, "I have told you this so that / my joy may be in you and / your joy may be complete" (15:11). It's as if obeying the commands of Jesus, living out in practice the commandment of love, will lead to joy. Too often we seek joy or happiness in and for ourselves. Jesus is telling us that if we make love and the works of love our priority, joy and delight will follow. Joy is the by-product of a life lived in the works of love and selfless generosity.

Friday of the Fifth Week of Easter—*Why we change*

Readings: Acts 15:22-31; John 15:12-17
Resp. Psalm: Ps 57:8-9, 10 and 12 (*L* 289)

Catholics, as we all know, reacted variously to the changes made by the Second Vatican Council in Catholic life and practice. Both priests and laity shared these reactions. In many cases it was understood that the changes would only be really implemented when an elderly pastor or bishop had moved on. The early Christians with whom our readings these days deal were mostly at one time Jews. They found it hard to imagine any kind of religious life, even following the man they believed to be the Messiah, which would involve dropping the customs and beliefs of their upbringing. Somehow, they imagined and hoped that belief in Christ could coexist with the observance of the whole Law of Moses. Finally, with help from the apostles who were involved with non-Jewish converts, the church decided that indeed the practices of the Jewish religion no longer held for those who put their trust in Jesus, in the name of Jesus. A number of things were involved: the difficulty of change, dropping secondary or unnecessary practices, and, finally, putting all one's trust in Jesus. The changes brought about in the liturgy and practices of the Catholic Church have some similarities. Much of what has been done was an effort to clear away developments that obscured the face of Christ in the church, that detracted from an essential emphasis on his saving power and presence. In our continuing discussions about change and adaptation, we need to keep as our priority too whatever helps ensure the central place of the risen Lord Jesus Christ in our lives as Christians.

Saturday of the Fifth Week of Easter—*To change or to accept*

Readings: Acts 16:1-10; John 15:18-21
Resp. Psalm: Ps 100:1b-2, 3, 5 (L 289)

"If the world hates you, realize that it hated me first. / If you belonged to the world, the world would love its own; / but because you do not belong to the world" (John 15:18-19). Perhaps we need to be worried about too easy accommodation to the world, being too comfortable with all that is in our world. There is an inevitable tension in the life of any thoughtful person between changing the world and living comfortably in it. Religions or philosophies of life can be divided into (1) those that challenge us to change or even overturn the order of things in our world and (2) those that try to help us live in the world as it is. This is an issue for all of us. If we are only and constantly intent on altering our world we can make life very miserable for ourselves and everyone else. If we do not want to change anything or make any such effort, we tend to leave the world miserable for many others. If we learn somehow to live with life as it is around us we are on one path to happiness; if this is our only concern we can appear quite selfish and

73

indifferent to the pain and suffering of the world. What to do? Each of us must determine within the confines of our own obligations and situation where the emphasis should fall in our life at any one moment. Our differences in this matter show up in daily life. One is up in arms over the way the school handles certain situations; another finds that to be a matter to accept and not worth a big fight. In our conscience and before the Lord is where we best make our own decisions about such matters.

Monday of the Sixth Week of Easter—*How we witness*

Readings: Acts 16:11-15; John 15:26–16:4a
Resp. Psalm: Ps 149:1b-2, 3-4, 5-6a and 9b (*L* 291)

Our witnessing to Christ is so pale, so low-keyed—to put it mildly! In saying this the idea is not that we should go looking for ways to make ourselves really obnoxious, to bring on the desired persecution that would make us more like the kind of witnesses Jesus speaks of in today's Gospel. But it does seem that our faith in the Lord could permeate us more fully, be more influential in our lives, at least to the extent that others see it as intrinsic to our identity. We may not be called to ringing doorbells, passing out religious literature, or preaching in the mall on Saturday afternoon, but in some way a genuine belief in the Lord requires that we let it flow over into some visible, audible consequences. We might suggest to a despairing, inconsolable neighbor that he or she try prayer; we might tell another miserable friend why we hope, why we have joy amid difficulties. We might put more effort into finding something to read for a confused or uninformed friend. We could invite a neglected acquaintance to a welcoming parish liturgy. We might meet the cynicism of fellow employees with some trust in the possibility of change, improvement. The ways of witnessing are as varied as our lives and opportunities.

Tuesday of the Sixth Week of Easter—*Religious experience*

Readings: Acts 16:22-34; John 16:5-11
Resp. Psalm: Ps 138:1-2ab, 2cde-3, 7c-8 (*L* 292)

We can't say to anyone or even to ourselves: "Go out and have a religious experience." Some definite awareness of God working in our life or around us comes as a gift; we don't work ourselves into it as people may rev themselves up by pumping iron or thinking positive thoughts. But it is undeniable that religious experience is very power-ful. The jailer in today's first reading, after witnessing the freeing of the prisoners, asks Paul and Silas, "what must I do to be saved?" (Acts 16:30). To see something as extraordinary as this certainly would have an impact on most human beings. But while we can't produce reli-gious experiences like this, we can be more receptive to seeing God at work around us and in ourselves. In the jailer's case a miracle seems to have produced faith. Often it's the other way around: genuine faith produces or is willing to see miracles where others see just natural hap-penings. The way a particular individual brightens up our life, makes us happy, chases the clouds away is like a miracle for some of us. Why not? Can't God be helping us through such people? Faith that God is all around us and in other people can result in our seeing God at work more often, can result in our having what we can call religious experi-ence. Religious experience here means a kind of verification of our faith. Seeing good come to us through others or through events confirms for many of us that there is truly a God who cares for us. God isn't forced on us but God is perceivable with some openness on our part.

Wednesday of the Sixth Week of Easter—*The right moment*

Readings: Acts 17:15, 22–18:1; John 16:12-15
Resp. Psalm: Ps 148:1-2, 11-12, 13, 14 (*L* 293)

Both readings today meet in the recognition that human beings can only absorb so much at any one time. T. S. Eliot said somewhere, "Humankind cannot bear very much reality"; we could say, not too much truth or insight. Paul, speaking to the Athenians, starts where they are with a reference to their altar, "To an Unknown God" (Acts 17:23). He goes on to speak of other beliefs of theirs which he also shares; thus far they are with him. When he gets to the resurrection of Jesus some of them sneered and others put him off till some other time. This was too much for them. Jesus recognizes a similar situation with his disciples: "I have much more to tell you, but you cannot bear it now. / But when he comes, the Spirit of truth, / he will guide you to all truth" (John 16:12-13). If we reflect on our life in Christ we must realize that there are certain truths that we have only come to appreci-ate with experience, often with hard and painful experience. There are other truths we hear repeatedly in preaching or in Scripture which still puzzle us, which still await the right moment to mean anything to us. There is for most of us a time, determined by circumstances and the maturity of our heart, when the mysteries of human life and of God become clearer to us. All that is to be expected and simply tells us to be earnest in listening and open through prayer and reflection on our life to what God has yet to teach us. When the Spirit comes he will guide us to all we need to know.

Thursday of the Sixth Week of Easter—
Joy and sorrow on the same street

The following are used when the Ascension of the Lord is celebrated on the Seventh Sunday of Easter.

Readings: Acts 18:1-8; John 16:16-20
Resp. Psalm: Ps 98:1, 2-3ab, 3cd-4 (L 294)

At any given moment in our world's history or our lives there is weeping and mourning in many places. And, often only miles away or less, there is rejoicing and the sound of people enjoying life. Jesus says to the disciples, "Amen, amen, I say to you, / you will weep and mourn, while the world rejoices; / you will grieve, but your grief will become joy" (John 16:20). Both on the bigger stage and in individual lives, mourning and joy are often only minutes apart. We may be celebrating a family reunion with lots of favorite foods and joy in seeing seldom-seen relatives. Down the street another family may be agonizing over the senseless beating death of a daughter or son. Or, that favorite grandmother dies two days before her grandson's wedding. Our society and country may be enjoying prosperity and peace while a few hours away by air whole peoples are involved in life and death battles, mourning the spouses killed in war, children dead of starvation. There's no way of completely avoiding grief in our lives, and we probably aren't able to completely forget about the pains and sorrows of others. Yet the resurrection of Christ can instill in us a deep confidence that God did not make us or our world for sorrow and pain. That deep confidence will probably not save us from tears or stave off clinical depression but perhaps it will serve to be some light breaking through the clouds, momentarily at least, to tell us that this will pass. "[Y]ou will grieve, but your grief will become joy" (John 16:20). As we share the Lord's body and blood here, we remember that we share not only his suffering, cross, and death—but also his resurrection.

Friday of the Sixth Week of Easter—*Why?*

Readings: Acts 18:9-18; John 16:20-23
Resp. Psalm: Ps 47:2-3, 4-5, 6-7 (L 295)

"On that day you will not question me about anything" (John 16:23). Probably the most frequent question we humans ask is, "Why?" It begins with those little children just learning to talk; so often their response to everything is, "Why?" And it goes on all through our lives. Mostly in difficult times, in pain and trouble, we ask "Why?" And during this life we ordinarily are going to be left unsatisfied regarding the most important matters. Why we lose someone in death, why a friend is seriously injured in an accident, why we can't get along with someone—often none of these have satisfying answers. Despite our deep desire for security and certainty, most of this life must be lived in faith and trust rather than in full knowledge and clarity. The words in today's Gospel do tell us that suffering, pain, and mourning do not have the last word; they reassure our faith. But they do not alter the fact that we may have to "grieve for a time" and be "sad for a time." The triumph of Jesus over death is the great model for us and ultimate assurance that pain and evil do not have the last word. But in the meantime they can certainly break our hearts and destroy our happiness. The follower of Christ is not spared the pains of ordinary human life, not delivered from them by his or her faith. As long as life lasts, the pains, the difficulties, the questions remain. The difference is that the Christian trusts deep down that the one who raised Jesus from the dead will also raise us from our pains and death (see Rom 8:11); by this we are strengthened. Then our "hearts will rejoice" and no one will be able to take our joy from us (John 16:22).

Saturday of the Sixth Week of Easter—*The witness of prayer*

Readings: Acts 18:23-28; John 16:23b-28
Resp. Psalm: Ps 47:2-3, 8-9, 10 (L 296)

Yesterday's Gospel told us that there will come a day when we will have no more questions to ask of the Lord (see John 16:23). Even the most devout Christian must have questions at times about how prayer works, how effective it is, about why we should pray. But one of the most trustworthy signs of a believer is the willingness to pray, to continue to pray. In many ways our beliefs and our morals are less convincing signs of our following of Jesus than our praying is. Belief can, at times, be so simply a mental thing; the morals we practice are often duplicated by many nonbelievers. But prayer shows a profound confidence there is a God and that this God is concerned about all that we pray about. Prayer is a practice that makes absolutely no sense apart from a genuine trust in God and in God's willingness to help. It's true that none of us may have a sure grip on how prayer works but a belief in it is essential. When cancer strikes, when someone loses a job, when a marriage is in trouble, when a teenager seems headed for disaster, when an accident or illness worries us, we pray. We trust that someway and somehow God will help. Our trust does not mean we have to expect God to change the laws of the universe—it will more likely be something much more subtle. Perhaps as a result of prayer someone for whom we pray learns how to deal with some disaster or big worry. We are probably better off in the long run not trying to fig-ure out what God might or should do and instead trust that God has ways of which we know so little. "[A]sk and you will receive, so that your joy may be complete" (John 16:24).

Monday of the Seventh Week of Easter—
Between despair and trust

Readings: Acts 19:1-8; John 16:29-33
Resp. Psalm: Ps 68:2-3ab, 4-5acd, 6-7ab (L 297)

The conversation in today's Gospel suggests that the disciples are being tempted by a false sense of security. They say, "Now you are talking plainly, and not in any figure of speech. / Now we realize that you know everything" (John 16:29-30). No need to ask questions. We be-lieve you came from God. They think that it will all be smooth sailing from here on. But, unlike some of the popular preachers and gurus of our day, Jesus does not readily proclaim that things are so simple, so clear, so painless. He says in response to all this: Do you really believe? It isn't going to be long before you will leave me to my suffering, while you will be scared and concerned about your own skins. Believing and trusting in God, in Jesus, is never easy, never without its testing. Faith must be re-won, gained, again and again. Just when we think we've figured out human life and have some absolute certainties, something comes along to shake us up, to show how difficult faith is. Just as we daily pray for forgiveness at Mass, so we can profitably pray daily for faith, for genuine confidence in God. It should never be taken for granted. "I have told you this so that you might have peace in me" (John 16:33). The Holy Spirit, whose coming we celebrate soon, can and does give us peace, a deep trust that Jesus has "conquered the world" (John 16:33), as he says. But it is never an easy peace. Our life as followers of the risen Christ is lived between despair and a too-cheap confidence. Our trust in God and Jesus has to be learned every day. When we share at this table, the Lord certainly helps us see that.

Tuesday of the Seventh Week of Easter—
Learning from puzzles

Readings: Acts 20:17-27; John 17:1-11a
Resp. Psalm: Ps 68:10-11, 20-21 (L 298)

One of the advantages of our two-year cycle of readings for daily Mass
and the three-year cycle for Sundays, introduced since Vatican II, is that
priests and people are all exposed to more of the teaching of Jesus, the
Gospel. Paul's claim in the first reading is that he has always proclaimed
"the entire plan of God" (Acts 20:27). Not all of it, by any means, is
equally intelligible or palatable to us at any one time. It serves as a
good corrective for our lopsided and often self-serving desires. In what
we hear today of Jesus' farewell address he says he has given human
beings the responsibility of handing on the message: "I revealed your
name to those whom you gave me out of the world. / They belonged
to you, and you gave them to me, / and they have kept your word"
(John 17:6). Our receptivity to the message is probably the greatest
disposition we bring to it. Not all of us do formal proclaiming of the
Gospel, but all of us must pray and hope to be open to it, to receive
it, and to allow it to work on our transformation. It's often helpful
to make more of an effort to accept especially those parts of Scripture
which seem to mean little to us or seem outrageously strange.

Wednesday of the Seventh Week of Easter—
Better to give (see Acts 20:35)

Readings: Acts 20:28-38; John 17:11b-19
Resp. Psalm: Ps 68:29-30, 33-35a, 35bc-36ab (L 299)

In all we've been hearing about St. Paul these past weeks, Luke has
been at pains to show him and his life as a parallel to that of Jesus, an
example par excellence of the follower of the Lord. A very significant
word used today by Jesus in his prayer captures perhaps the essential
of discipleship. The word is "consecrate" (John 17:17, 19). It can be
rendered as "sanctify" also (KJV). Jesus, in praying for his disciples,
says, "Consecrate them in the truth" (17:17). "I consecrate myself for
them, / so that they also may be consecrated in truth" (17:19). The
basic meaning of the word is: to set aside or—in this context—to be set
aside for the good of the world. The word "dedicate" also suggests its
meaning (see the Amplified Bible). What we have put before us daily
at Mass is the consecration of Jesus to the Father, his self-giving suffering and death. We assist at this ritual re-presenting of his sacrificial

suffering and death so that we may benefit from it by joining our own lives to his in self-giving. Paul quotes a saying of Jesus which we only find in Paul, "It is more blessed to give than to receive" (Acts 20:35). The phrase, "It is better to give than to receive," has entered into our day-to-day use. What stands out in Jesus himself and that great model Paul is this giving of self to God's work, to the good of the world and of our fellow human beings. For us too, it is better to give than to receive. And, paradoxically, it is in giving that we receive (a thought made famous by the "Prayer of St. Francis"). "Come, Holy Spirit, come! / And from your celestial home / Shed a ray of light divine!" (Sequence of Pentecost).

Thursday of the Seventh Week of Easter—*Unity in diversity*

Readings: Acts 22:30; 23:6-11; John 17:20-26
Resp. Psalm: Ps 16:1-2a and 5, 7-8, 9-10, 11 (*L* 300)

It is more and more apparent that any "unity" of Christians that is to be realized will have to coexist with differences in the way we worship, the way we are organized, and even in beliefs. Ideals of uniformity for all Christians stem from a much later period than the New Testament which knew much diversity. Christians can be united to God without sharing every practice, law, and dogma of every church. There is a unity of which Jesus speaks in his great prayer for unity which is like that between him and the Father. In this unity believers become one because of their union by faith with the Father and Jesus. We become one by reason of Jesus living in us and the Father living in him. This is a unity with God the Father and Jesus Christ which is different from organizational unity. Ultimate unity of Christians will have to be based in this union with Father and Son, in the Spirit. And this unity will accept differences, even disagreements, on a host of matters. The Catholic Church and many other churches have long accepted that baptism joins us to Christ. Jesus is saying in today's Gospel that joined to him we are also being indwelt by the Father and are all one in the Father and him. That is more important than whether or not we use a particular formula in our services, have a particular church government, or celebrate Easter on different dates.

Friday of the Seventh Week of Easter—*Self-questioning*

Readings: Acts 25:13b-21; John 21:15-19
Resp. Psalm: Ps 103:1-2, 11-12, 19-20ab (*L* 301)

Our words pastor and pasture are related in their Latin origin; both refer to the care of the flock. The pasture is the place where the livestock graze, and the pastor is the shepherd or one who cares for them. In today's Gospel Peter makes up for his triple denial of Christ by a triple declaration of love. The Lord says to him three times: feed my lambs, my sheep. In other words, be a good pastor. Our times with much help from the media have learned that pastors too can fail to care and instead be a threat to their flocks. By now we have all heard of cases of sexual abuse or exploitation by priests. Our times have also brought accounts of others in authority more out into the open, such as cases of parents who have practiced the same abuse. Whatever else may be involved, these cases point out that all—pastors, parents, teachers—need to guard against their own weakness and their own self-seeking in caring for the young, the weak, and the defenseless. Our positions in parishes or families or schools are positions of trust and great responsibility. Like everything else in human life the noble status of parent, priest, or teacher can be corrupted by self-seeking. Painful as it may be, in everything we do we need to question and purify our intentions with the help of the grace of God. Self-seeking can enter into anything. For that reason it's most appropriate that as we assist daily at this sacrifice of the Lord we ask to enter into his self-forgetting. Our union with Christ at this altar can, with our cooperation, transform us into the likeness of him who denied himself so profoundly (see 2 Cor 3:18).

Saturday of the Seventh Week of Easter—*Our influence*

Readings: Acts 28:16-20, 30-31; John 21:20-25
Resp. Psalm: Ps 11:4, 5 and 7 (*L* 302)

"What if I want him to remain until I come?" (John 21:22). These words of Jesus to Peter led the community of believers around John to think that John was somehow not to undergo death (see v. 23). And, we must admit, the words are not crystal clear to us either. The reality that John actually did die disturbed them considerably. In our day, despite pretty conclusive evidence over the centuries, we still find some of this amazement at death, especially in the case of a celebrity like Princess Diana or Elvis Presley. In one way it may testify to our deep longing for eternal life; we don't think an influential life should end. And we do go about trying to continue the influence through memorials of various kinds. The ending of John's Gospel assures his fellow believers of his abiding influence and even presence through the Gospel witness he has left. "It is this disciple who testifies to these things / and has written them, and we know that his testimony is true" (John 21:24). John has lived on in the midst of the Christian community for centuries through the influence of his writing. Every Christian believer, whether aware of it or not, has depended much on the testimony of others. The testimony of the New Testament writers has clearly been one very strong influence. In the lives of each one of us there are many such influences that have fed our faith and nurtured our hope. No matter how tempted we are to the self-made approach, none of us is what we are apart from influences that range from Gospel writers to parents, teachers, and friends. Accordingly we ask: what kind of witness or influence am I on those around me?

Ordinary Time

Monday of the First Week in Ordinary Time—
A person not a principle

The following readings may be joined to those of the next day when the Baptism of the Lord is celebrated on Monday of the First Week in Ordinary Time.

Readings: 1 Sam 1:1-8; Mark 1:14-20
Resp. Psalm: Ps 116:12-13, 14-17, 18-19 (L 305)

People who study theology can be tempted to overestimate the importance of that study. Certainly, an intelligent person who is able to understand physics or the development of the Russian empire should also make an effort to understand Scripture and the content of faith on a comparable level. But none of this study should ever fool us about the essence of being a Christian: following an inspiring person. The call of the first disciples in today's Gospel makes clear that Jesus did not get them from a theological school or any kind of university. They were fishermen, basically simple men who lived by the work of their hands. And that which they left everything to follow was not a set of principles or some theology but an impressive person. They had undoubtedly heard and seen him before but now, in response to his call, they abandon everything to follow him. Human beings are not moved by principles and theories as they are by a human being who exercises some attraction and who exemplifies great ideals. In ordinary secular life (if life is ever simply secular) we do our best out of love for someone or loyalty to someone. That is what inspires us in depressing moments or difficult times: the thought of this person I love, this person whose presence quickens my pulse and makes all the pains of life seem trivial. The martyrs did not die for an abstract principle but out of love for a person, the Lord. Prayerful reflection on the Gospels and all they say about Jesus helps us recognize and rejoice in the fact that our faith is not an intellectual exercise (accepting some truths) but a matter of following an inspiring person. The Christian is not a believer in a collection of truths but the follower of an incomparable and all-lovable individual, Jesus Christ.

Tuesday of the First Week in Ordinary Time—
Continuing to trust

Readings: 1 Sam 1:9-20; Mark 1:21-28
Resp. Psalm: 1 Sam 2:1, 4-5, 6-7, 8abcd (*L* 306)

Commentators on Scripture point out that people of New Testament times believed in the presence and power of devils all around them and especially as causes of illness and harm. The two readings today both suggest some of the frustrations and ills of ordinary human life which lend credence to the notion that some evil power is at work. Like Hannah many a human being has hopes that seem so often doomed to disappointment. Or there is present in our life or that of our family and friends illnesses like those attributed to unclean spirits by Jesus' contemporaries. Childlessness, cancer, unemployment, accidents— the list seems infinite. In Hannah's case, "the LORD remembered her" (1 Sam 1:19) and she had her son, destined to be Samuel. The man in the Gospel too was relieved of the presence of the demon in his life, whatever form it took. Other Gospel stories suggest that some of these cases looked a lot like mental illness or epilepsy. It would be wonderful if one could promise healing and solution to all our problems in exchange for trust in the Lord. But we all know from the example of faith-filled people who nevertheless suffer that there is no such simple arrangement. Can the fact that the Scriptures show us people getting responses from God help us to trust? And there are friends who attest to that; maybe another time of our life attests to it also. Part of the faith we pray for and work at daily is maintaining a trust in God even when the answer to our prayer is long in coming or never evident. Help us, Lord, to be less self-centered, less anxious about our own personal needs, and more willing to respond to the needs and suffering of those around us. "Let me not so much seek to be consoled as to console . . . " (Prayer of St. Francis).

Wednesday of the First Week in Ordinary Time—
"[Y]our servant is listening" (1 Sam 3:10)

Readings: 1 Sam 3:1-10, 19-20; Mark 1:29-39
Resp. Psalm: Ps 40:2 and 5, 7-8a, 8b-9, 10 (*L* 307)

When Eli finally understands that it is the Lord who is calling Samuel, he gives him good advice: "Go to sleep, and if you are called, reply, / 'Speak, LORD, for your servant is listening'" (1 Sam 3:9). We give so much value to talking, even, in a sense, to thinking, to all the ordinary activities, that there is little space left in our interior life for listening. But, like Mary's word to the angel, "May it be done to me according to your word" (Luke 1:38), the words Eli suggests can be taken as a model of our attitude in the face of God. To imagine that our thinking, planning, talking, doing are all that counts, is a pretty narrowly human-centered approach. Our usually self-seeking and self-absorbed will and mind need to stop and allow God to be heard, to make an impression. Too often our life consists of headlong movement supported by very little reflection but simply impelled by energy and, possibly, good will. Listening doesn't mean by any means that we expect to hear a divine voice address us but to be open to the much more subtle influence of God that comes when we pray and are quiet (see Ps 46:11). And, further, we need to be quiet to understand what the world around us, our families and friends, too, are saying to us. In the Gospel, too, we see this exemplified: Jesus went off to a lonely place to pray. Even the Son of God in the midst of his ministry realizes there must be some silence in order for him to hear God, to stay attuned to the Father. Every day there should be some time when we put aside the noise of the world around us and of our own hearts and minds to say, "Speak, LORD, for your servant is listening" (1 Sam 3:9).

Thursday of the First Week in Ordinary Time—*No magic*

Readings: 1 Sam 4:1-11; Mark 1:40-45
Resp. Psalm: Ps 44:10-11, 14-15, 24-25 (L 308)

It's hard to avoid the conclusion that both the Philistines and the Is-raelites regarded the ark of the Lord as having magical qualities. After a defeat by the Philistines, the Israelites decide that they would have fared better with the ark in their midst. The Philistines, hearing of it, are terrified that the next battle will mean defeat. As it turns out the Philistines inflict a disastrous defeat on the Israelites. This sign of the presence of God in their midst was thought of a bit too much like a mega-rabbit's foot. There remains the danger for us too of treating our signs of God's presence, the sacraments and our ritual, in a similar manner. Trusting in our baptism and the Eucharist, we can be lulled into inactivity. But the activity of Jesus reminds us that the presence of God is meant to be effective, to have results in the world around us—through our cooperation. Jesus healed the suffering but he did not heal all of them; there remains much for his followers to do. The power and presence of God in our midst, in the Eucharist, for instance, must be translated into such time-consuming and energy-absorbing deeds inspired by Matthew, chapter 25:31ff., as: visiting the sick and elderly, calling or writing the lonely and discouraged, leaving our cozy circle to spend time with the despised and unloved, consoling the griev- ing, greeting and possibly brightening the life of a depressed/bored friend, checking on a harassed relative. How the moral, physical, and social lepers fare at our hands tests the genuineness of our belief that God is with us around the altar, and in the bread and wine.

Friday of the First Week in Ordinary Time—*Conscience first*

Readings: 1 Sam 8:4-7, 10-22a; Mark 2:1-12
Resp. Psalm: Ps 89:16-17, 18-19 (L 309)

One commentary on the books of Samuel is entitled, *Let Us Be Like the Nations.* We hear that in our first reading in another translation as the elders speak to Samuel, "appoint a king over us, as other nations have" (1 Sam 8:5; cf. Deut 17:14). Parents have probably heard something similar from a child when a neighbor buys the latest toy for his little kids: "Can't we get one of those too?" An American newspaperman once wrote to the effect that if you let people do what they want, they end up imitating each other. We see it in teenage fashions where peer pressure almost dictates a uniform. Israel was governed by judges up to this point but now they want a king like everyone else. It sug- gests for us the issue of singularity and conformity. Our faith, our conscience at times requires some singularity of behavior on our part. Everyone knows how difficult that is when faced with a lot of contrary pressure from friends and neighbors. Though theoretically most of us are free to act as we think right, we are battered on the other side by a strong desire to fit in, to not stand out. Ideally in our own lives we would allow what God asks of us in our particular situation and with our specific capabilities to dictate what we do. Instead of looking over our shoulder to see what the trends are, we look within to know what God asks of us in the present moment in our life. Neither singularity nor conformity is primary but what conscience tells us. Though we hear that we are to be conformed to the pattern given us in Christ (see Rom 8:29), even that is different for each one of us.

Saturday of the First Week in Ordinary Time—
A gathering of sinners

Readings: 1 Sam 9:14, 17-19; 10:1; Mark 2:13-17
Resp. Psalm: Ps 21:2-3, 4-5, 6-7 (L 310)

There have been movements within Christianity that believed the church should be made up only of the obviously saved, people who apparently did not sin, the righteous. Or, as Jesus might say, "the self-righteous" (see Mark 2:17). Genuinely recognizable sinners were expelled from the community or even executed. The Catholic conception of the church, on the contrary, is of a gathering of people on their way to resurrection but who are all in some way sinners, all in need of God's mercy and mutual forgiveness. This is used by some as an excuse for not participating in the life of the church, in Mass. One hears the timeworn comment about those at Mass: "They're all hypocrites." This really means that the people at Mass are all sinners. We who are here know that. A hypocrite would be one who claims to be something he or she is not, that is, free from sin. One reason we're at Mass is just this: we are sinners and know we need help and forgiveness. We know we need the doctor, Christ. Andrew Greeley says somewhere to those looking for the perfect community or church, a group of people free from all sin, "Sure, look for it. And if you find it, realize that the moment you join it, that community is no longer perfect." No, being a member of the church means belonging to a messed-up group, an untidy gathering of people like you or me who continually fail to live up to the ideal. But we keep coming just for that reason; we need the help and forgiveness that flow from the offering of Christ.

Monday of the Second Week in Ordinary Time—
Responding to what is before us

Readings: 1 Sam 15:16-23; Mark 2:18-22
Resp. Psalm: Ps 50:8-9, 16bc-17, 21 and 23 (*L* 311)

On Saturday we heard that Saul was made king of the Israelites and today we hear of his rejection by the Lord. Five chapters have been omitted so it is not quite as abrupt as it may seem. Today's rejection of Saul is accompanied by famous words about the value of obedience over our personally chosen sacrifices. Obedience often raises in our minds the picture of submission to some authority, person in charge. It may be that in some circumstances but more often it will mean for most of us responding to the demands of our immediate environment, to the people with whom we are closely linked: a friend's need for help with a difficult job, a little assistance to an elderly family member who can't get around so easily, joining a community effort to do something about a local problem. Before we go looking for heroic sacrifices we're better off responding to the immediate needs of our neighborhood and family, of our friends and of fellow workers.

Tuesday of the Second Week in Ordinary Time—
A day free from gain

Readings: 1 Sam 16:1-13; Mark 2:23-28
Resp. Psalm: Ps 89:20, 21-22, 27-28 (*L* 312)

How do we observe the Sabbath? What does that old term "servile work" mean? What makes sense today? Jesus often had to face a similar discussion with some ill-intentioned people. The *Catechism of the Catholic Church* (2nd ed., 2000) sums up the Old Testament teaching (cf. Neh 13:15-22; 2 Chr 36:21) on the subject by saying it was conceived of as "a day of protest against the servitude of work and the worship of money" (§2172)—a day of protest against our enslavement to work and our headlong pursuit of money. We of the First World are certainly in no position to tell poor peasants whose physical survival depends on working every single day to take a day off. But can we expect people in our society to take the day off from work when for them it means falling behind everyone else in their business? What does the Sabbath, Sunday mean for us today? Is it a lost cause? Most of us who reflect at all on the issues can see the good of diminishing our slavery to work (true for many active people in our society). Just to spend some time not working, able to be with family and friends, to enjoy an unhurried meal, to play a game, to read a book or watch a movie—all can be restorative. To do things which earn us no money but which are good in themselves, enjoyable and restful, frees us, at least for the moment, from bondage to moneymaking. Unfortunately, some of these activities have taken over every minute of Sunday leaving worship a poor cousin. God rested after creation (Gen 2:2-3). God who gave us the example of the Sabbath deserves the prime time in our day of rest.

Wednesday of the Second Week in Ordinary Time—
The Lord's battle

Readings: 1 Sam 17:32-33, 37, 40-51; Mark 3:1-6
Resp. Psalm: Ps 144:1b, 2, 9-10 (*L* 313)

"[T]he battle is the LORD's" (1 Sam 17:47), David says to Goliath as he tells him his day has come. A dramatic story like today's of David and Goliath suggests comparisons with our own lives. Thinking of life as a battle is one of many images we use to understand these sixty, eighty, ninety years. We also speak of life as a workplace and very often as a journey—or even as a banquet or a cabaret, at least in Broadway musicals. We may not be very fond of the combat image but aspects of any life almost force us to accept it. The psalmist says, "I am for peace; / but when I speak, / they are for war" (Ps 120:7; NRSV). We can't always avoid it. No matter how pacific we ourselves are or wish to be, there are always going to be people and forces around us that demand some forceful response from us or even incite us to anger. Even if we don't care for terms like spiritual combat, we must recognize that there are elements of struggle in every human life, much of it within ourselves. St. Paul speaks for all of us when he tells of how his will and desires war against each other (see Rom 7:14-25). Some of the battles that go on within us are like continual skirmishes; they must be fought over and over again. Today's Gospel ends with the sounds of battle in the life of Jesus: ". . . The Pharisees . . . took counsel / with the Herodians against him to put him to death" (Mark 3:6). The Lord has gone through all this for us and is with us as we face our own battles. Like David we have the assurance that "[T]he battle is the LORD's" (1 Sam 17:47). We can be victors with and in the one with whom we have communion here at this table.

Thursday of the Second Week in Ordinary Time—*Envy*

Readings: 1 Sam 18:6-9; 19:1-7; Mark 3:7-12
Resp. Psalm: Ps 56:2-3, 9-10a, 10b-11, 12-13 (L 314)

The sequel to the David and Goliath story is another memorable and dramatic story. Coming out to greet the conquering heroes, the women of Israel sing a song for the occasion: "Saul has slain his thousands, and David his ten thousands" (1 Sam 18:7). One easily pictures the king smoldering with indignation and envy as this mere youth steals the spotlight. Very soon Saul is talking about killing David. We see here, undoubtedly a bit telescoped, the growth of envy into an intention to murder. Envy is traditionally listed as one of the seven deadly or capital sins by which is meant that from it flow all sorts of other vices. We see it here; such things as discord, resentment, hatred, distrust, all flow from the initial envy. Saul's frankness in talking about killing David is probably a surprise to us. Our envy tends to be secret, smoldering within and showing itself occasionally in an unkind word or a belittling of another. Angus Wilson has compared envy to some of the other capital sins saying that it has an "uglier face than Lust's bloodshot eyes, or Gluttony's paunch, or Pride's camel nose, or

Avarice's thin lips." The only antidote to envy is the love that is ours if we're open to the influence of Christ and his Holy Spirit. Good will and a desire for the good of others, practical love in other words, must nip the beginnings of envy and so cast it out before it grows and hatches other sins.

Friday of the Second Week in Ordinary Time—
Expecting the best

Readings: 1 Sam 24:3-21; Mark 3:13-19
Resp. Psalm: Ps 57:2, 3-4, 6 and 11 (*L* 315)

The account of the turbulent relations of David and Saul continues in today's reading from Samuel. Despite a reconciliation between the two, Saul is once again, several chapters later, in pursuit of David. Turbulence was not merely the quality of relations between the two men, it was also characteristic of David's whole life. As we know from elsewhere in Scripture, David models heroism and magnanimity as well as dastardly crimes and violence. Seeing his generous and reverential treatment of his foe, King Saul, in today's reading we are warned against putting any human being into some too narrow box. We are all capable of virtue and vice. Knowing that, we should be less willing to give up on others, less willing to predict for sure that they will fulfill our negative view of them. Genuine leaders in many areas of life are often characterized by their willingness to put some trust in a woman or man who has evidenced some real failings. Perhaps such trust was operative in Jesus' choice of the twelve apostles, a trust in what good they could do despite their weaknesses.

Saturday of the Second Week in Ordinary Time—
The pain of misunderstanding

Readings: 2 Sam 1:1-4, 11-12, 19, 23-27; Mark 3:20-21
Resp. Psalm: Ps 80:2-3, 5-7 (*L* 316)

In our exaltation of Jesus as the Son of God, the Word of God made flesh (see John 1:14), we often end up treating him only as divine, only as the Son of God. We think and speak of him as someone really not familiar with the genuine trials of ordinary human life. But if that human life is a model for us—and so commendable for sharing in human sorrows and joys—we need to take it more seriously in its details. The Gospel today tells us that his family at one time at least thought he was crazy, deranged. They came to him while he was surrounded by a crowd, hoping to take him away for his own good. Jesus felt, in other words, the depths of incomprehension by those closest to him by blood; he was misunderstood, thought to be "out of his mind" (Mark 3:21). Short of death itself, is there anything we humans can go through which is more depressing to us than this kind of incomprehension by those with whom we live? There is no sorrow or problem we go through with which Jesus cannot sympathize as a fellow human sufferer.

Monday of the Third Week in Ordinary Time—*Loneliness*

Readings: 2 Sam 5:1-7, 10; Mark 3:22-30
Resp. Psalm: Ps 89:20, 21-22, 25-26 (*L* 316)

In the verse preceding today's Gospel, the family of Jesus had come for him as they saw him being consumed by his mission. They said: "He is out of his mind" (Mark 3:21). Today misunderstanding takes a giant leap forward as he is accused of working in league with the devil. Throughout Mark's Gospel we hear of how uncomprehending those around him were—including his closest friends. In his truly human state Jesus experienced most profoundly our loneliness. In our loneliness we share his cross. Our desire for love and understanding seems a constant, but is it ever totally satisfied? We can never completely know another or be known by another. This is another example of how intimately the cross is woven into human life. The words of Jesus about taking up one's cross (Mark 8:34, for example) testify that the cross is built into human life; no one needs to go looking for it. It's there; it's always there in the fact that our self is never totally accessible to another human being. This is both the pain and the glory of being unique. Christian writers see in this an opening to more intimacy with God, an opportunity for growth, but one that is often hard to appreciate. In other words, the cross of loneliiness, the fact that we never feel completely understood, points us toward the one who knows and understands our hearts supremely, God who made them.

Tuesday of the Third Week in Ordinary Time—
Finding community

Readings: 2 Sam 6:12b-15, 17-19; Mark 3:31-35
Resp. Psalm: Ps 24:7, 8, 9, 10 (*L* 318)

As we heard a few days ago the family of Jesus did not constitute what we today would call a support group for his mission (Mark 3:21-22).

Elsewhere in the Gospels the Lord tells us that the acceptance of his message can pit family members against each other (see Matt 10:34–36). The incomprehension of the family of Jesus recorded earlier in chapter 3 of Mark is balanced here by his acceptance in another family, the company of those who do the will of God. Such persons are brothers and sisters and mother to him. This is some consolation for those whose faith in the Lord is not shared by their blood relations or who find it actively opposed in fact. Especially for the young, such opposition can be very difficult to bear. But everyone, no matter what age, needs some support and encouragement in such matters as faith and the practice of religion. Ideally the church community should provide this for believers. Large congregations particularly have a special difficulty in doing this; one can so easily be lost in anonymity. The small Protestant congregations that we often term sects are good at providing signs of concern and care for individuals. The challenge to us Catholics with large parishes is to find ways to provide signs of support and encouragement to members, to make the word "community" mean something. The task can use the best ideas any of us have on how to do this. It should begin with each one of us.

Wednesday of the Third Week in Ordinary Time—
Home or house

Readings: 2 Sam 7:4-17; Mark 4:1-20
Resp. Psalm: Ps 89:4-5, 27-28, 29-30 (L 319)

David has done or will do everything else but today it seems that he's to be denied the title of "builder." That is to be left to his son Solomon. Again and again obituaries tell us how some political leader, governor, bishop, or pastor was famed as a builder. He or she was the big push behind the domed stadium for the city, the new cathedral, or the parish grade school. But through the prophet Nathan, the Lord tells David that a permanent temple will be left to another to build. Instead God is building up David's house, that is, his line from which eventually will come the Messiah. God considers David's offspring, his house in this sense, more important than a material building. Builders in the church too must know that more important than the concrete or marble edifice is the building up of the community which will use it. Most of us will not be constructing cathedrals or stadiums but possibly a house for our family. We can recall the familiar distinction between a house and a home. A house, no matter how fine and well appointed, is no substitute for a home, no guarantee that it will be a home. A building to house parents and children is not, unfortunately, always the same thing as a home. A home has to welcome its children and allow for their messiness and energy. A home can actually be too elegant to allow for the familiarity and boisterousness of a real family. The best builders are those who enable parents and children to live and grow in love, peace, and mutual respect.

Thursday of the Third Week in Ordinary Time—
Giving and spending

Readings: 2 Sam 7:18-19, 24-29; Mark 4:21-25
Resp. Psalm: Ps 132:1-2, 3-5, 11, 12, 13-14 (L 320)

We don't really save time. We either spend it well or badly. The same can go for our talents, skills, education, and experience. They're most satisfying and fulfilling when we use them and exercise them—rather than somehow thinking we can hoard them. In fact, some of them, if not used, will atrophy, fade away, become unusable. In their own way, the short parables spoken by the Lord in today's Gospel also seem to say this. A lamp is purchased in order to shed some light, to illuminate the darkness—not to be hidden away in the attic or covered with a drape. The light we have to give to the world, each in our own way, should be used, spread generously. The enlightenment that our faith and trust in God gives us Christians is something many around us sadly lack. Our hope and the accompanying joy should be used to brighten other lives. The second parable stresses that it is in giving that we receive, that giving of all or anything we have is its own reward (see the "Prayer of St. Francis"). This is something we probably can only learn by enough experience. Giving what I have to share only enriches me on another level. Giving of self—in service, care, consolation, sympathy, counsel, encouragement—is, in many ways, the most perfect way in which we imitate the self-giving of Christ (see Phil 2) and carry out in daily life our offering of ourselves with Christ at Mass.

Friday of the Third Week in Ordinary Time—*Real celebrities*

Readings: 2 Sam 11:1-4a, 5-10a, 13-17; Mark 4:26-34
Resp. Psalm: Ps 51:3-4, 5-6a, 6bcd-7, 10-11 (L 321)

So often we think of the famous biblical character David as the beardless shepherd boy who kills the giant Goliath for his people; we picture him with a harp, a writer of psalms. We hear our Lord described as one from the "house of David" (Luke 1:27, 69), called the "Son of David" (Mark 10:47-48). But the full story as we have it in Scripture is by no means so clear and clean. Today we hear of a particularly heinous episode in his life involving adultery and murder. And there's more. True, at other times we have penitence and tears. What do we make of his prominence in Scripture? Perhaps he pictures on the large screen the ambiguities and inconsistencies in the life of any one of us. Over the whole period of our lives, isn't there some comparable collection of good and bad deeds? Or perhaps we have in David a lesson for all of us not to make heroes or at least models of behavior out of famous people. We have enough examples in our day of movie stars, professional athletes, and politicians who model adultery, slander, drug use and trafficking, spousal abuse, violence, and even murder. Whom do we point out as heroes to our children? Whom do we really admire? Possibly all of this tells us to look closer to home for imitators of Christ. In the gentle and thoughtful man next door, the sick and suffering child we know, the ever dependable young woman, the generous couple who lost their daughter in an accident, in our own husband or wife who is always there for us and the children. Christ shines forth in these faces, words, hands more than in the celebrities.

Saturday of the Third Week in Ordinary Time—
The many faces of David

Readings: 2 Sam 12:1-7a, 10-17; Mark 4:35-41
Resp. Psalm: Ps 51:12-13, 14-15, 16-17 (L 322)

Memorable stories cluster around the figure of David. We've heard here recently about his selection as king from among all his brothers, dancing before the ark, escaping Saul's envy, his generosity to Saul, his friendship with Jonathan, his killing Goliath with a slingshot, his heinous affair with Bathsheba, and God's great plans for his descendants (all in 2 Sam). Today we hear of his contrition for murder and adultery. He's one of the central figures of the Scriptures, and Jesus is often presented as the new David. You wonder at times what is consistent in this character, who is the real David. What makes him different from the soap opera celebrities who fill the media is probably the fact that through it all, the good times and the bad, he retains faith. He is aware of his dependence on God—that he is in God's hands and answerable to God. He praises God, petitions God, and asks forgiveness. Perhaps his sins and virtues are outsized pictures of what goes on in most human beings, a mixture of good accomplishments and embarrassing, even shameful failures. Much of the revelation we have received in Jesus Christ tells us that God will not break or forget the covenant and that we are justified in trusting God, whatever the storms or devastation that surround us.

Monday of the Fourth Week in Ordinary Time—
Times change

Readings: 2 Sam 15:13-14, 30; 16:5-13; Mark 5:1-20
Resp. Psalm: Ps 3:2-3, 4-5, 6-7 (*L* 323)

In these readings from Samuel we see David in every possible situation and with every possible emotional reaction. Today, as his son Absalom tries to take over the throne, David and his men flee. As an old enemy gloats over David's lot, the king takes it as only appropriate. "Perhaps the Lord will look upon my affliction / and make it up to me with benefits / for the curses he is uttering this day" (2 Sam 16:12). Though we know enough of David not to take him as the picture of virtue and the source of all wisdom, Scripture does give him some memorable lines. David's approach to his present straits reminds one a bit of a well-known passage in Ecclesiastes: "There is an appointed time for everything / . . . / A time to weep, and a time to laugh; / . . . / a time of war, and a time of peace" (3:1, 4, 8). We can hear in David's words the notion that good and bad alternate in any human life; some would say that joy and pain balance out over the course of the years. The poet Robert Southwell writes in a poem entitled "Time Goes By Turns" that "The saddest birds a season find to sing" (*The Poems of Robert Southwell, s.j.* [Oxford: Clarendon Press, 1967] 45). For us who trust in the presence and help of the Lord Jesus, there is always hope that a dark day or period of our life will eventually be brightened by signs of God's love, that resurrection will follow on our suffering and death. Very often we find that just allowing the passage of some time gives us a better perspective on today's worries or allows God to do us good. Like the man in the Gospel we have seen this happen enough to have reason "to proclaim what Jesus has done for us" (see Mark 5:19).

Tuesday of the Fourth Week in Ordinary Time—
Family situations

Readings: 2 Sam 18:9-10, 14b, 24–25a, 30–19:3; Mark 5:21-43
Resp. Psalm: Ps 86:1-2, 3-4, 5-6 (*L* 324)

The rebellion of David's son Absalom comes to nothing and Absalom is killed. In David's grief over his son's death we recognize the feelings of any parent faced with the death of a child. And the grief is there no matter what has transpired between parent and offspring. We've all heard: "He was still my son." Or, "Parents shouldn't have to bury their children." And, just like David, "If only I had died instead of you" (2 Sam 19:1). In today's Gospel too we see a parent distraught at the critical illness of his daughter; he throws himself at Jesus' feet for help. Families in the course of a few decades face a variety of problems and emotions: hurts and reconciliation, estrangement and noncommunication, misunderstanding and violent disagreement, breaking off of all relations and efforts to make up—all these and degrees of all these. Most often the bond of blood persists no matter what happens. Mistakes and pride on both sides make for an incredible variety of complicated situations within families, between parents and children, between siblings, between husband and wife. Like David any one of us is capable of oscillating even within the family, between tenderness and tantrum. Part of any solution for Christians must be to put ourselves and all the continuing problems of our family life at the feet of Jesus with loving and persistent trust.

Wednesday of the Fourth Week in Ordinary Time—
God in the daily
Readings: 2 Sam 24:2, 9-17; Mark 6:1-6
Resp. Psalm: Ps 32:1-2, 5, 6, 7 (L 325)

Despite the number of miracles and marvels Mark records, so many other touches in his Gospel compel us to see how different this Jesus is from fairy-tale wonder-workers. We've noted before how uncomprehending his followers are, how disappointing those closest to him can be. Today we hear of his rejection in his own hometown. Any imaginative writer trying to foist some wonder-worker on us would not weaken his case by telling us that even his relatives and neighbors wouldn't accept him. These scenes of rejection and misunderstanding of Jesus are most valuable for our faith. They show us a real human being, someone who lived in a particular place among specific people. Our Lord and Savior lived human life in all its grittiness and ambiguity. We have no reason to hesitate in bringing before him the problems of our lives, even those we are too embarrassed to tell others. And the reactions of his neighbors, even these encourage us; they show us limitations like those we experience. Aren't we often perplexed that God seems to come to us in such ordinary ways, with so little thunder and light? In order that Jesus may do anything in and for us we must be willing to see that occur in the nondramatic events of daily life, through ordinary people like ourselves. As he comes to us in bread and wine, so he comes through all the other ordinary elements of daily life.

Thursday of the Fourth Week in Ordinary Time—
The Gospel free of charge

Readings: 1 Kgs 2:1-4, 10-12; Mark 6:7-13
Resp. Psalm: 1 Chr 29:10, 11ab, 11d-12a, 12bcd (*L* 326)

Both readings today are sets of instructions, one of David to his son Solomon, the other of our Lord to his disciples. David offers noble advice to his son though our reading omits other instructions from David telling Solomon to take revenge on various enemies. That advice is more like that of a Mafia don. The instructions of Jesus to his disciples have none of that, of course, but they do show an awareness of how human sin could blemish their mission. The instruction to take no bag and no money suggests a well-justified fear of contaminating the message and mission with money. Outside of power the chief threat to good human behavior and to the mission of Jesus is wealth or the desire for it. The instruction to stay in the house that offers you hospitality is in a similar vein: don't be looking for better accommodations. The disciples must avoid even the appearance of making money on the Gospel or on healing. As with power, the history of Christianity has shown how the desire, really the lust for wealth, can corrupt the faith. The great division in Christianity between Catholics and Protestants stems, at least in part, from the intrusion of money into the mission of the church. From the papacy on down to the local priest, in many places the insistence on payment for every service in the Church has alienated believers. All this says: faith should not be a money-making matter.

Friday of the Fourth Week in Ordinary Time—
In his strength

Readings: Sir 47:2-11; Mark 6:14-29
Resp. Psalm: Ps 18:31, 47 and 50, 51 (*L* 327)

John's death at the hand of the local powers in Palestine shows us what is also to be the fate of his and our Lord. The Son of God, one who shares by right in the power and authority of the creator of the world, allows himself to be put to death by the power of mere human beings. In the story of John's martyrdom, as in the story of the passion of Jesus, we see the same type of local authorities, anxious to maintain their power and at the same time having some doubts— Pilate (Mark 15) and Herod (Mark 6:26). Isn't this close to the heart of the message of the life and teaching of the Lord? We triumph, we reach eternal life with God, not by the acquisition and exercise of earthly power but through suffering and death. How much more that speaks to us ordinary people. Most of us don't have enviable power; we aren't in competition with the CEO of General Motors or the president of the United States. But we do share daily in the suffering and death of the Lord in our own lives. We have illness to deal with, our own or that of people close to us; we have debts and obligations that hang over our heads; we have personality issues to deal with in the workplace; our marriage itself may be going through tough times; our job security may be an issue. Through bearing all these we come to new life and growth, hard as it may be to recognize that in the midst of bereavement, illness, quarrels, and tragedy. As we are present here at the daily offering of Christ, we have the opportunity to join our own suffering to his and to draw from his strength.

Saturday of the Fourth Week in Ordinary Time—
Growth in our conscience

Readings: 1 Kgs 3:4-13; Mark 6:30-34
Resp. Psalm: Ps 119:9, 10, 11, 12, 13, 14 (*L* 328)

Besides the struggle within each one of us between good and evil, generosity and selfishness, self-giving and self-seeking, there is in the Scriptures the same struggle. In the accounts of David and Solomon we see it. The authors tell us at one moment of fratricide, adultery, vengeance, and murder only to commend humility, patience, mercy, and forgiveness at another. The chosen people are told to slaughter their enemies at one time and later commended for taking care of the alien and the poor. Today, Solomon, who comes from a pretty violent background, gives us a model of prayer; he prays for an understanding heart and the ability to distinguish good from evil. What we see in the alternation of cruelty and kindness, love and vengeance, self-interest and ethics in the Scriptures seems to be the development of the chosen people's conscience. Solomon's prayer is commended because he doesn't ask for long life, riches, or vengeance on his enemies. It took the people of the pre-Christian period a long time to get rid of harems and accept monogamy; it is taking all the human race a long time to reject war as a solution to disputes, though at times we see some signs of progress. Throughout the Scriptures there seems to be a growth of sensitivity of conscience. We should not be surprised to see some of the same development within ourselves. And we should expect to see some progress in our sensitivity over the course of the years. May we allow Christ the Good Shepherd to teach us.

Monday of the Fifth Week in Ordinary Time—
The needs of others

Readings: 1 Kgs 8:1-7, 9-13; Mark 6:53-56
Resp. Psalm: Ps 132:6-7, 8-10 (*L* 329)

We could fault the people in today's Gospel for thinking of Jesus totally in terms of what he could do for them or their distressed family and friends. A busy pastor, counselor, teacher, parent can easily feel "eaten up" by the demands of others. At some time or other the besieged person must wish: if only I would be brought some consolation rather than being always at the mercy and call of those who are in such tough straits. But what can we expect from a sick person, someone in trouble, someone very worried or depressed? It's pretty difficult for most of us to forget ourselves when we are hurting so much. The injured person easily feels that the only event going on this day in the universe is my suffering, my problem. To transcend this and think of others is certainly ideal, and we shouldn't neglect the wisdom which tells us to forget our own troubles in concern for others. Still, the one who seems to be giving all the time understandably longs to be on the receiving end occasionally. All of us stand amazed at the generosity and constant giving of a Mother Teresa, of many of our mothers. We Christians believe that the power to give comes from Christ living in us or we living in Christ. He is the vine and we are the branches; we can do nothing without him (see John 15:5). Sometimes our weariness and self-pity may stem from the fact that we trust too much to self and too little to the Lord.

Tuesday of the Fifth Week in Ordinary Time—
Too many rules

Readings: 1 Kgs 8:22-23, 27-30; Mark 7:1-13
Resp. Psalm: Ps 84:3, 4, 5 and 10, 11 (*L* 330)

In almost any area of life we can become so wrapped up in the details of procedure that we forget what the basic purpose of the activity was supposed to be. The regulations in our church in recent centuries about how the priest was to say Mass (how far apart his hands should be, in what direction a particular finger should point, what to do if someone dropped the host, etc.) were examples of human regulations which really obscured the idea of the Mass as the Lord's Supper with his friends. In today's Gospel what Jesus seems most upset with is likewise the addition of all sorts of human regulations to the Law of Moses. The latter he seems to have supported. In all we do, whether it has to do with religion or not, we need to keep an eye on the essentials and not become so bound up in procedure that we kill the good originally intended. How easy it is to end all giving to the poor if we surround it with so many qualifications: they must be deserving, clean, nondrinkers, etc. Eventually we help only good middle class people like ourselves. Parents know how they must resist the temptation to hedge in their children's play with concerns and limitations based on fear. Enough of that and the child must stay indoors. The same has happened in the Christian religion at times: the avenues of God's love for others have been so regulated that only a thin trickle of love seems to come through. Our tendency to make rules based on our limited vision can kill almost anything from play to charity to worship.

Wednesday of the Fifth Week in Ordinary Time—
Purifying motives

Readings: 1 Kgs 10:1-10; Mark 7:14-23
Resp. Psalm: Ps 37:5-6, 30-31, 39-40 (L 331)

Without using elegant philosophical terminology Jesus corrects an age-old human tendency to blame the body or matter for sin, for evil. The idea that somehow there is a good part of the human being, the soul or spirit, and an evil part, the body, crops up throughout history, even in Christianity. Outside of Christianity there have been and are religious or philosophical systems which claim that the body or matter is evil. The language of this belief survives at times among us today. The body, the flesh, is the cause of sin; somehow the soul is free of it. In today's Gospel, Jesus continues the teaching of Genesis that the body, the whole person and our earthly environment, all this was created good. It's not what we eat that harms us or what the body somehow, of itself, does. No, Jesus says, wickedness, evil, sin come from deep within our heart. This teaching of Jesus places responsibility for sin—sexual sins, theft, murder, avarice, envy, deceit, arrogance, etc.—in the heart, in our choices. "All these evils come from within and they defile" (Mark 7:23). The direction of our hearts, our intentions, our purposes, in these lie good or evil. Such teaching aims to make us more responsible, to leave us less opportunity to "pass the buck." It wasn't the devil that made me do it or my body or my flesh or matter. We don't pray "deliver us from matter" but "deliver us from evil." And that comes from within. We are never finished with the need to ask the Spirit to purify, simplify our intentions, our desires, our motivation.

Thursday of the Fifth Week in Ordinary Time—*Our choices*

Readings: 1 Kgs 11:4-13; Mark 7:24-30
Resp. Psalm: Ps 106:3-4, 35-36, 37 and 40 (*L* 332)

Someone has suggested that the term "original sin" might be fittingly described as "the tendency of a good thing to go sour." While the Scriptures do give us examples of great individuals who persisted in faith and trust, who remained faithful to God no matter what, there are also many examples, even in high places, of unfaithfulness. In the Greek woman in today's Gospel we have an example of great trust in Jesus and persistent devotion to her suffering daughter. But with Solomon, as was the case with his father David, we have great men of Israel who fell away. It's true that today's reading from Kings keeps up the image of David as God's great servant. Both he and Solomon are seen in some of the Scriptures through the golden haze of memory. Taken in its entirety, however, the Scriptures tell us of the failures and betrayals of God by these famous kings. Their sins underline what we heard from Jesus in yesterday's Gospel about how important the heart with its intentions is. Within each of us lies the power to say yes or no to God. Our growth in Christ can be seen as a life-long struggle to become more generous, consistent, and faithful in our yes to God. Like Solomon and David the trajectory of each of our lives may also go through periods of unfaithfulness and periods of generosity. Only our receptivity to God's grace can assure our faithfulness.

Friday of the Fifth Week in Ordinary Time—*Amazing grace*

Readings: 1 Kgs 11:29-32; 12:19; Mark 7:31-37
Resp. Psalm: Ps 81:10-11ab, 12-13, 14-15 (*L* 333)

After curing the deaf man with the speech impediment, Jesus "ordered them not to tell anyone. / But the more he ordered them not to, / the more they proclaimed it" (Mark 7:36). Jesus was, according to some authorities, concerned not to arouse the crowd for the wrong reasons or to the wrong kind of acclaim. He was not trying to lead a revolution or enter politics. But, seeing what he had done, being amazed by it, the witnesses of his signs could not contain themselves. Can we sense in this old text a bit of a rebuke to us who take the Gospel so soberly, so much for granted even? Very possibly, most of us are not going to start our own crusade at the local shopping mall. But could we not evidence more in our behavior, our good cheer and generosity, our forgiveness and sensitivity, our compassion and concern, that the Gospel does strike us as Good News and affects everything we do? The great assurance that Jesus is near to us, that God truly and indefatigably loves us, this should amaze us and make us determined to share it. His gift, his grace to us, is truly amazing; may we realize that.

Saturday of the Fifth Week in Ordinary Time—
Do what we can

Readings: 1 Kgs 12:26-32; 13:33-34; Mark 8:1-10
Resp. Psalm: Ps 106:6-7ab, 19-20, 21-22 (L 334)

A number of elements in today's Gospel suggest much more than any one of us probably will get from it at one time. It is, for instance, almost an exact duplicate of another feeding (that of 5000 [Mark 6:34-44]); references to the language of the Eucharist are clear; and there are seven loaves, the sacred number for the people of the time. Very fruitful for us modern readers is the strong suggestion here that when faced with the needs of others, we must do what we can, with what we have. After Jesus had expressed his compassion for the crowd and made reference to their need for food, the disciples point out that it would be impossible to satisfy them, especially in such a remote spot. Jesus finds out what food they have and tells them to do what they can with that. The result: "They ate and were satisfied" (Mark 8:8), and still some food remained. The message seems to be that if we are generous with whatever limited means we have to help those around us in need, God will make up for our lack or inadequacy. It's the same old (and frequently heard) message of the Gospels: confidence and trust that our world and its needs are the concern not simply of us but of someone much more capable. Examples abound in the history of the saints of men and women who did what they could and trusted God—with equally amazing results. It's a lesson we only learn by experience, not from books.

Monday of the Sixth Week in Ordinary Time—
Signs for nonbelievers

Readings: Jas 1:1–11; Mark 8:11–13
Resp. Psalm: Ps 119:67, 68, 71, 72, 75, 76 (L 335)

"[They were] seeking from him a sign from heaven to test him" (Mark 8:11). Even though this Gospel reading follows immediately on the multiplication of loaves and fishes (from Saturday's Gospel), Mark pictures the enemies of Jesus as asking for some more spectacular sign. Jesus' answer expresses weariness and anger with their attitude. The Gospels often highlight the apparent unwillingness of Jesus' contemporaries to penetrate the signs he does. The fact that people still look for the more spectacular type of sign (for example, the face of Jesus appearing on a refrigerator door, a statue weeping, etc.) suggests a strong moral point. Would there be less of such looking for heavenly signs if Christians were more notable for their consistent concern for the hungry, the poor, and the abandoned? If our cooperation with the Lord in caring for the poor, the starving worldwide, the abandoned, were more characteristic of all of us, would that affect others more positively? Apparently, the miracle of the multiplication of loaves and fishes did not do it for these Pharisees. But we will notice throughout the Letter of James, which we begin reading today, that the care of the less fortunate is the touchstone for true faith (ch. 2). Possibly there will always be the human hankering for the more Hollywood-type signs, but it still seems a good idea for us followers of Christ to show more consistently the compassion and generosity of the Lord toward the poor. Wouldn't that be a compelling sign for everyone?

Tuesday of the Sixth Week in Ordinary Time—
The disciples were real people

Readings: Jas 1:12–18; Mark 8:14–21
Resp. Psalm: Ps 94:12–13a, 14–15, 18–19 (L 336)

If the Pharisees weren't difficult enough, the disciples themselves show up in today's reading as similarly obtuse regarding Jesus' signs. We often say of human leaders and celebrities that "It's lonely at the top." The Gospels very often picture Jesus as in a kind of isolation because of the unresponsiveness of all around him. Jesus shares here another condition of human life, one common even to those of us who do not sit on dizzying peaks. The picture of the slowness and incomprehension of the disciples is in two ways a consolation or help for us. (1)

Obviously, it provides company for us when we realize how slow or insensitive we have been to some God-given opportunity in our lives. We see in the disciples that even these stars of Christian beginnings had many slow moments. It may help us face our doubts and difficulties with faith and the following of Jesus by helping us realize that they may be a part of Christian life for most followers of the Lord. (2) Seeing the stumbling, unresponsive disciples so often and so clearly in the Gospels gives these writings a lot of credibility and suggests that the writers are very honest and reliable. If they were out to exaggerate and romanticize, they could have given us a different picture. If they are willing to present such an unflattering portrait of the disciples, then everything else they say gains in reliability too.

Wednesday of the Sixth Week in Ordinary Time—
True worship

Readings: Jas 1:19-27; Mark 8:22-26
Resp. Psalm: Ps 15:2-3a, 3bc-4ab, 5 (*L* 337)

The Letter of James is relentless in emphasizing that faith, religion, and worship are all empty without consequences in daily life. We who may attend Mass often, even daily, may need to hear at times warnings against taking that participation as some kind of magic ritual, a ritual that frees us from other obligations or takes their place. Assisting at the Lord's table is not a substitute for good action but should be the inspiring source and power of those actions. And they in turn are part of our service to God, our worship. James' famous lines are: "If anyone thinks he is religious and does not bridle his tongue / but deceives his heart, his religion is vain. / Religion that is pure and undefiled before God and the Father is this: / to care for orphans and widows in their affliction / and to keep oneself unstained by the world" (Jas 1:26-27). Clearly no one of us can solve all the problems of suffering, distressed people in our world. But James' words make clear that the love we celebrate at the Lord's table is genuine to the degree that it shows itself in some practical, concrete way in the street, at home, among friends or strangers, with the poor, the homeless, the ostracized. One of the most frequently heard criticisms of churchgoers is that we claim to be honoring God while being neglectful of God's suffering people. Today, as we hear James and the Gospel story about the cure of the blind man, we could well pray that our sight be improved, that we see more clearly all the implications of our worship.

Thursday of the Sixth Week in Ordinary Time—
God's standards

Readings: Jas 2:1-9; Mark 8:27-33
Resp. Psalm: Ps 34:2-3, 4-5, 6-7 (*L* 338)

Are the poor a nuisance or a challenge? Even if we are ready to help them or are concerned that they be helped, most of us do find their presence an embarrassment. We can link today's readings by joining together the poor and other rejected or despised people. James speaks of the first and Jesus shocks Peter by telling him that the one he calls the Messiah will be rejected and suffer. Both readings remind us of how uncomfortable the poor and the outcast make us feel. Like Peter, we hate to think that someone we admire could be among these people rejected by ordinary society. We all recognize that the rich, the wealthy, the powerful, can do a lot for causes, for us even. St. Benedict in urging his followers to receive poor guests as Christ tells them that the rich will always get respect and service because of the power their wealth gives them (Rule, 53:15). But both readings call us to a stance which goes against the ordinary practice of our culture; they tell us that no matter how much wealth and power rule the world, God prefers the poor and powerless. God's standards are different from ours. The test of our love of neighbor is how in practice we respond to the poor, St. James tells us. Like Peter we need, again and again, the help of God in learning to judge by God's standards rather than the obvious and easy ones of this world.

Friday of the Sixth Week in Ordinary Time—
Consequences of faith

Readings: Jas 2:14-24, 26; Mark 8:34–9:1
Resp. Psalm: Ps 112:1-2, 3-4, 5-6 (*L* 339)

Our two readings today are bound together by the teaching that faith and discipleship have consequences. The passage from the Letter of James is probably the most famous part of this letter. Because of these verses, Martin Luther had it removed from his Bible. He felt that the teaching about the necessity of works with faith was contrary to the teaching of his beloved St. Paul. To simplify for our purposes here, I think we can say that the two, Paul and James, are reconcilable. Without denying that faith had consequences, Paul was insisting on the element of trust in God. James says that genuine faith is not just a matter of believing a list of truths about God. Even the devil can do that and what good does it do the devil? Faith has to show itself, as his first verses make very clear, in the service of the needy and suffering. Jesus says that the consequences of faith in him, following him, will inevitably show up in demands made on ourselves, in the necessity of self-sacrifice, self-giving. The two are obviously close: in responding to the needs of others—the poor, the needy, the mourning, the suffering—we will find that our own preferences and desires may have to be abandoned or forgotten at least for the moment. To come after Jesus will involve denying ourselves. The consequences that life and circumstances present to us—the needs of those nearby—are the best and most obvious opportunities for us. Honesty will show us more opportunities on any day.

Saturday of the Sixth Week in Ordinary Time—
God in our past reassures us now

Readings: Jas 3:1-10; Mark 9:2-13
Resp. Psalm: Ps 12:2-3, 4-5, 7-8 (L 340)

Despite how spare the narrative in Mark is, he manages to convey well the impression of the spiritual yo-yo that is the life of the disciples. After the harsh realities of the preceding verses about the cross and suffering, three of the disciples now are jerked in another direction by seeing Jesus transfigured. And not only that but a voice reassures the embattled disciples, "This is my beloved Son. Listen to him" (9:7). If they had this reassurance in such a vivid way, you can expect that it would help them through the dark days to come (see the preface for the Transfiguration in *The Roman Missal: The Sacramentary*). Such experiences are rare. If we've been on the receiving end of an encouraging, energizing, reassuring experience of any kind in our religious life, we should be grateful and use it to help us maintain equilibrium in harsher times. More often our reassurance will come not so much from one isolated and glorious experience of God and God's love but from repeated experiences of how God has helped us through difficulty after difficulty. That should give us courage for the ones yet to come or that face us now. If God has been so faithful for so long, assuredly that will continue (see 2 Tim 2:13).

Monday of the Seventh Week in Ordinary Time—
Mystery but not magic

Readings: Jas 3:13-18; Mark 9:14-29
Resp. Psalm: Ps 19:8, 9, 10, 15 (L 341)

Again, there are a number of provocative remarks in Mark's account of the cure of the mute boy. There is the exasperation of Jesus with unbelief; there's the little exchange about "if you can" (9:22). And there are the famous words of the father, "I do believe, help my unbelief!" (9:24). Today let us stay with the final words of Jesus to his disappointed disciples: "This kind can only come out through prayer" (9:29). We don't require that Jesus engage in prayer every time he performs an exorcism or cure; after all, he is in direct contact with the power of God. But there may well be the implication here that the reason the disciples were ineffective in exorcising the mute and deaf spirit is that they were taking for granted powers that rightfully belonged only to God. It may be a warning to ministers of religion against an automatic approach to the dispensing of God's grace in the sacraments and liturgy. We mortals can only cooperate with the power of God doing good in our world if we realize that we are dependent on God and that we demonstrate that by prayer. Without prayer on our part, the rituals of our religion come off as magic. And the lesson is relevant for all of us in the exercise of our faith: nothing is automatic. God depends on and uses our effort, our dependence, and our trust. And the serious projects and concerns of our lives, despite all the human means available, still depend on God for their success. No matter what sophisticated techniques we bring to some difficulty in a relationship or in a group like the parish itself, for instance, these matters should be entrusted confidently to God's loving care in and through prayer.

Tuesday of the Seventh Week in Ordinary Time—
Let's not talk about it

Readings: Jas 4:1-10; Mark 9:30-37
Resp. Psalm: Ps 55:7-8, 9-10a, 10b-11a, 23 (*L* 342)

We rightly see Mark's Gospel as spare; even discussions and discourses in their rare appearance are brief, laconic. But Mark's clipped comments on what is happening are often pregnant with insight into human nature. Two such comments stand out in today's Gospel. Earlier Jesus had shocked the disciples with words about his passion and death (9:31-33); here he repeats that with a brief reference to his rising also. "But they did not understand the saying, / and they were afraid to question him" (9:32). True, the prediction is incomprehensible to them; what kind of a miracle worker and man from God is this who will be put to death? They seem to have some inkling of what he is saying but "they were afraid to question him" (9:32). They really didn't want to hear any more about such a distasteful subject. If they questioned him, he might give them more detail and emphasize more what they didn't want to hear: that their hero was not going the way of triumph to triumph. And then, when, back at Capernaum, Jesus asks them what they were discussing, "they remained silent" (9:34). They didn't want him to talk any more about his passion and they didn't want to talk about their discussion. They were embarrassed to tell him that they were looking ahead to the time when he would no longer be there and trying to decide who would be in charge. They had good reason to be unwilling to talk about it with him, since he was initiating them into his approach that was totally contrary to the way of power. As we assist, even daily, at the representation of the death and rising of Christ here we too need to ask for help in understanding the "power-less" way of Jesus.

Wednesday of the Seventh Week in Ordinary Time—
In other *words*

Readings: Jas 4:13-17; Mark 9:38-40
Resp. Psalm: Ps 49:2-3, 6-7, 8-10, 11 (*L* 343)

In our part of the world, in our Christian tradition, we have a long history emphasizing the importance of true teaching. Religious institutions have tried to state exactly what the truth is about God, relations in the Trinity, our relation to God, etc. Along with this has gone condemnation of those who think differently. There are other ways of thinking, of course, which stress how hard it is to put divine truth in our merely human words, how our words are always really just circling around the mysterious truth. It has taken centuries for Christians to even begin to embrace the generously tolerant view stated in our Lord's words: "whoever is not against us is for us" (Mark 9:40). Given the difficulty human beings have in expressing God and our relation to God, it certainly makes more sense not to claim too much for our formulations. Others should be appreciated for the good they do to others regardless of whether they do "not follow us" (9:38) as the disciples say. Today's Gospel is one of the roots of an attitude which recognizes that God's action in others is not limited by our definitions of where and how God can work. Christians need enough confidence in the Lord to accept the fact that God may work through people who believe quite differently than we do. The beliefs and formulations are, after all, so influenced by our history, background, language, that these statements are bound to be limited in their relevance. "There is no one who performs a mighty deed in my name / who can at the same time speak ill of me" (9:39). We should applaud the good others do and not expect them to mimic our words about divine matters.

Thursday of the Seventh Week in Ordinary Time—
"The Lᴏʀᴅ hears the poor" (Ps 69:34)

Readings: Jas 5:1-6; Mark 9:41-50
Resp. Psalm: Ps 49:14-15ab, 15cd-16, 17-18, 19-20 (L 344)

As we look at the history of humankind and even at life around our world today we must be struck at the terrible injustices that have been perpetrated over and over again for the sake of greed. Less than a hundred years ago in our own country women and children worked twelve, sixteen hours a day for pennies in unhealthy and dangerous conditions, restricted even in their use of bathrooms while clothing manufacturers and others profited from their enslavement. Today the same thing continues in various parts of the world where children spend the whole day weaving or assembling articles under similarly inhumane conditions. James voices some of the indignation this should rightly arouse in all of us: "Behold, the wages you withheld from the workers / who harvested your fields are crying aloud; / and the cries of the harvesters / have reached the ears of the Lord of hosts. / You have lived on earth in luxury and pleasure" (Jas 5:4-5). The words of Jesus about cutting off hands or feet or plucking out offending eyes must certainly pertain above all to the sins committed in the cause of greed throughout history. Christians today, as sometimes in the past, should be in the forefront of those who challenge and protest inhumanity in the name of the accumulation of wealth. Social justice, not only in our own country but anywhere in our world, deserves the support of Christians in whatever way we can give it.

Friday of the Seventh Week in Ordinary Time—*Absolutely*

Readings: Jas 5:9-12; Mark 10:1-12
Resp. Psalm: Ps 103:1-2, 3-4, 8-9, 11-12 (L 345)

Our reading from James today ends with a plea from the writer that we let yes be yes and no be no without equivocation. After hearing constantly the slippery language of many of our public figures, we cannot but appreciate some straightforward language and a clear stand. In the Gospel today, too, we hear in the words of Jesus a clear, unambiguous teaching about divorce. "Whoever divorces his wife and marries another / commits adultery against her" (Mark 10:11). It's impossible to deny the attractiveness of such clear and absolute stances. But . . . but . . . but. As Matthew's treatment of the same matter of divorce shows, the early Christians felt the need for some qualification of this teaching. In Matthew Jesus makes an exception (5:32). St. Paul, too, makes provision for marital situations that are not so simple (see 1 Cor 7). It would indeed be nice if all married couples would stay together and cooperate peacefully and wisely in rearing their children. But we all know of circumstances where the violence of one party makes that impossible. We know of situations where staying together would endanger the mental and physical health of the family. Human relationships, in marriage or out, fail. We'd all like absolutes for the simplicity and directness they seem to give to life. But is all this tenable? Do we ever live in a world where things are so simple and plain? Are the only true absolutes maybe injunctions to our children like: look both ways before you cross the street and eat your vegetables? Whatever we make of the absolute words of Jesus here about marriage and divorce, we must let the realities of daily life have their say. Is perhaps the only absolute in Christian life: "You shall love your neighbor as yourself"? (Mark 12:31).

Saturday of the Seventh Week in Ordinary Time—
Patience and the little ones

Readings: Jas 5:13-20; Mark 10:13-16
Resp. Psalm: Ps 141:1-2, 3 and 8 (L 346)

"Let the children come to me; do not prevent them" (Mark 10:14). One thinks of the people who are probably the most important and essential to our world: parents and teachers. Who gives more to the welfare of our life and our world than the men and women who so patiently introduce the wildly energetic little ones to life together in this world, to mutual respect, to all the skills necessary for living and working? We have special days to honor mothers and fathers, and most appropriately. But teachers and caretakers of little children deserve much more respect and reward in our society than they get. You see them leading groups of little ones safely across streets, accompanying their noisy, even screaming, little charges on buses. On a crowded bus you see the teacher ask the little boy to surrender his seat to an elderly person, teaching even outside the classroom. As you sit on the bus and hear the din of their shrill little voices and wild laughter, you cannot but be amazed at the patience and concern the accompanying teacher shows. Most of us would be worn out within minutes by the work of caring for these little bundles of energy. The teachers get nowhere near the salaries of professional athletes and executives, but can you possibly put a figure on the invaluable work they do? Anything we can do to help them in their work, to show our appreciation, is most appropriate. As Jesus tells us to learn from the openness and dependence of little children how to receive the kingdom, so we can all learn from the generosity and patience of their teachers.

Monday of the Eighth Week in Ordinary Time—
This too will pass

Readings: 1 Pet 1:3-9; Mark 10:17-27
Resp. Psalm: Ps 111:1-2, 5-6, 9 and 10c (*L* 347)

First Peter is helpful in reminding us of the *inspirational* or *motivational* power of our belief in the resurrection of Christ. The writer speaks of the "living hope / through the resurrection of Jesus Christ from the dead" (1 Pet 1:3). Further, he tells us, "In this you rejoice" (1:6) for this faith tells us there is more to reality than what our eyes can see. Amid the comfort and relative prosperity of the "have-nations" there's a reluctance to emphasize too much the influence of our hope in eternal life. Our society and culture point us to expect "everything" from technology, science, and a high standard of living. The question of the rich man in today's Gospel, "what must I do to inherit eternal life?" (Mark 10:17), is left in the dust by the questions that are implicit in our lives. Aren't these the questions we are in effect asking: What must I do to have a longer, healthier life? What must I do to assure my comfort and security? What must I do to be sure of enough resources for a comfortable retirement? We can't deny the importance of these concerns. Christian life is not lived solely in another world; it begins in and amid the cares and work of this world. Yet the full Christian life is lived with an unavoidable tension between this life and the world to come. Both the sorrows of human life and the perils implicit in wealth are good reasons to keep the resurrection, eternal life, before our minds and hearts. In regard to the sorrows, this hope assures us that these and life's other evils will ultimately pass; in regard to riches, this hope tells us not to put our security in them. They too will pass.

Tuesday of the Eighth Week in Ordinary Time—
Happiness follows

Readings: 1 Pet 1:10-16; Mark 10:28-31
Resp. Psalm: Ps 98:1, 2–3ab, 3cd-4 (L 348)

The addition of the words "with persecutions" (Mark 10:30) to the promises made by Jesus in response to Peter's remark is significant. Without it there could be the suggestion that the following of the Lord is a sort of bargain. Jesus would be saying: "You follow me and you'll have all this." The words about persecution add a tougher dimension, another reminder of the Cross. We who so often live our Christian lives in relative tranquility and safety are unworthy to comment on what these words meant to those who suffered and died for their following of Christ. They suggest a truth about human life. An old Hindu legend speaks of a sort of wishing tree. Those who wish on the tree receive what they ask for and the opposite. Homes, brothers, sisters, children, property—and persecution (see Mark 10:29). Our blessings are probably never unmixed. A young woman gets a well-paying job but feels strongly the lack of someone with whom to share her good fortune. A married man with a wife and three little children senses that these limit his enjoyment of sea cruises. Good things by their nature seem to rule out other good things. The words of Jesus remind us that the most important goals of human life, holiness, love, good relationships, when realized, do not necessarily coincide with some simple and bland happiness. Happiness is a sort of flourish added to some other goal of life. Holiness or integrity is first even if it entails suffering, struggle. Genuine happiness follows and does not exclude some admixture of the challenging elements of human life.

Wednesday of the Eighth Week in Ordinary Time—
The ever-present self

Readings: 1 Pet 1:18-25; Mark 10:32-45
Resp. Psalm: Ps 147:12-13, 14-15, 19-20 (L 349)

How hard it is for us to leave ourselves or our self-interest out of anything we do! Whether it's a relationship, a job, or position, self intrudes everywhere. In its worst form we turn almost anything we do or are involved in into a way to feed ourselves, to please "me." Right after hearing Jesus speak of his coming suffering and death, a couple of disciples, not unlike us, turn the focus to themselves. "[W]e want you to do for us whatever we ask of you" (Mark 10:35), James and

John say to Jesus. They ask for positions of honor when he comes into his glory. Eventually Jesus tells them and us that among his followers the goal must be to "be the slave of all" (10:44). All of us probably exercise some kind of authority in however limited or wide a sphere: in the home or office or business or some service organization. It is so easy to make the preservation of the dignity of the position or the power or our self-image the focus while forgetting those we should be serving. We want to make our "importance felt" (Mark 10:42; NAB, 1st ed.), as Jesus says. Joined to the Lord in this Eucharist we can with his help learn to model our daily exercise of authority on the one who "did not come to be served but to serve" (Mark 10:45). May our prayer and communion help us to daily purify our actions of the taint of self-seeking.

Thursday of the Eighth Week in Ordinary Time—
I see; I follow

Readings: 1 Pet 2:2-5, 9-12; Mark 10:46-52
Resp. Psalm: Ps 100:2, 3, 4, 5 (L 350)

This section of Mark's Gospel began with the cure of a blind man (8:22-26) and ends with the cure of the blind beggar Bartimaeus. To him who wants to see Jesus says, "Go your way; your faith has saved you" (10:52). The next act in Mark's Gospel is in Jerusalem. The point of the two cures seems to be to highlight the spiritual blindness of the disciples and of ourselves. Faith, Mark tells us, cures us of blindness and enables us to see, no matter how provisionally, the truth of the way of Jesus. The next step is to fall in behind him and share his way, the way that will lead through suffering and death to resurrection. This is the basic sequence in Christian life: we must bring some faith and trust to the encounter with Christ. This in turn gives us insight into the meaning of Christ. We are called, as First Peter puts it, "out of darkness into his wonderful light" (2:9). Following from that, for the completion of a Christian life, must come the practical following of the Lord. "Immediately he received his sight / and followed him on the way" (Mark 10:52). And that way, we know from Mark, is to Jerusalem, to suffering, death, and resurrection. The early Christians called their movement "The Way" (Acts 9:2). This is the way, the way through suffering and death to glory. Any other way, the way of power and aggrandizement, for instance, is the wrong way. When Christ says, "I am the way" (John 14:6), we see what he is saying. Despite our resistance to the idea, we have to admit that suffering, pain, opposition, difficulty are built into human life. If we share them with him in faith, they become our way to eternal life. Let us not take for granted what happens daily at this altar; that saving mystery is put before us each time so that we can more fully enter into it.

Friday of the Eighth Week in Ordinary Time—
Just do it: pray

Readings: 1 Pet 4:7-13; Mark 11:11-26
Resp. Psalm: Ps 96:10, 11-12, 13 (L 351)

Successful or not, prayer is to Christian life as breathing is to physical life. Prayer is mentioned once in the first reading today and several times in the Gospel. Nothing surprising there, I suppose, since we are, after all, hearing the inspired Scriptures. But it is too easy to take prayer for granted, to expect that the preacher or the Scriptures should talk about it and implicitly to dismiss it. That's the preacher's job, or what do you expect to hear from the Scripture? But, perhaps even the most observant Christian needs to be reminded that there is no genuine Christian life without the practice of prayer, some personal involvement in prayer. It is not enough that we attend services where someone else can be trusted to lead us in prayer or do it for us. Prayer is absolutely essential as an act which we voluntarily do for at least two very basic reasons: (1) It is a recognition of our creatureliness, that we come from God; why religion if this is not true? (2) It is a recognition of our needs and deficiencies, another intrinsic component of religion. Away with concerns about how to pray; as the younger generation might put it on the back of a T-shirt, "Just do it."

Saturday of the Eighth Week in Ordinary Time—
Open doors, open ears

Readings: Jude 17, 20b-25; Mark 11:27-33
Resp. Psalm: Ps 63:2, 3-4, 5-6 (L 352)

In the Gospel, for the next few days, we witness Jesus' encounters with various groups who are out to trick him, to somehow weaken his hold on the masses of people who are impressed with him. One surmises that the chief priests, scribes, elders, Pharisees, Herodians, etc. all saw him as a threat and were at a loss about how to stop him. All this is of interest in understanding the events of the Savior's life, but we need also to see some immediate significance for our lives as his followers. One lesson we can learn concerns the unwillingness of Jesus to speak more bluntly and directly to these people. Instead he tells them stories where they can draw their own conclusions. He is not going to verbally bludgeon people into receiving him. Doesn't all this illustrate the truth that Jesus or God can only work in us if we show an open attitude, if we offer a willing, receptive heart? That is not to be presumed too easily. All of us tend, often too early in life, to settle on some nonnegotiable certainties that prevent us from being shaken up or being open to change. The groups mentioned above had their minds pretty well made up and were not going to be upset by some upstart from the countryside. As we hear the stories of these encounters we can ask ourselves if we are sufficiently open to questioning our own way of doing things, our own certainties and longtime practices. Do we allow our encounters with Jesus in Scripture, in the Eucharist, and with others to really change us or suggest questions? Jesus will not force entry into our hearts and lives; he will not overwhelm us with his presence and power. We must open the door.

Monday of the Ninth Week in Ordinary Time—
Living up to our dignity

Readings: 2 Pet 1:2-7; Mark 12:1-12
Resp. Psalm: Ps 91:1-2, 14-15b, 15c-16 (*L* 353)

Though Second Peter claims to be a letter like First Peter, it is more of a pep talk about resisting erroneous teaching about the Second Coming and being aware of the great dignity given the recipients, given us, by faith. We could add, by our baptism. Our entrance into the Body of Christ has given us, Second Peter says, the necessary and saving knowledge which should inspire what we do, how we act. More than that, we have "come to share in the divine nature" (1:4). To paraphrase an early Church Father (St. Irenaeus, *Against Heresies*, 3.10) *Christ became human like us, that we might become divine like him.* Even if we allow for some dramatic language, this still refers to the essential Christian teaching that tells us we share God's life by faith and baptism. We have been elevated above what the author calls "the corruption that is in the world" (2 Pet 1:4): greed and self-seeking. Daily, practical Christian life, then, means acting in accord with what we really are, acting like sons and daughters of God, rather than simply consumers or hairless animals. We've all heard of family heads who urge their children to live up to the family's honor. In such a context, this can refer to some pretty external matters but for us Christians living in accord with what we are as God's family can be an incentive to good lives in Christ. Living up to our dignity as Christians does not mean stuffy concern for appearances but a joyous awareness of the fact that God loves us and has so elevated us by that love. For instance, if we know God loves us and lives in us we might be more concerned that the joy we know appear in our lives, words, and attitudes. That joy is nourished when we share at this table of God's Son.

Tuesday of the Ninth Week in Ordinary Time—
Who or what governs us?

Readings: 2 Pet 3:12-15a, 17-18; Mark 12:13-17
Resp. Psalm: Ps 90:2, 3-4, 10, 14 and 16 (*L* 354)

Unless we live under a militantly anti-Christian government, the ordinary presumption for us Christians must be that civil authorities have a right to respect and that we can obey our country's laws. The effort to test Jesus in today's Gospel raises the issue of civil authority. The topic is indeed complex but not totally chaotic. The words of Jesus are famous: "Give to Caesar what belongs to Caesar. And give to God what belongs to God" (Mark 12:17; NIV). In one sense, of course, everything is God's, governments and civil authority included. On the other hand, in many areas of human life we recognize that even you and I and parents and teachers have been entrusted with some bit of God's governance; God does not directly take care of changing diapers and teaching computer science. Nor does God take direct charge of traffic or highway maintenance or settling disputes over property. All these are among the many functions involved in the good order of the world that are entrusted to human beings. The response of Jesus to his testers takes for granted that ordinarily there need not be any conflict between being a good citizen and being devoted to God. But again, having said this, we must recognize that the state is not God and can be questioned. Alert and conscientious citizens may need to challenge it in whatever ways the circumstances require and there is plenty of room for differences of approach. Do we challenge unjust policies at the polling station by demonstrations or by even more drastic actions like civil disobedience?

Wednesday of the Ninth Week in Ordinary Time—
He has robbed death of its power (1 Tim 1:18; NAB, 1st ed.)

Readings: 2 Tim 1:1-3, 6-12; Mark 12:18-27
Resp. Psalm: Ps 123:1b-2ab, 2cdef (*L* 355)

In today's Gospel Jesus deals with the group called Sadducees for the only time in Mark's Gospel. And their brief appearance here fits what we know of them elsewhere. They were wealthy and powerful Jews of the time who accepted a limited number of biblical books and claimed that there was no teaching about afterlife in them. Therefore, in asking Jesus about the woman who married seven brothers in succession and whose wife she would be in the resurrection, they are really trying to make fun of the resurrection. If all seven brothers and the woman rise to another life, will she be the wife of Harry or Frank or Bill, etc.? Jesus says that resurrection is nothing so crass; life will be transformed, not just a continuation of this one. And Jesus argues that the fact that the living God speaks of himself as "the God of Abraham, the God of Isaac, and the God of Jacob" (12:26; Exod 3:6)—people who are all dead—means that they must be living too. Resurrection is the source of our hope, confidence, and joy as Christians. No matter how little we know of the "mechanics" of it, we know from Scripture that because of it evil, suffering, pain, and death do not have the last word. Second Timothy says, "Christ Jesus . . . destroyed death and brought life and immortality / to light through the Gospel" (1:10). God works to carry through the day.

Thursday of the Ninth Week in Ordinary Time—
Instead of do's and don't's

Readings: 2 Tim 2:8-15; Mark 12:28-34
Resp. Psalm: Ps 25:4-5ab, 8-9, 10 and 14 (L 356)

The query addressed to Jesus by the scribe seems to have more sincerity to it than the tricky questions put before Jesus earlier. The scribe asks about which is the greatest commandment (cf. Matt 22:34-40). Apparently other Jewish teachers of the time had debated this question and answered it by saying, for instance, that the commandment to honor your parents is the greatest. Jesus evades getting into legalistic arguments about "which" commandment by commending love of God and love of neighbor. These two demands are much more fundamental than any commandment to do or not do this or that. They require an attitude which is unrelenting in its demands and contains any other possible moral commandment. If we were truly to love God and neighbor, the right behavior would follow. As St. Augustine put it, "Love and do what you will." The motivation and inspiration of love would carry us through every situation. In one sense the commandment to love God does not require us to do anything specific, yet reflection and

117

prayer will eventually suggest to us that it requires everything. So often, perhaps regularly, the problem in our morality is not a lack of knowledge but the motivation to live in a manner consistent with our relation to God. People know it's wrong to kill and steal; what they lack is the proper attitude, the desire and the will. We seem to lack more often the motivation to live morally than the knowledge that something is wrong or the will. The murderer doesn't plead, "Oh, gosh, I had no idea that murder was wrong. Why didn't someone tell me?" A loving relation to God, nourished by reflection and prayer, is probably more effective for ethical living than repeated do's and don'ts.

Friday of the Ninth Week in Ordinary Time—
How we read the Bible

Readings: 2 Tim 3:10-17; Mark 12:35-37
Resp. Psalm: Ps 119:157, 160, 161, 165, 166, 168 (*L* 357)

There is always danger that we take Scripture for granted; that we think we understand it because we've heard it often. Take that phrase from today's first reading: "All Scripture is inspired by God and is useful for teaching" (2 Tim 3:16). "All Scripture" here can only mean all or part of what we usually call the Old Testament. When this phrase was written the New Testament was in the process of being written and not all available yet. If we really think about it, most of us twentieth-century Christians will find it hard to see how today's Gospel is "useful" from our point of view. The way of arguing there is quite foreign to us. It means to make a point about how the Messiah, Christ, is more than just a descendant of the great king David; he is also God. A little thought about what is said in Second Timothy and in Mark should make it clear to us that Scripture indeed has great potential for our "training in righteousness" (2 Tim 3:16) *but* Scripture is not self-evident. Much as many would like to believe that we can just open the sacred book, put our finger down, and find the solution to alcoholism, desertion, or depression, Scripture requires some study, some help from experts, attention to the community of believers. Our approach to getting value from Scripture must be a combination of prayerful reading and a willingness to look for help.

Saturday of the Ninth Week in Ordinary Time—
The widow's giving

Readings: 2 Tim 4:1-8; Mark 12:38-44
Resp. Psalm: Ps 71:8-9, 14-15ab, 16-17, 22 (*L* 358)

There was a song quite a few years ago sung by Frank Sinatra entitled "The Tender Trap" and it was about marriage. In flippant terms we can see marriage as a "trap" which draws two people into the kind of self-giving and sacrifice most of us would otherwise avoid. Love and attraction bring a man and a woman into a life where, if there are children, they must inevitably give up some of their freedom, time, and comfort, to take care of dependent little human beings. They have no choice about getting up in the middle of the night for a sick child even though they may have serious responsibilities the next morning on the job. Parenting means giving, like the widow in today's Gospel, giving of what we may seem almost to lack: time and energy. Parents are often not giving of their surplus of energy and time; they are already, as we say, "run ragged." The widow—and parents—remind us all that true giving, true sacrifice, is not of what we have left over, but of what we could use for our comfort or convenience if we didn't give it. Statistics on giving to charitable causes show that the poor widows still give the most; people of lower income give more proportionately than do the wealthy. As we assist at this remembrance of the self-giving of the Lord, we pray to be strengthened in our own self-giving.

Monday of the Tenth Week in Ordinary Time—*Fulfillment*

Readings: 1 Kgs 17:1-6; Matt 5:1-12
Resp. Psalm: Ps 121:1bc-2, 3-4, 5-6, 7-8 (L 358)

Where does one begin talking about the Beatitudes, this first part of the Sermon on the Mount, read as today's Gospel? One way is to note how the ideals given here by Jesus are in such contrast to those of our society; how different the values here are from those illustrated in "The Lives of the Rich and Famous" or in the heroes of *People* magazine or the *Wall Street Journal* or a health and fitness magazine. In what we see and read, good looks, material success, aggressive takeovers, lavish lifestyles, and earthly fulfillment are preeminent. What Jesus says God blesses are attitudes and conditions that we should just as soon think of as little as possible. Sure, the newspapers or the television news occasionally will highlight a person of extraordinary selflessness or heroism or even suffering. But generally, we only reluctantly think of these things. Fulfillment for our society has to come within the span of our earthly lives. We are to be pitied if we don't have cushy retirement or reach our potential in a well-paying, powerful position. Jesus puts forcefully before us the fact that our fulfillment, our happiness may very likely be deferred but it is most sure for those who suffer, experience sorrow, are persecuted, are merciful, are generous, are peacemakers.

Tuesday of the Tenth Week in Ordinary Time—
Hospitality wins out

Readings: 1 Kgs 17:7-16; Matt 5:13-16
Resp. Psalm: Ps 4:2-3, 4-5, 7b-8 (*L* 360)

The story about Elijah and the widow suggests a point similar to that made in the stories of our Lord's multiplication of loaves and fishes. Generosity toward others and trust in God should be the fixed stars in our world. As yesterday with the Beatitudes, we see here an example of what could be called the Spirit's overturning of worldly values. Prudence and self-concern would dictate to the widow to take care of herself and her son, to trust in whatever resources she had. Instead hospitality or concern for others wins out and she gives what little she has to Elijah. As with the "[f]ive loaves and two fish" (Matt 14:17) in our Lord's miracle, the willingness to share what little we have is rewarded beyond expectation. "Give, and it shall be given to you" (Luke 6:38; NAB, 1st ed.). Trust and God will take care of you. Such generosity and trust are hard to muster, unimaginable for most of us, possibly. The lesson seems to be one which our world—and we in it—finds so hard to comprehend. Share what you have and you will not be disappointed. The Spirit must help us live this way, in this manner. It requires more prayer, more receptivity on our part to the Spirit's power. Allowing the Spirit to work this in us would truly make us "the salt of the earth," "the light of the world" (Matt 5:13, 14).

Wednesday of the Tenth Week in Ordinary Time—
God will come through

Readings: 1 Kgs 18:20-39; Matt 5:17-19
Resp. Psalm: Ps 16:1b-2ab, 4, 5ab and 8, 11 (*L* 361)

If today's first reading were being presented on television it would fittingly carry a warning: Do not try this at home. It surely is dramatic. The Books of Kings show us repeatedly the wavering and actual unfaithfulness of God's people by which their authors justify the great trial to come, their exile from the Promised Land. Today's action-filled episode shows the Israelites "in black and white" how superior is the God whom they have not trusted. Both the story itself and the type of literature we have here make that one point and do not give the disciple of Christ or the believer in God any warrant for testing God. Don't try this at home! In an earlier reading we heard of how Elijah was able to command a drought and it came (1 Kgs 17:1). The god Baal who seemed such an attraction to the Israelites was supposed to be the god who controlled such things, so Elijah's action was a defiant challenge. In today's episode we see Elijah's claims verified by, you might say, an experiment. Again, one you shouldn't try at home! Scripture regularly warns against testing God but it does encourage us to learn from experience and steady faithfulness how close God is and how concerned for us. That is something we can and must try at home, in the office, at school, on the job, on the street, or on vacation. Though no immediate excitement or miracle is promised, the Lord does say, "whoever obeys and teaches these commandments / will be called greatest in the kingdom of heaven" (Matt 5:19).

Thursday of the Tenth Week in Ordinary Time—
People, profit, and power

Readings: 1 Kgs 18:41-46; Matt 5:20-26
Resp. Psalm: Ps 65:10, 11, 12-13 (L 362)

Anger, abusive language, and contempt—don't they seem standard fare in many a discussion in our country, in many a talk show? Our culture, the spirit of public discourse today, takes anger, abusive language, and contempt for minorities and the weak for granted, and it tempts us all to accept that. But the teaching of Christ requires so often that we be countercultural, that we refuse to go along with what is fashionable when it is so opposed to Christ's teaching. Greed and excessive profit taking are still the favored vices of our world. Our world, its great buildings and cities, its famous people, are, in many ways, closely linked to the drive for wealth. The difficult mission of Christians is to temper the fever of greed and to speak out for sensitivity and generosity in speech and talk, to illustrate in our own lives and words respect for all our fellow human beings. In a world so populous as to be overwhelming to most of us, the Lord still teaches us that each human being has a God-given dignity and deserves respect. People are above profit and power.

Friday of the Tenth Week in Ordinary Time—
Where God is found and heard

Readings: 1 Kgs 19:9a, 11–16; Matt 5:27–32
Resp. Psalm: Ps 27:7-8a, 8b-9abc, 13–14 (*L* 363)

The fascinating story of Elijah's encounter with God, no matter how odd some of its components, is the kind of story that lingers in our imagination. "[T]he Lord will be passing by" (1 Kgs 19:11) God tells Elijah. But the Lord is "not in the wind," "not in the earthquake," "not in the fire," but in a "tiny whispering sound" (19:11, 12). It's another reminder to us not to look for the Lord solely in the dramatic and unusual but that the Lord may well be revealed in the quiet and unremarkable, in the most ordinary things. But what the story may be telling us most of all is not that God is more available in the microscopic than in the macroscopic, that God prefers the small to the large, but that God cannot be limited by our expectations of where and how God can appear or be revealed. So often, if we look back on our lives or on some particular moment we're struck by how God worked and was present in something we would have avoided if at all possible. The presence of God, God's activity in our life, is more evident the more we leave ourselves open to the possibility of God's presence where we might least expect it. Let's not close the doors too early.

Saturday of the Tenth Week in Ordinary Time—
Honest and open

Readings: 1 Kgs 19:19–21; Matt 5:33–37
Resp. Psalm: Ps 16:1b-2a and 5, 7-8, 9–10 (*L* 364)

Though this section of the Sermon on the Mount is very brief and given in the context of taking oaths or swearing by something or someone, still it touches matters basic to human life and relationships. Honesty and straightforward speech are not to be taken for granted in our society. In our day and our speech, oath-taking has become for the most part simply a vehement way of speaking. When we say, "By God" or "By all that's sacred" we're usually just repeating some bit of jargon. But originally an oath was taken to bolster one's statement and to assure the hearers that you were speaking in utmost seriousness. About the only serious oath we hear in our world is "So help me God" in certain civil contexts. We may say "I swear" when a friend asks us to verify or confirm that Jerry did indeed quit his job at Seagate. So, oaths have a relatively small place in our society; we try, instead, by all kinds of legal stratagems to assure that if someone is not telling the truth, the consequences will be felt. But fundamentally what Jesus is asking of his disciples, therefore of us, is that we be of such transparent and honest character that others know that when we say "Yes" we mean "yes" and similarly with "No" (see Matt 5:37). Honesty in thought and speech, simplicity, directness, and straightforwardness are virtues too often taken for granted when, in fact, they may be missing from much of our conversation. When you think of it, a habit of honesty in speech is probably closely related to a lack of selfishness. We are simple and honest because our primary concern is not to protect ourselves.

Monday of the Eleventh Week in Ordinary Time—
Another measure than the world's

Readings: 1 Kgs 21:1-16; Matt 5:38-42
Resp. Psalm: Ps 5:2-3ab, 4b-6a, 6b-7 (L 365)

We use that famous line about "An eye for an eye and a tooth for a tooth" (Matt 5:38; see Exod 21, 24; Lev 24:19-20) in our language to signify vengeance, retaliation. Actually in the Law of the Jews it was an attempt to limit retaliation. Instead of gouging out both eyes of enemies, smashing all their teeth, this law was urging restraint and limitation. An eye for an eye, no more! Don't do worse to your foe than your foe has done to you. The New Moses, Jesus, goes much further: "offer no resistance" to injury (Matt 5:39), Jesus is attempting to push the Law of Moses further along the path of compassion. The actions of Ahab and Jezebel in the first reading go further along the path of cruelty and self-seeking. Not only do the two plot to get this piece of property but they also kill the rightful owner to boot. We can read of and witness the same ruthlessness on the part of the powerful throughout history and among the tyrants of our day, too. Seeing such callous injustice to others on the part of the powerful must make ordinary people at times think that it's just we peasants who practice any self-restraint or forgiveness or kindness. As a famous member of the powerful of our time has said, "Only the little people pay taxes." We've already been told at the beginning of the Sermon on the Mount, in Matthew, that the little people, the mourning, the poor, the meek, the hungry—these are the truly blessed (see 5:3-9). What is big or little in the eyes of the world is pretty irrelevant when it comes to our relation to God.

Tuesday of the Eleventh Week in Ordinary Time—
Loving like God

Readings: 1 Kgs 21:17-29; Matt 5:43-48
Resp. Psalm: Ps 51:3-4, 5-6ab, 11 and 16 (*L* 366)

Few phrases in the Gospel have been used to cause worry and fear as much as the final words of today's radical statements by Jesus. "So be perfect, just as your heavenly Father is perfect" (Matt 5:48). Or, in the more familiar and even more frightening language, "you must be perfect . . . as your heavenly Father is perfect" (see the Amplified Bible). Taken out of context and thrown around as a general principle for Christians, it is bound to leave us feeling like continual losers or failures. The injunction to be perfect like God has led to a lot of gritting of teeth and self-torment for every little failure. It has led at times in some forms of Christian spirituality to an atmosphere where people are very willing to cry over their faults but never able to laugh off their foibles. But it makes no genuinely Christian sense out of its context. The Gospel throughout presupposes that we will sin, that we do not become perfect, that we need forgiveness and the healing of God's grace. We are to be perfected like our heavenly Father, Jesus tells us, insofar as we try to give our love to everyone, irrespective of color, distance, nation, or character. To be perfected as the Lord asks is to be perfected in how indiscriminately and generously we love others. To be perfect like God is to greet not only our nice neighbors but everyone, to do good to not just those who do us good (tit for tat) but to all we possibly can.

Wednesday of the Eleventh Week in Ordinary Time—
Without a mirror

Readings: 2 Kgs 2:1, 6-14; Matt 6:1-6, 16-18
Resp. Psalm: Ps 31:20, 21, 24 (*L* 367)

"[D]o not let your left hand know what your right is doing" (Matt 6:3). Much religious teaching the world over sees this kind of freedom from self-consciousness as basic. The most popular religious book of India teaches that one should do one's actions without thought of reward or even of outcome. In various traditions there are as many ways of putting this. For instance, one should put all one's heart and attention into what one is doing at the moment without looking over one's shoulder to see how one is doing or what others think. We should be so devoted to doing well what is before us that we don't have time to think about what the reward will be or to worry about the results. In Jesus' teaching, as we hear it today, the emphasis is on doing what is good, right, pleasing to God, without looking for acclaim, praise, or recognition. It would be like a college student hearing with great surprise at graduation that he or she was graduating summa cum laude. She had only been concerned for four years to do each day's work as well as possible and wholeheartedly. Wouldn't it be ideal if we could be so intent on doing what our conscience and situation in life ask that we do not worry about the crowds, the publicity?

Thursday of the Eleventh Week in Ordinary Time—
The root of all good (cf. 1 Tim 6:10)

Readings: Sir 48:1-14; Matt 6:7-15
Resp. Psalm: Ps 97:1-2, 3-4, 5-6, 7 (L 368)

Elijah and Elisha were two wonderworkers of ancient Israel who seem so mysterious to us. Yesterday's reading from Second Kings had spoken of the two, so today the reading from Kings is interrupted to bring us a hymn of praise to the two from Sirach. They are most significant to us as pictures of what God was to do for all through the risen Christ. Three aspects of their lives especially point to our Lord: (1) bringing the dead back to life, (2) ascending to heaven, and (3) bringing about the day of final reconciliation. Christ has risen, ascended to his Father, and now works through the Holy Spirit to reconcile all people, to raise all to new life in God. The Our Father concentrates our attention and energies on cooperating with the work of the risen Lord. God's name will be holy before all, the kingdom will come, the will of God will be accomplished insofar as we allow the power of the risen Christ to operate in forgiveness. If greed or the desire for wealth is the root of all evil (1 Tim 6:10), then a willingness to forgive, to let go of the grudges and hatred that cause so much suffering is the root of all good.

Friday of the Eleventh Week in Ordinary Time—
What finally counts

Readings: 2 Kgs 11:1-4, 9-18, 20; Matt 6:19-23
Resp. Psalm: Ps 132:11, 12, 13-14, 17-18 (L 369)

What do we really value, what will last? What is our treasure? Where is our treasure? Things that can be counted like wealth, money, the things we collect, are no real substitute for what really counts. Jesus warns here, as so often in the Gospels, against counting on earthly securities that we accumulate for ourselves. What we can really count on, he tells us, is a treasure we lay up in heaven where it cannot decay, dissolve, or be stolen. For Athaliah, as for many of the power-hungry sovereigns we hear about in the Books of Kings, in Shakespeare, and in our daily news, what really counts is power and control. Nothing in the bloody tale of Athaliah is all that foreign to us; within recent years we heard of the member of a royal family who killed off almost all the other members. Clearly, power and control are not treasures we lay up for ourselves in heaven. One must live on a superficial level without self-knowledge to think that something external to ourselves can be what counts most. It would be hard to get to the heart of this matter any more concisely than Thomas G. Long does in his commentary on Matthew (Thomas G. Long, *Matthew* [Louisville, Ky.: Westminster John Knox Press, 1997]): "What our hearts really desire, of course, is to count—to count for something and to count to someone." In other words, our true treasure must be found in a clear conscience and the knowledge that we have spent our life and energies in the service of love.

Saturday of the Eleventh Week in Ordinary Time—
See the birds and the lilies

Readings: 2 Chr 24:17-25; Matt 6:24-34
Resp. Psalm: Ps 89:4-5, 29-30, 31-32, 33-34 (L 370)

We who are here for Mass today are very fortunate. This most beautiful Gospel text is not used on any other Sunday of the year nor the similar one in Luke's Gospel. Too bad we can't all hear its message more often! The words are the strongest and most attractive of encouragements to trust and confidence. And surely many of us need that daily as we are tempted to become all tied up and worried about this or that problem, at home or with relationships or on the job. It tells us in moving ways to retain some perspective on all the worrisome elements of our life. Aren't life and health more important than the external we fuss about? Doesn't God have a greater and deeper care for us than we can possibly have? See the birds of the air and the flowers of the field, how they live. We can become so impressed with our own importance or indispensability to some endeavor that we deprive ourselves of sleep, snatch our meals on the run, neglect family and friends, God. "The unbelievers are always running after these things" (Matt 6:32; NAB, 1st ed.). But God knows we need food, drink, clothing, and shelter. Cannot our faith and trust help us relax a bit and live with a bit more carefree attitude? This is not an invitation to become a vagabond but to keep a sense of perspective about the relative importance of the elements of our life.

Monday of the Twelfth Week in Ordinary Time—
A little self-questioning

Readings: 2 Kgs 17:5-8, 13-15a, 18; Matt 7:1-5
Resp. Psalm: Ps 60:3, 4-5, 12-13 (*L* 371)

"Israel sinned"; "they venerated other gods"; "they . . . were . . . stiff-necked"; "They rejected [God's] statutes, / the covenant" (2 Kgs 17:7, 14, 15). The first reading may seem to provide us with ample reason for self-congratulation. After all, it was the ancient Hebrews who sinned, practiced idolatry, turned their backs on the covenant, and were so stiff-necked—not us. But it's just that sort of self-righteous judgment our Lord advises us against. The Scriptures, especially the history of the failures of the Hebrews to live up to the covenant, are not given us to bolster our own sense of spiritual contentment. Better to use the example of the Israelites to examine our own lives. How faithfully do we live up to our status as sons and daughters of God, members of God's family? The idols may not be golden calves (see Exod 32), but how do we look on our ambitions, wealth, or the desire for it, our own time and comfort? Have we perhaps become rigid in our conviction that we know and obey God's will for us? True, our Lord's teaching was not given simply to terrorize us or make us, as we say, nervous wrecks. It does, however, require a constant and adjustable willingness to suspect that we are as likely as the rest of the human race to become prematurely content with ourselves. The specks aren't just in other eyes.

Tuesday of the Twelfth Week in Ordinary Time—
Competing for the gold

Readings: 2 Kgs 19:9b-11, 14-21, 31-35a, 36; Matt 7:6, 12-14
Resp. Psalm: Ps 48:2-3ab, 3cd-4, 10-11 (*L* 372)

"Do to others whatever you would have them do to you" (Matt 7:12). In urging the Golden Rule, Jesus is also supporting and commending the Jewish Law. The same teaching is found elsewhere in Jewish thought of the time and before Jesus. In fact, he says, "This is the Law and the Prophets" (7:12). Jesus gives an incentive for us by telling us later in this same Gospel that the good we do to others, the naked, hungry, sorrowing, etc., is done to him (25:31-46). Not only is this teaching about doing to others what you would have them do to you

127

found in the Jewish religion, it appears in other religions. Jesus is careful in the Sermon on the Mount to state that he is fulfilling, not rejecting, the wisdom of Judaism (see 5:17). All this tells us not to attempt to build up our faith by putting others down. There is much to value in other religions, other faiths. The Second Vatican Council said that the Church rejects nothing of the truth or holiness found in other religions. We are to respect these religions. Christians, in other words, are happy to find their values and wisdom echoed or paralleled elsewhere. The Golden Rule can be a genuine bridge to other faiths, a guide to behavior that all can proclaim. Above all, it is a legitimate area for competition. None of us need fear overdoing the Golden Rule.

Wednesday of the Twelfth Week in Ordinary Time—
True prophets

Readings: 2 Kgs 22:8-13; 23:1-3; Matt 7:15-20
Resp. Psalm: Ps 119:33, 34, 35, 36, 37, 40 (*L* 373)

Jesus speaks today to a subject that has been most difficult and messy throughout the history of the Christian faith: false prophets, or how we are to evaluate people who claim to bring a special message from God. As long as there have been individuals claiming to speak on God's behalf, to bring God's message, there has been the problem of knowing whether they are genuine. Early Christian documents show the earliest followers of Jesus wrestling with the problem. They came up with a standard which ruled against prophets who asked for money or anything for themselves. But even that is not as simple as it sounds. There is so much room for self-deception on the part of the speaker or the hearer. The more we think about it, the more it seems clear that no one of us can make the final judgment; discussion by many members of the Christian community and attention to the full voice of tradition are both required. Possibly the safest course for all of us is not to jump too eagerly and quickly on the bandwagon of some new prophet, some person claiming special visions or messages from God or Mary (or another saint). Along with that we need to look for what leads to more charity, more attention back to Jesus and his words, more service of others.

Thursday of the Twelfth Week in Ordinary Time—
Truly human

Readings: 2 Kgs 24:8-17; Matt 7:21-29
Resp. Psalm: Ps 79:1b-2, 3-5, 8, 9 (*L* 374)

Some have argued about whether the Sermon on the Mount is intended for the disciples alone or for everyone, for all Christians or for those dedicated to a specific kind of religious life such as monasticism. Can't we believe that it must be meant for all of us? Otherwise Jesus could have made it clear that it was only for the elite. Too, why give it so much space in Matthew's Gospel if it's a handbook for a small group? One commentator offers a compelling judgment: "The commands of the Sermon describe what it means to be fully human, not just what it means to be religious" (Thomas G. Long in *Matthew* [Louisville, Ky.: Westminster John Knox Press, 1997]). This fits with the great dignity that Scripture gives to the human being. Psalm 8 puts it well: "What are humans that you are mindful of them, / mere mortals that you care for them? / Yet you have them little less than a god, / crowned them with glory and honor. / You have given them rule over the works of your hands, / put all things at their feet" (vv. 5-7). And after the book of Genesis describes the creation of man and woman, "God looked at everything he had made, and he found it very good" (Gen 1:31). Looking at the Sermon on the Mount in such a context, it tells us that to be forgiving and considerate of others, to serve rather than dominate, to be in solidarity with the suffering and poor, is to be truly, genuinely human. When we're ruthless, self-seeking, and revengeful we're poor pictures of what a human being should be.

Friday of the Twelfth Week in Ordinary Time—
Misery calls to everyone

Readings: 2 Kgs 25:1-12; Matt 8:1-4
Resp. Psalm: Ps 137:1-2, 3, 4-5, 6 (L 375)

Matthew's Gospel is thoroughly grounded in the Jewish tradition of Jesus. In it we hear protestations by Jesus himself that everything he does and says is in continuity with the religion of his family. Jesus himself and Matthew's Gospel are good examples of being rooted in a specific religious tradition. That could, of course, result in a very narrow perspective. We've all run into people whose religion seems to have narrowed their view of life, their sympathies. As a result, some of our contemporaries like to practice an open attitude, which means they accept everything around them with no discrimination and feel that to do so would be "judgmental." Yet, there is a way—we see it in great saints and generous souls—of prizing one's own tradition and being appreciative of others. Above all mercy and love should know no boundaries; human misery should call all of us to help. Yesterday some comment was made about how the Sermon on the Mount may be meant as modeling the genuinely good human being, not just the Christian. In today's Gospel, after coming down from delivering the Sermon, Jesus performs the first of several signs that show that his sympathies and mission go beyond his fellow Jews and those considered full members. Today he cures, even touches, a leper. Following this he cures a Gentile and a woman. All three represent people whom we would call marginalized. If our religious tradition is, like the Christian, basically broad in sympathies, our devotion to it should not prevent us from helping the marginalized in our world: the poor, the homeless, the immigrant, and those of another color.

Saturday of the Twelfth Week in Ordinary Time—
Suffering is never far away

Readings: Lam 2:2, 10-14, 18-19; Matt 8:5-17
Resp. Psalm: Ps 74:1b-2, 3-5, 6-7, 20-21 (L 376)

The picture of fallen Jerusalem in the Lamentations could be a picture of some part of the world at any given time. If there is at the moment no country victimized by another, there is at least one suffering from famine, internal strife, or racial or religious unrest. It's a wonder of our human consciousness that even though, with the help of the media, we may be very much aware of suffering in Ethiopia, Albania, or China, we are still able to go to sleep. Commenting on the ministry of Jesus, Matthew quotes Isaiah: "He took away our infirmities and bore our diseases" (8:17; see Isa 53:4). Christian belief is that Christ truly entered into human suffering and misery and ultimately delivers us from it. But we always risk thinking of that too much as magic: that all we must do is pray and trust, and the Lord will repair all that is wrong with our world. The more complete message about our redemption by Christ is that we are God's instruments in alleviating the suffering, famine, disease, pain, and terror of our fellow human beings. While being alert to possibilities of helping the global situation, we are all capable of doing something about the local situation: the loneliness, poverty, strife, abuse, in our own neighborhood or community.

Monday of the Thirteenth Week in Ordinary Time—
Solidarity

Readings: Amos 2:6-10, 13-16; Matt 8:18-22
Resp. Psalm: Ps 50:16bc-17, 18-19, 20-21, 22-23 (L 377)

For most of this week we will hear the frank and ferocious words of the prophet Amos. He pulls no punches in indicting the injustices of Israel's and our society. We may, in fact, be discouraged at seeing how similar are the injustices against the poor in our world and then. The slightest acquaintance with conditions around the world today show us the poor still being enslaved for others' profit or being expected to live a subhuman life because of others' disregard and cruelty. We ask, hasn't anything changed? We can, it is true, point to improvements, no matter how spotty and shaky. But the deep-seated greed that lurks in all of us needs to be fought continually by people who speak on behalf of justice and of the poor and powerless. We need prophets, people who speak up for the poor and act against injustice, people like Dorothy Day, Martin Luther King, and Mother Teresa. There are always enough of us who speak up for self-interest and the comfort of our own economic class. The words of Jesus in the Gospel, addressed to two different individuals, stress the Son of Man's solidarity with the poor and the urgency of his mission. Come, he says, forget about personal comfort and join me now in bringing good news to the poor (see also 4:19; Luke 4:18).

Tuesday of the Thirteenth Week in Ordinary Time—
In God's hands

Readings: Amos 3:1-8; 4:11-12; Matt 8:23-27
Resp. Psalm: Ps 5:4b-6a, 6b-7, 8 (L 378)

Quite a contrast between the two readings today! The first pronounces God's judgment on an unjust people and threatens severe punishment. The Gospel reading, on the other hand, encourages us in the storms of our lives with the power and concern of the Lord. Taken altogether the various parts of Scripture, written, sometimes, over six hundred years apart, give us many different faces of God. Any one image of God, if it alone is in our minds, limits God too much, can omit various aspects of God. There is a God who judges; there are limits to what human be-havior God tolerates; and there is a God who, pictured in Jesus, wishes to calm the storms of life. Hearing and reading less familiar parts of the Bible, like today's reading, helps us avoid thinking we have God too well-packaged. God is always more than what we can imagine; God is always more, for instance, than some kind of a servant at our beck and call. As Jesus teaches by resting placidly in the boat during the storm and by his words, we are right to call on God and to trust God. But, as the Our Father teaches, our petitions need to always be accompanied by our recognition that God's way of doing things is different than ours, God's plans may be other than what we would like at the moment. Our faith and trust need to be so complete that we feel free to trust God without spelling out exactly what God must do.

Wednesday of the Thirteenth Week in Ordinary Time—
From words to acts

Readings: Amos 5:14-15, 21-24; Matt 8:28-34
Resp. Psalm: Ps 50:7, 8-9, 10-11, 12-13, 16bc-17 (*L* 379)

From the student who spouts a lot of ecologically sensitive stuff while still trashing the environment to the entrepreneur who is concerned for the poor but not to the point of paying them a living wage, we all tend to miss or conceal the implications of our beliefs. We can let worship be a sedative rather than a spur to action and love. In it we can profess our faith and trust in God, our belief that all belongs to God, and that we are stewards of God's world and so easily not live up to that in daily life and practice. That this can happen does not argue against worship but simply points out that there is no automatic way to make us humans moral and worthy sons and daughters of God apart from our cooperation and will. Neither congregation nor celebrant can rest from the effort to relate what goes on in worship to what goes on in daily life, in business, education, the family, government, social life, etc. "[L]et justice prevail at the gate" (Amos 5:15). Genuine self-giving and sharing in Christ's sacrifice is accompanied by love and justice: "let justice surge like water, / and goodness like an unfailing stream" (Amos 5:24).

Thursday of the Thirteenth Week in Ordinary Time—
Hard tasks

Readings: Amos 7:10-17; Matt 9:1-8
Resp. Psalm: Ps 19:8, 9, 10, 11 (*L* 380)

It's hard for most of us to imagine what a prophet's life would be like. When Amos says he is no prophet, he is separating himself from a group so called whom he considered corrupt. But from the message he gives to the priest Amaziah it is clear he feels compelled to prophesy, to hand on God's message. Surely most of us do not feel comfortable in warning, threatening others, or even in making great claims such as Jesus made. "[Y]our sins are forgiven" (Matt 9:2), he says. We'd rather not call attention to ourselves and especially not call hostile attention to ourselves. Some courageous souls among us are willing to combat, take on our culture and common practices, and at times denounce them. The nearest thing to being a prophet for most of us, however, may have to do with simply telling someone the truth, helping others face reality. A new lieutenant in the army must discipline, even recommend dishonorable discharge for two soldiers caught using cocaine. A doctor has to break the news of a terminal illness to the patient or the family. A teacher has to tell a student that his or her work is just not up to standard. No one likes to bring the bad news but, as experience often shows, it may be the key to a real awakening for the one who receives it. The truth can make us free (see John 8:32); facing it can help us avoid greater difficulties further along the way.

Friday of the Thirteenth Week in Ordinary Time—
The human web

Readings: Amos 8:4-6, 9-12; Matt 9:9-13
Resp. Psalm: Ps 119:2, 10, 20, 30, 40, 131 (*L* 381)

An eloquent passage from Amos on the exploitation of the poor comes at us today with the story of the call of Matthew the tax collector. The tax collector who was thought of as skimming off a share for himself is an example of how the poor especially can be exploited by officials and institutions. But we shouldn't point the finger too eagerly at everyone else and let ourselves off the hook. In our worldwide economy we all, to some degree, are beneficiaries of the exploitation of the people who produce, for instance, our inexpensive coffee, who serve us in restaurants and hotels, who bring us discount prices. The "great" prices we get at the discount store may be at least partially due to the low wages of the employees. Apart from research for which we have no time we cannot know how totally we are involved in the exploitation of others. One of the psalms asks forgiveness for our "unknown faults" (Ps 19:13). Strictly speaking, we only have genuine sins if we know they are sins. But unknown sins can certainly refer to situations where we are not really aware of what good or evil we do with our lives and time. We drink our coffee and sprinkle our sugar, unaware of how little those who pick the coffee beans or harvest the cane (or beets) get of the price we pay for a pound. It may not be such a bad idea to ask forgiveness, at least at times, for our "unknown" sins while we also work for economic justice.

Saturday of the Thirteenth Week in Ordinary Time—
Joy in the life of Christ

Readings: Amos 9:11-15; Matt 9:14-17
Resp. Psalm: Ps 85:9ab and 10, 11-12, 13-14 (L 382)

With the help of the exultant and final passage from Amos, we have a good occasion today to stress the joy of life in Christ. The last words of the very sober and even grim book of Amos are about the joy and excitement of the days when God will triumph, the age of the Messiah. And Jesus explains that his disciples cannot fast while he is with them; they should rejoice. Fasting is for periods of mourning and repentance. True, our life, even after the Lord comes into it, can be crushed with sorrow and pain. Undoubtedly! And, true enough, Jesus is not with us in the same way that he was present to his disciples. But our faith and trust that—in Jesus—God has shown us most clearly that we are loved (see John 3:16) and God wants only the best for us, shouldn't this be evident in more joy, more enthusiasm about our life in Christ, our life with Christ? A complaining and self-pitying mood certainly reflects poorly the presence of Christ in us. There is nothing wrong in praying that the Lord with whom we are united in this celebration will increase and intensify our joy in his presence.

Monday of the Fourteenth Week in Ordinary Time—
God and the beloved

Readings: Hos 2:16, 17c-18, 21-22; Matt 9:18-26
Resp. Psalm: Ps 145:2-3, 4-5, 6-7, 8-9 (L 383)

Many a Christian today is surprised to hear that God's relation to humans, to those who believe in God, is compared in Scripture a number of times to that of a lover and beloved, husband and wife. This first of a series of readings from Hosea speaks of God wooing back the bride of his youth who had been unfaithful. Our faith relation to God in most of its particulars is helpfully compared to such a relationship. Our relation has to begin with some risk and some attraction, possibly with an introduction by someone else. Our parents, for instance, may first have told us about God. We get to know God better by reflecting on his words (the Scriptures), by spending time with God in quiet, and in the sacraments. The relationship, like all our relationships, may have its ups and downs. It may have to be reaffirmed after we have strayed. The final state of the relationship is much like that of a couple who have firmly settled on each other, who promise to be there for each other. What we expect to find in marriage or in an intimate friendship is that the other will be there for us in every circumstance. God—over and over again in Scripture—assures us of that presence and power in sorrow and joy, fervor and doubt; what often needs work is our faithfulness and responsiveness. God is always there, responsive to the least bit of new effort on our part. May we be more and more available for God's work.

Tuesday of the Fourteenth Week in Ordinary Time—
What idols?

Readings: Hos 8:4-7, 11-13; Matt 9:32-38
Resp. Psalm: Ps 115:3-4, 5-6, 7ab-8, 9-10 (*L* 384)

When we hear talk of idolatry in Scripture we don't have to go looking for statues and images of winged animals or idealized human beings. Idolatry, even in the absence of these in our lives, remains a genuine peril for all of us. We can easily make self, our comfort and tranquility, our peace and prosperity, into idols. They become this when we devote our greatest efforts and our best energy and time to them while giving considerably less attention to the service of God and love of our neighbor (see Matt 22:37-39). In the Gospel we hear Jesus say to his disciples, "The harvest is abundant but the laborers are few" (Matt 9:37). Working for God's reign in our world in whatever capacity we can do that is a way to lessen the temptation to idolatry. Working for a better neighborhood, a safer one, working for economic and social justice, working for peace, working for the spread of the values of Christ, all these take us away from simple self-absorption. Rather than spend a lot of time worrying whether or not we're idolaters, we can make that an irrelevant question by using our talents and energies for the harvest the Lord speaks of. Nothing helps us turn from self and selfish concerns about our comfort and contentment more than to work for and to interest ourselves in the service of others. In working for others and serving the kingdom of God we discover the meaning of life.

Wednesday of the Fourteenth Week in Ordinary Time—
Faithfulness

Readings: Hos 10:1-3, 7-8, 12; Matt 10:1-7
Resp. Psalm: Ps 105:2-3, 4-5, 6-7 (*L* 384)

We need stories about loyalty and faithfulness. Is it because they are in such short supply among us humans that we dote on stories and movies about loyal dogs and dolphins? Stories about us humans so often seem to glorify the fact that someone's dream has come along and this someone feels free to abandon an earlier commitment to be fulfilled by this new love. Undoubtedly, there are miserable human relationships from which people deserve to be delivered. But it would be inspiring to see a case where people like you and me face the difficulties of genuine faithfulness and come through them. Throughout the Gospels and, for that matter, the whole of Scripture, God's loyalty to the chosen people is striking. No matter how often they go after other gods and idols, God always invites them back. In today's Gospel Jesus even tells his apostles—at this phase of their work—not to go to the Gentiles but to make a real effort at being heard by the people of Israel, "the lost sheep of the house of Israel" (Matt 10:6). We have heard lately in the Gospel readings about the unfaithfulness of their leaders but Jesus only very slowly and reluctantly will cease his effort to be heard and received by them. God's covenant means faithfulness on God's side no matter what (see 2 Tim 2:13). Once chosen and loved, always chosen and loved. Isn't there some room for similar steadfastness in our relationships? Can our friends find in us the loyalty that is put before us daily at this altar?

Thursday of the Fourteenth Week in Ordinary Time—
Prefer nothing to Christ

Readings: Hos 11:1-4, 8e-9; Matt 10:7-15
Resp. Psalm: Ps 80:2ac and 3b, 15-16 (*L* 386)

In telling the disciples how to act when they go forth with his message, Jesus is entrusting them with his work, asking them (us, the church) to be the vehicles for his continued loving action in the world. "Cure the sick, raise the dead, / cleanse lepers, drive out demons" (Matt 10:8). When we call the church the sacrament of Christ we mean that through and in the church Christ and his saving power are made manifest; the church should be transparent so that Christ is seen and shines forth in its activity. The church is to serve Christ and point to Christ, not to be an obstacle to his work or to make itself the center of Christian life. We sometimes hear language that suggests a bishop or pastor is appointed to serve the pope or the church. That may be susceptible of a good interpretation, but it would be better if we put Christ at the center. Too much emphasis on church and hierarchy can look like a kind of idolatry. All of us who make up the church from pope to you and me are Christians to the extent that we point to Christ and through and with him serve God (see John 13:1–17). Part of the appeal of the saints is undoubtedly their Christ-centered spirituality. One of his most famous and always applicable expressions of this comes from the Rule of Saint Benedict: "Prefer nothing whatever to Christ" (72:11; *RB 1980* [Collegeville: Liturgical Press, 1981]).

Friday of the Fourteenth Week in Ordinary Time—
Snakes and doves

Readings: Hos 14:2-10; Matt 10:16-23
Resp. Psalm: Ps 51:3-4, 8-9, 12-13, 14 and 17(L 387)

"[B]e shrewd as serpents and simple as doves" (Matt 10:16). Putting together in our minds such seemingly contradictory advice is hard. The context in which Jesus speaks these words may be some help. He speaks of how those who witness to their belief will face persecution and opposition. Just being simple-minded is not going to be enough. Christians need some distance from and even suspicion of what the state is up to in their regard. On the one hand, states like to use religion for their purposes. On the other, the state can be very resentful of any criticism based on the teaching of Jesus. Christians should not be naive about what the state or society may do about our faith and our expression of it. We need to be on guard, and that often means simply not regarding the government as above criticism or infallible. But, given all that, we are not to be violent in our response or fall into the worldly mode of secular societies and governments. In this sense, we are to be "innocent as doves" (Matt 10:16; NAB, 1st ed.), devoid of revengeful thoughts or retaliatory measures. In his own teaching and behavior the Lord has illustrated this for us. He was certainly "shrewd" (Matt 10:16) in his verbal response to his enemies; he was surely innocent in not resisting their cruelty. Perhaps we need to learn these lessons in regard to matters of daily life, dealings with our neighbors and local institutions. Here at this altar the lessons are put before us daily.

Saturday of the Fourteenth Week in Ordinary Time—
From the altar to the street

Readings: Isa 6:1-8; Matt 10:24-33
Resp. Psalm: Ps 93:1ab, 1cd-2, 5 (L 388)

We all seem to have our own particular expectations of worship, of what should come from our attending the Eucharist. Should it be some great experience? Should it be a time for withdrawal from the noise of our life? Should we expect to be fired up by it for our life and work? Should it renew our solidarity with others? No matter what we feel or think, priests, liturgists, and musicians know that it is difficult, if not impossible, to satisfy everyone in the congregation. In today's first reading the prophet Isaiah claims to have seen God in the Temple; at least occasionally we have been similarly moved. And, daily we touch the sacramental Body of Christ. Those of us who persist in our participation in the Eucharist have answered for ourselves in some way these questions about what worship means to us. Worship is, no matter how colored, the center of Christian life, and from it should flow all the good of Christian activity. Isaiah's vision was not just a private consolation for him; at the end of this episode we hear him responding to God's call with "Here I am . . . send me!" (6:8). In some way or other, each of us too must leave the place of worship with a sense of mission, with the conviction and, it is to be hoped, the strength and spirit to make a difference this day in the world around us. Lord, we have received your gifts and blessing; let us share them with those we meet.

Monday of the Fifteenth Week in Ordinary Time—
Prophets and the poor

Readings: Isa 1:10-17; Matt 10:34–11:1
Resp. Psalm: Ps 50:8-9, 16bc-17, 21 and 23 (L 389)

Abraham Heschel says somewhere that no one ever invited a prophet home for dinner a second time. The harsh message and language of the prophets is certainly not the pleasant chitchat one hopes for in a relaxing evening with friends. To expose the injustices and fraudulence of our society, even of our religion, is what the prophets do in season and out. After a few sessions of this from a zealous friend, we're likely to say, "Give me a break." The Jewish prophets were not called "the conscience of Israel" for nothing. They, and Jesus in continuity with them, don't let us forget that worship and prayer must have implications in daily life, especially in regard to the weaker elements in our society. No other emphasis in religion, be it sexual purity, Mass attendance, membership in religious societies, participation in certain devotions, none of these can substitute for concern for the poor and those we call "marginalized." "For the Jewish prophets, our standing with God depends upon where we stand with the poor, and no private faith and piety, be they ever so pure and sincere, can soften that edict" (Ronald Rolheiser, *The Holy Longing* [New York: Doubleday, 1999] 175).

Tuesday of the Fifteenth Week in Ordinary Time—
Surrounded by gifts

Readings: Isa 7:1-9; Matt 11:20-24
Resp. Psalm: Ps 48:2-3a, 3b-4, 5-6, 7-8 (L 390)

"[I]f the mighty deeds done in your midst / had been done in Tyre and
Sidon, / they would long ago have repented in sackcloth and ashes"
(Matt 11:21). If the miracles worked for you and me in Melbourne,
Yonkers, Lagos, or Regina—or wherever we live—had happened in
places that had never heard of God, these places would have been af-
fected, would have reformed. We can expand miracles here to mean
all the great things that have happened and do happen in our lives:
the signs of God's love that we have in other people's kindness, the
beauty of a baby, the faithfulness of spouses and friends, the security
and comfort we enjoy. Sensitive, grateful hearts don't need extraordinary signs in the heavens or alterations in nature. They can see in the
ordinary world that surrounds us constant evidence of God's care and
love. What is needed is a general attitude on our part which does not
take the good around us for granted and sees that basically everything
we have is a gift. We have no prior claim on all these good things.
Possibly, we need to compare a bit of our lot to that of the less fortunate who surround us or who appear on our television screens or are
begging in our streets. "There go I but for the grace of God." A person
availing herself of a food shelf pointed out to one of the workers: "It
just takes a few weeks without your regular income and you could be
where I am." May we see and appreciate all the miracles of loving care
that surround our lives and which we so easily take for granted. May
they drive us to live and work generously with the power of Christ for
the less fortunate.

Wednesday of the Fifteenth Week in Ordinary Time—
Dependent

Readings: Isa 10:5-7, 13b-16; Matt 11:25-27
Resp. Psalm: Ps 94:5-6, 7-8, 9-10, 14-15 (L 391)

Assyria was one of a number of superpower enemies of Israel in the
centuries before Christ. If it wasn't Assyria, it was Babylon or Persia
that was swallowing up the little biblical land of Israel. The prophet
Isaiah pictures God as using Assyria to punish the unfaithfulness of
his people. Assyria serves as the instrument of God's anger and punishment. But while Assyria serves this purpose, God has not become a

big buddy of Assyria. Assyria is out like most superpowers for domination and power, not to be God's instrument. The pride and self-sufficiency of Assyria is a danger and a sin as much as the unfaithfulness of Israel. The essential point of God's message through the prophet is that all human power and ability to do anything, good or bad, comes from God. We would not be able to save masses of people from starvation and massacre any more than we could massacre whole peoples or starve them apart from a power that comes from God. As one can learn by bringing up the topic of our dependency on God in a college classroom—or probably, to most adults—dependency has become a bad word. So many of our contemporaries think of dependency as some sick state of immaturity from which we should be delivered. In the Bible, dependency means just the simple fact that all we have and are comes from outside ourselves, and it is not our creation. To recognize that, to accept it, to even rejoice in it, and thank and praise God for it should be part of our basic position in relation to God. It is one of those truths that Jesus says are often more easily accepted by the simple than by the foolishly self-sufficient (see Matt 11:25).

Thursday of the Fifteenth Week in Ordinary Time—
My burden is light (see Matt 11:30)
Readings: Isa 26:7-9, 12, 16-19; Matt 11:28-30
Resp. Psalm: Ps 102:13-14ab and 15, 16-18, 19-21 (L 392)

Like a good teacher, Jesus alternates as the situation demands between castigation and warning, on the one hand, and assurances that he is the Good Shepherd (see Ps 23), our refuge and comfort in distress (see Pss 7 and 9, for example), on the other. Today's very brief Gospel selection is just such a piece of consolation, comfort, and encouragement. Some of us may need to hear this more often than others. We respond to different sorts of invitations and challenges; some of us respond better when not overtly challenged but when we're encouraged. Others work better when "called to arms." But even the most defiantly energetic must have moments when he or she looks for a bit of rest and consolation. We can't deny that the Gospels are unrelenting in presenting the real challenges that Jesus offers to our life and activities. If we heard only the warnings and somber rebuttals to the Pharisees and others, we could be forgiven for seeing the following of the Lord as a very tough matter, something only for the strong. But, as is so often the case in even ordinary human affairs, what looks harsh and demanding is simply the external face of something reassuring and encouraging. We discover by experience that things are not as forbidding as they seem. "Take my yoke upon you and learn from me, / for I am meek and humble of heart; / and you will find rest for your selves. / For my yoke is easy, and my burden light" (Matt 11:30).

Friday of the Fifteenth Week in Ordinary Time—
Compassion

Readings: Isa 38:1-6, 21-22, 7-8; Matt 12:1-8
Resp. Psalm: Ps Isa 38:10, 11, 12abcd, 16 (*L* 393)

In yesterday's Gospel Jesus spoke his famous and oft-quoted words about the nature of following him: "Come to me"; "I will give you rest"; "I am meek and humble of heart"; "my yoke is easy, and my burden light" (Matt 11:28, 29, 30). Today we hear the Pharisees complaining about his hungry disciples picking grain on a Sabbath. In Luke's Gospel Jesus speaks of how they lay impossible burdens on others and do nothing to ease them (11:46). It was recognized by the humane law of the Jews that the hungry were in their rights to take from another's field. The Pharisees make a big deal about it being done on the Sabbath as if it were some kind of forbidden servile work. Jesus, while he honors and fulfills the law of Moses himself, does get disturbed by the prescriptions and refinements that people like the Pharisees have added to it; "human precepts" (Matt 15:9; see Isa 29:13) he calls them. They add harsh and inhumane demands as part of a misguided effort to be more religious. Jesus, as if to illustrate the passage about his easy yoke and light burden (see Matt 11:28-30), rebukes this effort to be strict and legalistic. What God asks, he says, is not the piling up of impossible and petty regulations, but compassion and concern for the burdens of others. "I desire mercy, not sacrifice" (Matt 12:7; see Hos 6:6). We can measure our devotion to God—if we must—not by how we add new external practices, but rather by how we grow in compassion. Is our religion helping widows and orphans, the poor and the weak? (see Mal 3:5; Jer 22:16, for examples). That is what God asks, not more observances.

Saturday of the Fifteenth Week in Ordinary Time—
God's way of doing it

Readings: Mic 2:1-5; Matt 12:14-21
Resp. Psalm: Ps 10:1-2, 3-4, 7-8, 14 (L 394)

Someone has said that all people are divided into two groups: those who divide humankind into two groups and those who don't. One such division of the human race comes to mind as we hear the Scriptures, a division of people into the aggressive and contentious on the one hand and, on the other, the gentle or meek. Among his contemporaries Micah singles out the unjust who spare no ingenuity, time, and thought to get what they want, primarily other people's possessions. Jesus, as described by Matthew with the help of the prophet Isaiah, represents the opposite type. "He will not contend or cry out, / . . . A bruised reed he will not break, / a smoldering wick he will not quench" (12:19-20; see Isa 42:1-4). Our world writes up the former in its magazines and adulates them in other media; generally it sees the unasser-tive and quiet as stupid and lacking in gumption. But in God's eyes it is all part of the mystery of the Cross, of how God brings about his ends. Instead of relying on naked human power and aggression, God relies on the power of a non-contentious approach, the power of the Cross and suffering, the power of weakness (see 1 Cor 1:27; 2:2). We may all be tempted to regard money, power, and assertiveness, even brutality, as the way to get things done. Assisting at the altar, at the sacramental representation of the suffering and death of Jesus tells us day after day to put our trust in God's way of doing things (see Ps 62:9).

Monday of the Sixteenth Week in Ordinary Time—
Do right, love kindness, and walk humbly (see Mic 6:8)

Readings: Mic 6:1-4, 6-8; Matt 12:38-42
Resp. Psalm: Ps 50:5-6, 8-9, 16bc-17, 21 and 23 (L 395)

Complaints about empty, external worship occur in several prophets and it would be easy to assume that the last verse from Micah in today's reading is a rejection of the earlier mentioned sacrifices and offerings. "Only to do the right and to love goodness, / and to walk humbly with your God," this is "what the Lord requires" (6:8), Micah says. But a more careful reading of the text and its context suggests rather that sacrifices, offerings, while part of worship, are complete when they lead to a life of justice (the right), steadfast love (loving goodness), and humble walking with God. Offerings and sacrifice are good but no one offering or gift to God exhausts God's claim on our whole existence. To do the right here means carrying out all the implications of my place, my lot in life. It requires that we learn what is asked of us where we are. "[T]o love goodness" (6:8) seems a generalized translation of a word asking for loyalty to God and our fellow human beings. Another translation reads: "To love kindness" (NRSV). "To walk humbly with your God" (6:8) means obedience to whatever God requires, whether in worship or in behavior. Our participation in worship, in the Eucharist, enables us to live in Christ a life of justice, steadfast love, and humble obedience to God.

Tuesday of the Sixteenth Week in Ordinary Time—
Family problems

Readings: Mic 7:14-15, 18-20; Matt 12:46-50
Resp. Psalm: Ps 85:2-4, 5-6, 7-8 (L 396)

Thoughts about the family are inevitable after hearing today's readings. Micah speaks of God's people, a family with which God has had an age-old agreement, the covenant. Jesus speaks of the ideal family in the Gospel: those who do the will of his heavenly Father. Faithful response to God's faithfulness is what confirms us as God's family. But, most interestingly, the selection from Matthew also brings out inherent difficulties with and in families. Without this reminder, the idea of God's family could easily be an airy, ideal, off-in-the-clouds concept. No matter how happy they look, how ideal we may think them, all families have their defects, defects traceable to the individual members. The problem between Jesus and his earthly family is incomprehension, lack of understanding. In Mark's Gospel we get the suggestion that not only did his immediate family not understand Jesus, they were afraid that he was going off the deep end (3:21). Could we say that we need the support and comfort of the family but that the family also inevitably brings with it problems? Possibly all of this would be more acceptable to us if we did not idealize the family too much. Certainly we should have high ideals for our family, high hopes, but along with these we need to realize that like every other element in human life, the family too has inherent difficulties. Like Israel in its relation to God, family life calls for redemption and, on our part, the exercise of the qualities put before us in the Eucharist: compassion, forgiveness, self-denial, patience, love. May we take the lessons home with us.

Wednesday of the Sixteenth Week in Ordinary Time—
No excuses

Readings: Jer 1:1, 4-10; Matt 13:1-9
Resp. Psalm: Ps 71:1-2, 3-4a, 5-6ab, 15 and 17 (*L* 397)

In a way, the farmer in today's parable sounds like a sort of scatter-brain or at least a bit haphazard in sowing the seed. But the point for us seems to be that God's word is scattered among all types of hearers, with accordingly different results. Jesus and Jeremiah, whose book we begin reading today, both experienced this often-disheartening truth that their word would not always be well received. Jeremiah must have anticipated some of this frustration, not to mention the violence that would greet his prophesying, as he sought to get out of his call. More or less, he says to God, Lord, couldn't you find someone else? I'm one of those people who consider public speaking only slightly less terrifying than death; I'm no good at it; I've never had a course. Besides, "I am too young" (1:6). Who's going to listen to a mere kid? But God settles it all for Jeremiah by telling him that he will be with him: "Have no fear before them, / because I am with you to deliver you" (1:8). Can't we assume that each of us has something to offer the world—a gift or ability? True, it may take some time to understand what our particular gift is; that's part of maturing. But with the help of prayer, self-examination, and the advice of those who know us well, we can figure out what our gift is. We shouldn't wait till we're eighty to start using it. Once we know what it is, we may see that with it we can do something for the world around us, for others. Saying we're too young or haven't had the necessary training can be an excuse for laziness or inertia.

Thursday of the Sixteenth Week in Ordinary Time—
Sticking with it

Readings: Jer 2:1-3, 7-8, 12-13; Matt 13:10-17
Resp. Psalm: Ps 36:6-7ab, 8-9, 10-11 (*L* 398)

In our own personal lives we can all look back and see how diffi-cult faithfulness and fulfillment of promises have been at times. Our two readings today both echo this theme. Jeremiah speaks of how the Lord's people have gone back on the fervor of their youth, the pioneer days of their relation with Yʜwʜ. Jesus puts it in terms of an unwill-ingness to listen or to see, to respond to the Lord: "they have closed their eyes, / lest they see with their eyes" (Matt 13:15; see Isa 6:10). While romance often surrounds the initiation of a commitment as in a wedding, the fulfillment of that faithfulness is often a very ordinary, even plodding, affair. The promises of marriage made so generously and often in the beauty, health, and optimism of youth have to be fulfilled in illness and poverty, depression and dullness, routine and boredom. The test and proof of our commitment to God, family, friends, and responsibilities will often be to continue our service, our care, our work, even when the "fun" seems gone. If we have made our commitment in sound mind and with thought, we know that it is worth the effort and that the satisfaction will be on a deeper level.

Friday of the Sixteenth Week in Ordinary Time—
Attentiveness

Readings: Jer 3:14-17; Matt 13:18-23
Resp. Psalm: Ps 31:10, 11-12abcd, 13 (L 399)

Whoever may have been the hearers of the parable about the farmer sowing seed in various kinds of soil, the parable can certainly be taken to heart by any of us who now hear it. A certain kind of Buddhism makes "mindfulness" or attention the essential heart of religion (see, for example, Thich Nhat Hanh, *The Miracle of Mindfulness* [Boston: Beacon Press, 1987]). We might articulate things differently, but this parable can underline for us how vital is the attention we give to the word of God, how vital is our receptivity. Indeed why should so many things have to be repeated for us over and over again and in so many different ways? Viewed ideally it makes no sense. Yet we all realize how difficult it is for us to give our full attention to anything: a parent, a child, our work, a piece of music, even our food. In fact, we often purposely try to do several things at one time to avoid "wasting," as we say, all that time and concentration on one thing. Someone has said that there is no moment so rare as one where we want to be where we are doing what we are doing. Our attention is most often scattered all over at any one moment. To stay with just one example, one situation: wouldn't it be wonderful and extraordinary if when we come to Mass we could bring our whole self, our whole attention? Think of what greater effect the Word of the Lord could have if our minds and imaginations were free from all the other worries and distractions that keep us from really being attentive. Possibly we should begin making gentle efforts to give our whole attention to what we hear in the daily readings without fighting violently against our distractions but simply trying to refocus again and again. "[T]he seed sown on rich soil / is the one who hears the word and understands it" (Matt 13:23).

145

Saturday of the Sixteenth Week in Ordinary Time—
No rabbit's foot

Readings: Jer 7:1-11; Matt 13:24-30
Resp. Psalm: Ps 84:3, 4, 5-6a and 8a, 11 (L 400)

One has to admit that some of the prophets' writings are downright obscure to people of the twenty-first century. Either their references are unknown or, in some cases, the text has not been well preserved. But today's piece from Jeremiah, his sermon about the Temple, is powerful and clear. He cries out against superstitious trust in the Temple by his fellow Jews. They would like to believe that the temple itself and their presence in it is enough to protect them from enemies and to please God. It's as if you or I were to regard the physical presence of this church building or of the Eucharist or our being here as one huge rabbit's foot. It's something we hear in other prophets and it's apparently an age-old problem: how to maintain the proper link between the church building and its ceremonies, on the one hand, and our behavior and morals on the other. Jeremiah reminds his hearers—and now us—that we come to church, to Mass, to prayer, because all this is extremely important for uniting us to God. Ideally from this should flow our respect for others, our concern for "the needy and the poor" (Prov 31:9), our involvement for the betterment of our world. Prayer and churchgoing can be simply superstition, a misplaced trust in some action or place, unless they are accompanied by serious work to carry out the implications. "Only if you thoroughly reform your ways and your deeds; / if each of you deals justly with his neighbor; / . . . / will I remain with you in this place" (Jer 7:5-7). You must recognize my presence on the street and in your homes if you are to find me here (see Matt 25:31-46).

Monday of the Seventeenth Week in Ordinary Time—
Faith in what we do

Readings: Jer 13:1-11; Matt 13:31-35
Resp. Psalm: Deut 32:18-19, 20, 21 (L 401)

A former student works as a Peace Corps volunteer in a very poor country of Africa with children who did not qualify for better schools. The hope is that through education these children will be able to better their own lives eventually, that they could learn a skill that would help them break out of the poverty and drudgery of their environment. The volunteer must struggle every day to motivate them and to motivate himself as he faces apparent resistance or at least inertia. Most of us, if not in our occupation at least in some other facet of our lives, must face situations where we need to trust that the little we are doing or are able to do is of some value, that something will come of it. The parable of the mustard seed probably tried to encourage Christ's disciples in their difficult efforts to spread the word of Jesus. The Peace Corps volunteer, any of us who must persevere in work and action where results are slow in coming or hard to see, need faith that doing our work now with our whole heart and generously is itself valuable, whether we see the results or not. How often parents of rebellious and surly adolescents must doubt the value of their love and work. How often, too, life shows that the love given in such circumstances does eventually have good results. "It is the smallest of all the seeds, / yet when full-grown it is the largest of plants" (Matt 13:32).

Tuesday of the Seventeenth Week in Ordinary Time—
God works in many ways

Readings: Jer 14:17-22; Matt 13:36-43
Resp. Psalm: Ps 79:8, 9, 11 and 13 (*L* 402)

The scene behind Jeremiah's words is probably a time of drought and accompanying starvation as well as a time of war, the worst of all possible worlds. In our time the peoples of Somalia and others have had the same awful combination. We tend to see El Niño involved with drought and power politics and warlords involved with war. Jeremiah and the people of his time saw God more directly implicated: "Have you cast Judah off completely? / . . . / Why have you struck us a blow / that cannot be healed? / . . . / You alone have done all these things" (Jer 14:19, 22). Are we right and the Israelites wrong? It isn't that simple. For instance, science has shown us most of the elements involved in the production of our weather. We see God working in our world through other people, events, happenings, scientific laws, rather than directly. But there is certainly no reason why we cannot see with faith how God works in our lives through no matter how many other people and events. To thank God for the way things have worked out to make our job more pleasant or tolerable, for how someone's illness has been cured—all that is still most appropriate. It means that with our faith we are able to see God working through all that happens in our lives (see Rom 8:28). Interpreting our world and events around us in faith is one way that faith becomes more concrete. Looked at this way, the world and our life are full of God's care and presence.

Miracles, in many ways, are events in which by faith we see God working good for someone. We see God present in the bread and wine and in this congregation in order to be able to see God present everywhere.

Wednesday of the Seventeenth Week in Ordinary Time—
The gift of God

Readings: Jer 15:10, 16–21; Matt 13:44–46
Resp. Psalm: Ps 59:2-3, 4, 10-11, 17, 18 (L 403)

"Familiarity," the old saying goes, "breeds contempt." We can say that familiarity breeds a misplaced certainty that we understand something or have exhausted its possibilities. This is so often the case with Scripture; we've heard and read the same passages over and over again and too easily think there's nothing more to learn. Today's very simple-appearing parables are typical of this but with a bit of help they can surprise us. Both parables are about a man and something very precious for which he is willing to give all he has. But there are differences in the two parables. In the first the man seems to really stumble across the buried treasure. He wasn't really looking for anything special but all of a sudden something extraordinary shines across his life. You think of cases where the birth of a baby or falling in love simply bowl someone over; the person is changed, gains an entirely new perspective, and happily gives him or herself to this treasure. The two events mentioned, falling in love and the birth of a baby, can be the kind of events that awaken in us an awareness of God's gifts to us, an awareness that there is truly this great Someone from whom so much good comes and to whom we owe so much. In the other parable, the man is on a search for something precious. Possibly he has been studying, praying, hoping for some answer or enlightenment and what he finds seems and is the answer to his prayers. This is another way in which we find God and the kingdom of God, and give ourselves to it. Let us hope that in one way or the other we will discover and cherish the gift of God (see 1 Tim 4:14; 1 Pet 4:10).

Thursday of the Seventeenth Week in Ordinary Time—
Turning around

Readings: Jer 18:1-6; Matt 13:47-53
Resp. Psalm: Ps 146:1b-2, 3-4, 5-6ab (L 404)

While the image of ourselves as clay in the hands of God, the Great Potter, seems to say that we are passive in God's hands, at the mercy of

God, the passage from Jeremiah offers more. "Whenever the object of clay which he was making / turned out badly in his hand, / he tried again, / making of the clay another object of whatever sort he pleased" (18:4). Our passage argues both for God's willingness to give us another chance and for our freedom to start again. We speak of "false starts" and "getting off on the wrong foot" in our lives, of endeavors or approaches that are wrong or don't work. Fortunately, we see around us and perhaps within ourselves good examples of how human beings can change directions and start a new life. Think of the teenage and college-age hellions who have become conscientious and tender fathers, loving and giving mothers. Think of the periods and behaviors in our own lives that we are embarrassed to even think about today. It's right too that we remain open to new possibilities for ourselves even if it isn't a matter of turning from a life of corruption and sin. And we can become more patient with diversity around us, more understanding of people whose clay is different from ours.

Friday of the Seventeenth Week in Ordinary Time—
Grace is all around us

Readings: Jer 26:1-9; Matt 13:54-58
Resp. Psalm: Ps 69:5, 8-10, 14 (*L* 405)

Reactions to Jesus in his native place underline for us what should be a truism: the mob or the crowd is fickle. One shouldn't put too much stock in its adulation or approval; it can all change tomorrow. But we also see here the grumbling of neighbors about the pretensions of a local from the same background as theirs who is presuming to teach them and even dazzle them with his works. We know his father, the carpenter, they say; we know his mother and brothers and sisters. They're no better than we are: "'Where did this man get all this?' / And they took offense at him" (13:56-57). It's all part of our unfortunate tendency to want stupendous signs in the heavens and to be unable to hear God's message when it comes in an ordinary wrapper. One conclusion we heard over and over again after the horrors of September 11, 2001, was about how heroic the ordinary people around us were. They led those crippled out of crumbling buildings; they gave their lives fighting fire and catastrophe. Heroes were all around us, in the most ordinary-seeming people. Celebrating here at Mass the presence of God in the food of daily life tells us repeatedly that we find God in the simple elements of daily life. We needn't look for God or for heroism or great generosity in some television spectacular or some cosmic disturbance. God is at work and present in the people and circumstances of our humdrum life. Grace from God may sit at the desk or counter next to us, may flow from a sick and demanding member of the family, or from a selfless man or woman carrying out ordinary responsibilities without grumbling or fanfare. After meeting Jesus in the words, food, and people at this gathering we are prepared to meet him throughout the day in other ordinary situations.

Saturday of the Seventeenth Week in Ordinary Time—
Solidarity with saints and sinners

Readings: Jer 26:11-16, 24; Matt 14:1-12
Resp. Psalm: Ps 69:15-16, 30-31, 33-34 (L 406)

On first reading the Scriptures, many are bowled over by all the unusual happenings, the number of miracles. But longer acquaintance and a closer look at the texts show us great realism about human nature. Despite outsized characters like Samson or events like the passage through the Red Sea, the people of Scripture are not simply cartoon heroes and villains. The characters of the Bible are not all black or white. They hesitate between good and evil; they struggle within about what to do. It wasn't a case of the good Jeremiah being surrounded by a crowd of homicidal maniacs; he had his defenders. Even Herod, who easily matches our picture of a villain, shows a flickering of conscience and some hesitation in his judgment of Jesus. He suggests that Jesus is John the Baptist returned to life, and that this is why he does such remarkable things (see Matt 14:2). Elsewhere in the Gospels we find evidence of a mix of belief and unbelief in the disciples, of good intentions and self-seeking—just like you and me. Perhaps seeing all this in the characters of the Bible can encourage us to reflect on our own divided natures, on the muddied character of our intentions and desires. And doing that, perhaps we can become more understanding and forgiving of others around us. We are all in the same boat insofar as we need the constant help and forgiveness of God in our lives.

Monday of the Eighteenth Week in Ordinary Time—
One step is enough for me

Readings: Jer 28:1-17; Matt 14:22-36 (Year A) or Matt 14:13-21 (Years B and C)
Resp. Psalm: Ps 119:29, 43, 79, 80, 95, 102 (L 407)

Hearing about two prophets, Hananiah and Jeremiah, with two different messages, our sympathies may well be with the people of the time. That a prophecy is comforting doesn't guarantee that it's true any more than the fact that a prophecy is unsettling guarantees its truthfulness. Who to believe, Hananiah or Jeremiah? Hananiah promised a good outcome for the king and people of Judah; Jeremiah said that there was no such rosy prospect. From our angle and time in history we may feel justified in believing Jeremiah. But at the time it was probably not all that clear. Possibly for us the most practical approach would be to take the emphasis off knowing what will happen and put it on "trust in the Lord" (Ps 4:6). On the cross the Lord says, "into your hands I commend my spirit" (Luke 23:46; see Ps 31:6). His words express a general and total trust in God at the moment of seeming abandonment and suffering. That must be our aim: to trust God completely about all the details of the future while we do what we can with the strength God gives. Supporting our trust must be the conviction that God cares for us more than we can imagine. Cardinal Newman (d. 1890) expressed it beautifully for all of us: "The night is dark, and I am far from home— / Lead Thou me on! / Keep Thou my feet; I do not ask to see / The distant scene—one step is enough for me." Lord, we live amid the storms and trials of life; we trust in you (see Ps 31:15), the one sure center of our life, and say with Peter, "Lord, save me!" (Matt 14:30).

Tuesday of the Eighteenth Week in Ordinary Time—
Present to our desperate moments

Readings: Jer 30:1-2, 12-15, 18-22; Matt 15:1-2, 10-14 (Year A) or Matt 14:22-36
    (Years B and C)
Resp. Psalm: Ps 102:16-18, 19-21, 29 and 22-23 (*L* 408)

Jeremiah speaks of both punishment and compassion from Yhwh in today's reading. Part of the compassion and consolation is that the people will again be close to God. To their leader God says: "When I summon him, he shall approach me; / how else should one take the deadly risk / of approaching me?" (30:21). Jesus' words to the disciples terrified by the lake storm are [or were in Sunday's Gospel]: "Take courage, it is I; do not be afraid" (Matt 14:27). And to Peter, "Come" (14:29). The composition of the Bible extends over nearly a thousand years and includes changes in thinking about God. For us the final truth about God appears in God's image, God's Word come to earth (see John 1:14), Jesus. His message is that in him God is near and available to quiet our fears. "[I]t is I; do not be afraid" (Matt 14:27). "Come" (14:29). Even at three in the morning (the time of the disciples' scare), waking and unable to sleep, worried about tomorrow, our children, our health, "The Lord is near" (Phil 4:5). "[H]e came toward them, walking on the sea" (Matt 14:25). The Lord is not only near but is always moving in our direction. It may not be so much a matter of our finding him but of recognizing the Lord's nearness. In our quieter, less troubled moments, developing a sense of God's presence can ultimately be some help in our more desperate moments.

Wednesday of the Eighteenth Week in Ordinary Time—
God chose them

Readings: Jer 31:1-7; Matt 15:21-28
Resp. Psalm: Jer 31:10, 11-12ab, 13 (*L* 409)

"I will be the God of all the tribes of Israel, / and they shall be my people" (Jer 31:1). Though there are places in the Hebrew Scriptures where God becomes the God of Gentiles too, this is not one of them. Jeremiah is primarily concerned with the chosen people, the nation chosen by God to bring the world a message and way of living. The Gospel today shows Jesus faithful to this too. Only gradually does he move his mission to non-Jews. The non-Jewish woman in the Gospel provokes Jesus into curing her daughter but not before Jesus underlines the priority of the Jews. It may be particularly hard for us today to appreciate that God approached the world through one particular people, but that mystery remains. Jesus was a Jew and went first to his Jewish contemporaries with his message. Though most Jews ended up rejecting Jesus as the Messiah, God, St. Paul tells us, has not rescinded their status (see Rom 11). There is no excuse for the anti-Semitism, the anti-Jewish behavior of Christians over the centuries, and being a follower of Jesus means rejecting it today. God could have chosen the Welsh or the Mongolians; God had to start somewhere. But, in point of fact, God started with the Jews. That alone should assure our respect for this people. Part of our worship and following of Jesus the Messiah, the Christ, must be respect for his people, the Jews. The tendency, so continual in the history of the West, to find some Jewish conspiracy behind every problem or difficult situation must be opposed by Christians. And efforts to attack or persecute Jews must be opposed by the followers of Jesus.

Thursday of the Eighteenth Week in Ordinary Time—
Change from within
Readings: Jer 31:31-34; Matt 16:13-23
Resp. Psalm: Ps 51:12-13, 14-15, 18-19 (*L* 410)

Peter is probably no different from any one of us in his rejection of the Messiah's way of suffering and death. Even if we cringe a bit at the overaggressive types among us, we still feel that legitimate power can accomplish something. But the following of Jesus will require for all of us, as it did for Peter, a conversion to the way of suffering and death, something that must be wrought within us by God's grace. The church of the Middle Ages tried to use violence and massacre, a crusade they called it, to rid Europe of the Cathari, a strange and deviant sect. Fortunately there were some good men and women who hoped to use instruction and prayer, knowing that only grace could change hearts. The famous passage we heard today from Jeremiah also stresses that the right relation to God, the covenant, is a gift of God to willing and receptive hearts. "I will place my law within them, and write it upon their hearts" (31:33). Written laws and external force can do little without the influence of God gently moving us from within. The ideal of our Christian life is that with time, reflection, regular and personal contact with God, with prayer, God's desires for us will become our second nature. However haltingly, we must be moving in our life as disciples of Christ to a closer union with the heart and spirit of Jesus so that God's intentions and desires become ours also.

Friday of the Eighteenth Week in Ordinary Time—
Surrender

Readings: Nah 2:1, 3; 3:1-3, 6-7; Matt 16:24-28
Resp. Psalm: Deut 32:35cd-36ab, 39abcd, 41 (*L* 411)

That the prophet Nahum is happy over the fall of the city of Nineveh is pretty obvious in the first reading. The oppressive empire had been a source of suffering for Israel. In our own day, too, we have seen the fall of a huge and terrifying empire and the great relief this brought. Great empires and their leaders are the exact opposite of the approach of Jesus. And while they may be able to make the trains run on time, they bring no one lasting happiness. There is no profit for them in gaining the whole world by force; in the process they destroy themselves (see Matt 16:26). None of us is going to compete with an Alexander the Great or a Stalin, but on our own level we can at times be persuaded that power plays, ingenious strategies, cunning, and self-seeking are the obvious ways to happiness. Jesus teaches a paradox which sounds like nonsense to the world of politics and power seeking. "Whoever loses his life for my sake will find it" (16:25). By surrendering to the power and life of God in us we attain—better yet, are given—a fulfillment we ourselves could never have devised. Salvation in the Bible and Christian tradition is not something one attains as the result of a series of seminars or the practices of some guru. It is "the gift of God" (Eph 2:8) to those who open themselves in poverty of spirit to allow God to work in them.

Saturday of the Eighteenth Week in Ordinary Time—
We live by faith

Readings: Hab 1:12–2:4; Matt 17:14–20
Resp. Psalm: Ps 9:8-9, 10-11, 12-13 (*L* 412)

Obvious though it may be, it nevertheless merits underlining: what separates believers from nonbelievers is just that, belief, faith, trust. Any one of us who looks deeply and with clear sight into ourselves must see how often we're tempted to live, not by faith, but by our own powers, strategies. The last verse of the reading from Habakkuk turns up several places in the letters of Paul and it reads this way in the Letter to the Galatians: "the one who is righteous by faith will live" (3:11). Luther took this up with a vengeance in his criticism of what he saw as the church's teaching that one could rely on one's good deeds. Faith (trust) seems to be from one aspect a matter of opening ourselves to the power and strength of God, of letting a superior force work in our lives. Jesus tells the disciples in the Gospel that the reason they could not expel the boy's demon was that they had "little faith" (Matt 17:20). With trust God's power would have worked through them. With all the emphasis there is in our lives on education, planning, and self-development, today's reading reminds us that we cannot put our basic trust in them. They help; they are necessary for the working of this world; but the son or daughter of the Lord lives by faith (see Hab 2:4; Gal 3:11).

Monday of the Nineteenth Week in Ordinary Time—
Beyond us, yet with us

Readings: Ezek 1:2-5, 24-28c; Matt 17:22-27
Resp. Psalm: Ps 148:1-2, 11-12, 13, 14 (*L* 413)

Ezekiel and Matthew tell us much about God's way with us humans and what God is like. In exile, on the shore of a Babylonian river, the prophet Ezekiel receives his call from Yʜᴡʜ. In what follows he strains to say something intelligible about the indescribable God. But the passage is full of words like "resembled" (1:27) or "had the appearance of" (1:26) something. With his colorful and even bizarre images Ezekiel succeeds in telling us how unimaginable God really is. In the story about the temple tax we learn something else about God's approach to us. Matthew shows us Jesus being careful about his identity in order not to provoke a premature confrontation. He does not stand on his rights and say, "This is my father's house; you can hardly expect me to pay for its support. The children of a king are not taxed to support the ruler." Rather, Jesus carefully avoids sparking a controversy with his fellow Jews or pushing them to make a decision now. Throughout the Gospels, Jesus tries to lead people to see who he is by demonstrations of his power to heal and comfort—signs of God's caring presence. Between Ezekiel and Matthew we get a balanced picture of the God of the Bible. Ezekiel shows us how God is above and beyond our comprehension; we cannot say exactly what God is but only approximate God's nature by images. Matthew, on the other hand, pictures the sensitivity, gentleness, and consideration of God as they have been shown to us in the Son. Our God has both the loftiness and mystery we see in Ezekiel as well as the tenderness and closeness we see in Matthew. That same God is present here. We venerate the mystery of God but trust God's loving understanding of us.

Tuesday of the Nineteenth Week in Ordinary Time—
Children in an adult world

Readings: Ezek 2:8–3:4; Matt 18:1-5, 10, 12-14
Resp. Psalm: Ps 119:14, 24, 72, 103, 111, 131 (*L* 414)

It's tough listening to these readings from Matthew, especially for those of us who must leave here to go to a rough, competitive business climate or work situation. This repeated teaching of Jesus in Matthew seems so counter to the atmosphere in which we live and work. We're told that self-assertion is not the way to fulfillment, even that the way there is through the Cross. And today maturity seems to get a slap in the face as Jesus commends children as models for all of us. The answer to "Who is the greatest in the Kingdom of heaven?" (18:1) is: "children" (18:3) and those who make themselves "lowly" (18:4; NAB, 1st ed.). We spend years in school—and life itself—learning to grow up, to become responsible, learning how to "fend for ourselves." And then we're told that "unless you turn and become like children, you will not enter the Kingdom of heaven" (18:3). What do we do? How do we reconcile the Gospel and the real world? Some opt for dropping out. But that can't be practical advice for most of us. There is no easy answer to these questions. The words of Jesus seem to ask that at least we soften the hardball approach of the marketplace, that we manage somehow to prize human values over economic, that we let the example of Jesus temper our combativeness. Only those involved in the world of tough competition *and* concerned about the following of Christ can truly solve these problems. Help us, Lord, to know how to "become like children" (18:3).

Wednesday of the Nineteenth Week in Ordinary Time—
We leave; God doesn't

Readings: Ezek 9:1-7; 10:18-22; Matt 18:15-20
Resp. Psalm: Ps 113:1-2, 3-4, 5-6 (*L* 415)

The Gospel stresses the presence of God in the community, in believers: "where two or three are gathered in my name, / there am I in the midst of them" (Matt 18:20). The picture of the presence of the Lord leaving the Temple on a vehicle of cherubim, wings, and wheels is memorable, dramatic. Yʜᴡʜ is abandoning his people to their punishment. While it may be dramatic and picturesque, we are better off reminding ourselves that it is a picture and that the reality in our case may be different. Does God really ever leave us? (see 2 Tim 2:13). Isn't it that we abandon, desert, ignore, forget God? The responsibility is ours. We make real the presence of God in our midst, in our lives, by our willingness to live in peace and work for peace with others. Possibly it's better to think that by our indifference, coldness, and lack of attention, we are effectively walking out the door and abandoning the true center of our being where God dwells. Whether it's Ezekiel or ourselves we are often limited by spatial images. God is present everywhere, especially, as the last words of the Gospel tell us, in our fellow human being gathered in God's name. Yet the reality is that we can live oblivious of that, absorbed in the trinkets and trivia of our world, undervaluing the truly human and divine elements in our midst. God is here, in these people, but we look elsewhere.

Thursday of the Nineteenth Week in Ordinary Time—
Our willingness to forgive

Readings: Ezek 12:1-12; Matt 18:21–19:1
Resp. Psalm: Ps 78:56-57, 58-59, 61-62 (*L* 416)

"Enough is enough." That phrase, used so often in ordinary life, sounds profoundly reasonable to most of us. You know the next line: "There comes a point when you just have to say no; you can't be taken any longer for a fool." We've all had neighbors who borrow machines or tools and return them with some new defect, something missing. We have sons or daughters, spouses who regularly return our car without gas, who leave the kitchen a mess. "Enough is enough." Peter felt the same way and thought he was being pretty generous when he asked, "how often must I forgive him? / As many as seven times?" (Matt 18:21). Jesus, of course, responds that he must forgive indefinitely, "seventy-seven times" (18:22). How are we to do it? It seems not only impossible but also likely to disrupt the working of daily life. It seems to destroy the idea of accountability. Possibly the answer is that the parable and the teaching of Jesus here are concerned with what goes on in my heart; I must be free of rancor and the thought of revenge. That I will be forgiving says nothing about the responsibility I and others have to not offend in the first place. Parables make one point; they do not try to cover every facet of an issue. Other parables about the good use of our talents, for instance, make the point that you and I should do whatever we do as well as possible, honestly, with integrity, with respect to others. Our forgiveness by God is conditioned by our willingness to forgive (see 6:12).

Friday of the Nineteenth Week in Ordinary Time—
Living out commitments

Readings: Ezek 16:1-15, 60, 63 or 16:59-63; Matt 19:3-12
Resp. Psalm: Isa 12:2-3, 4bcd, 5-6 (*L* 417)

We may think of problems with fidelity in marriage as simply typical of our time, but listen to the disciples after hearing Jesus' tough teaching on marriage and divorce: "If that is the case of a man with his wife, / it is better not to marry" (Matt 19:10). Evidently they were used to the possibility of divorce. To now hear the severely uncompromising words of Jesus about the indissolubility of marriage strikes them as extreme. How could anyone enter into marriage if there was no out? The remark tells us a lot about how far Jesus had to bring them along in order to accept his teaching. It tells us also how difficult faithfulness or commitment is and has been for human beings. Ezekiel has God speak of Israel as his bride but also of her unfaithfulness and his willingness to "remember" and "set up an everlasting covenant" (16:60). Our times may glorify "hanging loose" and avoiding entanglements, but the problem is much older. Should we despair of the possibility of a lasting commitment? No. Obviously Jesus presents a permanent union as the ideal. All of this reminds us that any commitment we've made requires a daily renewal; it cannot be taken for granted. We all have a number of commitments that we try to live up to, some more serious than others; some possibly serve as practice for the really big commitments of our life like marriage or religious profession. At this altar we have put before us day after day the supreme example of total commitment. "He loved his own in the world and he loved them to the end" (John 13:1); "even [to] death on a cross" (Phil 2:8). Through our participation here we can learn and absorb the strength and generosity to live out our commitments to husband, to wife, to children, to our job, to our neighbors and friends, to God (see Matt 22:37-39).

Saturday of the Nineteenth Week in Ordinary Time—
Responsible to the gift

Readings: Ezek 18:1-10, 13b, 30-32; Matt 19:13-15
Resp. Psalm: Ps 51:12-13, 14-15, 18-19 (L 418)

We may be more sophisticated about it, but the desire to push away responsibility seems to be a pretty consistent trait of our species. From the story of Adam and Eve on we see it. In another age people blamed the devil; today we hear responsibility being laid on our astrological sign (Scorpio, Capricorn, etc.) or on our genes, environment, or upbringing. It is a complex issue: various factors do influence responsibility. The Israelites of Ezekiel's time had the proverb we heard today which laid the blame for their problems on their ancestors. But it's gone far enough, God says through Ezekiel. People are responsible for their own actions. "I will judge you . . . each one according to his [or her] ways" (18:30). Each of us must assess our degree of responsibility; we alone know the influences, past and present, that affect us for good or bad. No one else can substitute for our conscience. Given the psychological climate of our day we may need to accept a bit more responsibility than seems the norm in our society. But, after we've hammered this home to ourselves, we have today's Gospel to consider. On the other side of the coin, "the Kingdom of heaven belongs," Jesus tells us, "to such as these" (Matt 19:14): those who receive it like children receive most things, as a gift. Even our ability to be responsible, to respond to the Lord, is first of all something we receive from God (see 1 John 4:10, 19). We're responsible, you might say, for the use of what we've received from God.

Monday of the Twentieth Week in Ordinary Time—
To be free

Readings: Ezek 24:15-23; Matt 19:16-22
Resp. Psalm: Deut 32:18-19, 20, 21 (*L* 419)

You'd probably not choose today's readings as feel-good reading. They certainly don't support the idea that people come to Mass to escape reality and have their sweetest dreams confirmed. God comes off as very upset with Israel in the selection from Ezekiel. He is pretty rough on Ezekiel too; he tells him his wife will die and he should not express grief for her. This seems to refer to the destruction of Jerusalem and implies that its citizens are so bad that they would dishonor the city by mourning for it. The Gospel, no matter how we limit its strong demands, seems to ask an awful lot or, at least, to be pretty negative about things for which many of us work. Not much here to really put anyone at ease or to serve as a sleeping pill. The young man in the story considered joining the disciples who accompanied Jesus on his trips and took part in his mission. For that the man's possessions would have been a serious obstacle. The truth, of course, is that no matter what we do with our lives, possessions can be like extra baggage which just weighs us down. They cause us a lot of worry and concern, both in accumulating them and protecting them. Thus they really limit our freedom. Raising a family or carrying on our business requires that we have certain things, of course. The things themselves are not evil. It is only an excessive desire for them and attachment to them which results in them strangling us. Giving God and persons the priority can limit the damage.

Tuesday of the Twentieth Week in Ordinary Time—
Security and dependence

Readings: Ezek 28:1-10; Matt 19:23-30
Resp. Psalm: Deut 32:26-27ab, 27cd-28, 30, 35cd-36ab (*L* 420)

The prince of Tyre, of today's first reading, has not had an immense impact on history; he doesn't appear in crossword puzzles. Yet his pride and self-satisfaction in his wisdom and wealth were sufficient to merit a very harsh reprimand from the Lord through Ezekiel. Is the point perhaps that we do not have to be a Caesar or a Hitler to be tempted to think of ourselves as gods? Even our down-home satisfaction with our possessions and achievements—even that—may be enough to warrant God's rebuke. No matter on what scale we operate, we are all susceptible to the desire to put ourselves in place of God (see Acts 12:21-23), to in actuality put all our trust in what we have or can do. Religion, faith in God is founded in a basic sense of our dependence on God, a realistic recognition that we come from God and continue in existence because of God. Scripture does not teach a crippling dependence on God, a perpetuation of immaturity, but an honest acceptance of that fact that we are not our own creator. Our pursuit of security and adequate means never, in God's mind, negates our need for God. For the Christian, the necessary pursuit of the means for our own and our family's sustenance never becomes the sole and absolute purpose of life. We only contribute to what remains basically God's work, sustaining our life.

Wednesday of the Twentieth Week in Ordinary Time—
An antidote to self-seeking

Readings: Ezek 34:1-11; Matt 20:1-16
Resp. Psalm: Ps 23:1-3a, 3b-4, 5, 6 (*L* 421)

Even in our contemporary world, in country after country, including our own, we hear daily of people with serious complaints about their leaders, the "shepherds" of that reading from Ezekiel. Leadership, public office, brings with it opportunities for service, for bettering the lives of others. Apparently, it also brings with it opportunities for profit and gain for the leaders themselves. Ezekiel accuses the leaders of his day and place of seeing their flocks, their constituents, only as means to their own benefit and comfort. What is the solution to such an age-old and universal problem? Is it in term limits, careful surveillance of fees and gifts, and lie detector tests? These are only bandages on a much deeper problem. How do we, how does anyone, control the intrusion of self-seeking into anything we do? Self-seeking can find an opening in any position, any work, civil or religious, large or small. No one of us is exempt from the effort needed to contain selfishness or from the need to be strengthened in self-giving by the example and power of the Lord. The Eucharist is the place where we offer self and work with Christ to God and receive the power in this sacrament of his passion and death to die more consistently to our self-seeking. In what happens at this altar we have put before us the supreme example of self-giving and service of others.

Thursday of the Twentieth Week in Ordinary Time—
Resisting inertia and dullness

Readings: Ezek 36:23-28; Matt 22:1-14
Resp. Psalm: Ps 51:12-13, 14-15, 18-19 (L 422)

Isn't the whole purpose of the liturgy with its readings and celebrations to encourage our renewal, to push us to move, to change, to get going? Some whole seasons are devoted to this; the most important feasts of the church year are invitations to new birth, to renewal. And throughout the year we are nudged, as if by a friend really concerned about our good, to begin again, to allow ourselves to be renewed. Today's beautiful and oft-quoted passage from Ezekiel is typical: "I will give you a new heart and place a new spirit within you, / taking from your bodies your stony hearts / and giving you natural hearts. / I will put my spirit within you and make you live by my statutes" (36:26-27)—an echo of Pentecost: "Come, Holy Spirit, fill the hearts of your faithful / and enkindle in them the fire of your love" (Alleluia verse). At almost any time of the year we need reminders that life can be more fervent, more generous; we need not surrender to torpor. Even the hot, slow days of summer or of a tropical clime need not flatten our spirit, leave us stagnating. We may move at a slower rate in heat and humidity, but the Spirit can still be crisp inside—sometimes. It may not be easy, I admit, but in the words of Scripture we have daily encouragement to new beginnings and the strength of God's Word to move us.

Friday of the Twentieth Week in Ordinary Time—
Faithfulness not excitement

Readings: Ezek 37:1-14; Matt 22:34-40
Resp. Psalm: Ps 107:2-3, 4-5, 6-7, 8-9 (L 423)

"Dry bones" (Ezek 37:4) taking on flesh and sinew first and then coming alive with spirit—this is a famous picture from the prophet Ezekiel, the text for a great African-American spiritual. Ezekiel wrote these words to encourage a dispirited people. Israel, he said, will rise from present misery to a new national life. Dry bones or a lifeless desert, a dead rocky terrain, these picture the emptiness and dryness we feel at times in our Christian life. Everyone who takes life in Christ seriously has felt some consolation and joy in prayer and worship. Then come periods, often pretty long, when all seems drudgery, as bad as any boring job we have ever had. We plod through prayer, attendance at Mass, our daily routine, feeling like lifeless robots. Our faithfulness brings no rewards. The fact is that we cannot command our feelings; they come and go for reasons often hard to understand. We cannot force them. At times of dryness in our life in Christ, when we feel no love or joy, we probably should offer this to God as part of our sharing the cross of Christ (see 1 Pet 4:13; Col 1:24). As we all know from relationships or from marriage, faithful carrying out of duties and responsibilities is more of a sign of our deep-down spirit than our feelings. We can command our faithfulness but we cannot command our feelings. Mother Teresa said that God wants our faithfulness, not our success; we could add, God wants our faithfulness whether or not it's exciting and consoling.

Saturday of the Twentieth Week in Ordinary Time—
Who lives in the Temple?

Readings: Ezek 43:1-7ab; Matt 23:1-12
Resp. Psalm: Ps 85:9ab and 10, 11-12, 13-14 (*L* 424)

In Ezekiel's vision, he saw the glory of God enter the Temple. "[T]he temple was filled with the glory of the LORD" (43:5). Supposing that to be literally true, that doesn't leave much room for the glory of human beings. But that is the temptation and abuse against which Jesus speaks in the Gospel referring to how the Pharisees and scribes lay burdens on others and seek position and prestige for themselves. The danger for those who are supposed to serve the glory of God and facilitate our meeting with God is that they use their office for self, to enhance and glorify self. While the words of Jesus are directed at these specific historical groups, the scribes and Pharisees, we do well to extract from them something of pertinence to ourselves. Obviously the strictures of Jesus are applicable to the church's counterparts to the scribes and Pharisees: priests, bishops, and popes, but the rest of us face the same seemingly eradicable foe: self-seeking. Self and self-seeking are always alert to opportunities for, what else? For self. The philosopher Nietzsche wrote somewhere that even when we deny ourselves we are patting ourselves on the back for just that self-denial. Possibly his words leave too little room for the truly selfless and the possibility of self-forgetting but we must admit that emptying ourselves of self is a life-long task and a very difficult one. That difficulty is one always valid reason for asking forgiveness at the beginning of every Eucharistic celebration. Dethroning self is never easy. Is it ever accomplished? God not only should fill "the temple," the church, with God's glory, but God also desires to fill us with life and divine vigor. After all, Saint Paul tells us that we too are temples of God (1 Cor 3).

Monday of the Twenty-First Week in Ordinary Time—
Love and law

Readings: 2 Thess 1:1-5, 11-12; Matt 23:13-22
Resp. Psalm: Ps 96:1-2a, 2b-3, 4-5 (*L* 425)

Careless reading or listening to Jesus' woes against the scribes and Pharisees has at times fueled anti-Jewish attitudes among Christians. Read more carefully the text appears as addressed to some of the Jewish religious leaders, not to everyone. We should not believe too easily that every Jew of the time practiced the Jewish faith as did those whom Jesus criticized so strongly. It's the same with us. One can't blame every Christian for the vices and sins that seem such occupational hazards for church leaders. We've all heard of church leaders who are unfaithful to commitments, skim money from church funds, waste time and energy on incidental and petty matters, and worse. It's always more profitable to turn the warnings at ourselves rather than spending effort in finding out who else is guilty. All religion and all of us who aim to live as Christ's followers need to be wary of the tendencies Christ denounces. We can spend valuable energy splitting hairs over how to fulfill a law. If I go to a wedding on Saturday afternoon, does that fulfill my Sunday worship? Or we worry uselessly over whether someone stands, sits, or kneels during the service. Or we can make fulfilling laws to be the whole point of Christian life when they are only justified insofar as they help lead us to God. As we've heard recently in these daily readings, the center of the following of Christ is love of God and love of neighbor (see Matt 22:37-39). How do my worries help to deepen love? It may seem pretty grand and on the big scale, but we can judge the value of all we do by whether or not it serves the cause of love. We come here basically to have our love made stronger.

Tuesday of the Twenty-First Week in Ordinary Time—
Life and love now

Readings: 2 Thess 2:1-3a, 14-17; Matt 23:23-26
Resp. Psalm: Ps 96:10, 11-12, 13 (L 426)

Agitation and terror about the end of things regularly seizes people, and just as regularly there seem to be preachers on television or elsewhere who feed the fear. As we came to the year 2000 there was more of this than usual. The words of our Lord about how we will not know the time of the end or of his coming should encourage us all to put our energies and talent into doing here and now what life, family, friends, our world need. Worry about an unknown future event is simply a distraction from real life. Even in our own limited experience there is continual evidence of how misleading are the prophets of terror. Immediately before the Persian Gulf War there were preachers all over the country bringing in big crowds with assurances that the "final battle" would now take place in the Middle East. One local preacher told the young people in his congregation that they would not have to worry about growing old; it would end before that! More helpful for our future, our destiny with God, is that we recall the essential tradition of our faith: God loves us, and today is the time to respond to that love. "May our Lord Jesus Christ himself and God our Father, / who has loved us and given us everlasting encouragement / and good hope through his grace, / encourage your hearts and strengthen them / in every good deed and word" (2 Thess 2:16-17).

Wednesday of the Twenty-First Week in Ordinary Time—
A word for work

Readings: 2 Thess 3:6-10, 16-18; Matt 23:27-32
Resp. Psalm: Ps 128:1-2, 4-5 (L 427)

When year after year one sees the tizzy and turmoil into which college students lead themselves during exam week, one gains a greater appreciation of regular work and regular living habits. Students who have spent the months and weeks before exams in unproductive pursuits or unorganized activity find themselves trying to salvage the semester with a huge burst of work and energy during the last couple weeks. They try artificially to keep themselves awake with caffeine, neglecting not only sleep but also regular meals. Some come dangerously close to breakdowns, others just expose themselves to illness. What a more satisfying and rational life they'd have if every day included regular work, regular meals, recreation. But they see that regularity as inevitable in the settled routine of adults. For now, they seem to want none of it. But with St. Paul and much of humanity we can see a great value in regular work, some regular habits. They help us share Paul's independence, knowing that we have been doing our share for our own support. And more subtly the regularity of daily work keeps us in contact with the reality of our world, with the reality of other people's lives. Regular work keeps our feet on the ground and our hearts open to our fellow human beings.

Thursday of the Twenty-First Week in Ordinary Time
Our high calling

Readings: 1 Cor 1:1-9; Matt 24:42-51
Resp. Psalm: Ps 145:2-3, 4-5, 6-7 (L 428)

In a century and world where human life and dignity have been so often destroyed or degraded, one is struck by the high vision St. Paul has of us. Respect for ourselves and for others presumes some such valuing of being human. St. Paul, writing to the Corinthians, reminds them—and us—that we have been consecrated, made sacred, in our union with Christ Jesus. We are called to be a holy people. God has given us divine favor, assured us of eternal love, again in the Son who came among us, died, and rose. We have been "enriched in every way, / with all discourse and all knowledge" (1 Cor 1:5). We are "not lacking in any spiritual gift" (1:7); God strengthens us to keep us "blameless" (1:8; NAB, 1st ed.). Finally, God has called us to a relation of "fellowship with . . . Jesus" (1:9). Wouldn't it be good for us to confront the often dull and uninspired reality of daily life with these facts of faith? Authorities tell us we hardly ever exhaust the potential of our brains and other capacities. Similarly, we so often allow the gifts of God in Jesus to rust or lie unused in ourselves. There's nothing wrong with praying for more fervor, more spirit, more fire and generosity in our daily life, in our devotion to God, and our concern for neighbor (see Matt 22:37-39).

Friday of the Twenty-First Week in Ordinary Time—
Wise foolishness

Readings: 1 Cor 1:17-25; Matt 25:1-13
Resp. Psalm: Ps 33:1-2, 4-5, 10-11 (*L* 429)

"What kind of fool do you think I am?" is an oft-asked question. Some variation of that is found in both readings today. And we are left with the question too of what kind of "foolishness" (1 Cor 1:18) we are talking about. Elsewhere (in Matthew 5:22) Jesus promises dire punishment for calling another a fool though we should notice that he himself speaks of "foolish" people in today's Gospel (Matt 25:3ff.). In the passage from Matthew it seems to mean one who rejects wisdom out of ill will. In the Gospel before us about the wise and foolish virgins, "foolish" seems to refer to people who do not take sufficient care for the future, who don't look ahead enough. In the reading from the First Letter to the Corinthians, Paul uses the word "foolishness" to describe the reaction of worldly and reasonable people to the Gospel he proclaims. In the New Testament the most deadly of these kinds of foolishness may be the kind of which Paul writes. A crucified Savior is foolishness to the worldly wise of whom Paul speaks. "How could someone be a savior and at the same time be crucified?" they ask. Their world, and so often ours too, says that the only way you get anything accomplished is by power and force. Yet, the message of Paul and the crucified Savior is just the opposite: Christ conquers by undergoing the Cross; "the weakness of God," Paul says, "is stronger than human strength" (1 Cor 1:25). It's a message which our world never seems to get and which we Christians too find very hard to live by. Possibly, it's only by continual and repeated presence at the ever-renewed sacrifice of Jesus that we can come to any genuine appreciation of this central paradox of our faith. Help us, Lord, to overcome our foolishness.

Saturday of the Twenty-First Week in Ordinary Time—
Let them be well worn

Readings: 1 Cor 1:26-31; Matt 25:14-30
Resp. Psalm: Ps 33:12-13, 18-19, 20-21 (*L* 430)

While today's parable may have had application to more local problems of the time of the Gospels, for us it is significant as continuing the theme of yesterday's parable about the ready and the unready bridesmaids. Today's parable adds the idea that those waiting for the return of the Lord or who must expect their own ultimate end have been given certain abilities and should make the best use of them. The word for the denomination of money given the servants was "talent" (Matt 25:24), and in time it came to mean not money but the capabilities you and I have. As St. Paul urges elsewhere, in the body of Christ we all serve different functions, we all have differing gifts to be used "for building up the body of Christ" (Eph 4:12; see vv. 1-16). We might reflect here too that happiness and some satisfaction with life itself flow from the good use of what we have. Our talents are not simply given to us as private ornaments but for the good of all. One of us may have a gift for sympathetic listening and encouragement, something that helps the self-pitying. Another may have continually good spirits, good cheer to be shared with the less exuberant. Another may have great practical gifts, actually understand how machines work, and be a great boon for the more clumsy among us who can be completely stymied, for instance, by a stuck window. Others are well organized and help the rest of us get things done. Another may not be organized but have an infectious spirit of spontaneity which rescues others from boredom. We bring these gifts to the altar—and wherever we go—to offer their good use to God through and in Christ. May they show signs of wear and tear when we eventually return them to God who gave them.

Monday of the Twenty-Second Week in Ordinary Time—
Beyond reason

Readings: 1 Cor 2:1-5; Luke 4:16-30
Resp. Psalm: Ps 119:97, 98, 99, 100, 101, 102 (*L* 431)

As we grow into adulthood, in the course of our education, we often go through a phase of strong emphasis on what we consider plain, clear reason. We may enjoy seeing how reason can clarify matters, demolish others, expose inconsistencies. We think that both good and bad things should be explainable, comprehensible to us. The conduct of civil matters and the running of our country—or even of our household—certainly all benefit from the use of reason. But if we're fortunate and continue growing we usually come to see the limitations of reason. Life and our experience teach us that there are deeper truths. Paul speaks today of such truths. The life of the Lord who humbled himself to human conditions (see also Phil 2:5-8) and underwent public execution demonstrates that weakness and submission, self-forgetfulness, can, paradoxically, lead to new life, growth, deeper happiness. The scene from Luke's Gospel today, an early episode in the public life of Jesus, shows us in abbreviated form the pattern of his life: a favorable reaction, followed by doubt and downright hostility, an attempt to kill him, "But he passed through the midst of them and went away" (Luke 4:30). As we know, the plots of people to destroy the Savior are turned by God into his way to victory, resurrection, something reason would never have expected.

Tuesday of the Twenty-Second Week in Ordinary Time—
A new way of looking

Readings: 1 Cor 2:10b-16; Luke 4:31-37
Resp. Psalm: Ps 145:8-9, 10-11, 12-13ab, 13cd-14 (*L* 432)

We speak of the "eyes of faith" (see Acts 26:18), the ability to look at and evaluate the world, our experience, in terms of the standards given us in God's revelation. St. Paul's talk today about "the one who is spiritual" (1 Cor 2:15), and "the Spirit of God" (2:11) refers to this also. One of the qualities accompanying faith, that comes along with our receiving the Lord into our lives, is a new way of looking at what otherwise are the "same old things." A distressing, nagging family or office situation can become, with God's Spirit, a means for growth, for hope and trust—rather than simply anger and anxiety. The situation may be "the same old thing" in terms of what is happening, but we can begin, at least, to look at it from the perspective of the Spirit, of God. The weariness and boredom of our work or life itself can be altered, become an opportunity—at least to some degree—once we look for the hand of God in it. Faith does not—and it seems fraudulent to speak too easily as if it did—just change that situation in the office or the attitude of our children or neighbor, but it can give *us* a new way of looking at those situations. Perhaps it *primarily* gives us a new attitude. We can see that all this can, in God's mind, work to the good, in ways we may not see (see Rom 8:28). It gives us hope, protection against giving up. Lord, may your Spirit in us help us to see our world, our life, our family and friends, and our work in relation to your love and presence.

Wednesday of the Twenty-Second Week in Ordinary Time—
The human element

Readings: 1 Cor 3:1-9; Luke 4:38-44
Resp. Psalm: Ps 33:12-13, 14-15, 20-21 (*L* 433)

Paul berates the Corinthians about their attachments to particular individuals who may have been their teachers in the faith. He tackles a difficult subject and one which is still with us. Today's equivalent for many of us Catholics deals often with our preference for Father McGillicuddy over Father Tartini. Paul speaks in ideal terms and tells the Corinthians and us that neither one is of any special account and that to push your allegiance to one over the other is immature. After all, God gives us grace, affects us through the sacraments, through the priests as well as through other ministers in the church. They are simply God's instruments. But very realistically, we can't deny we like Father Tartini's manner better or Father McGillicuddy's sermons better; we feel more comfortable with one or the other. We may like the one more than the other because he's nearer our age or isn't our age. Even the athletic build of one may give him an edge as far as we're concerned. There are many human factors which can't simply be dismissed or glossed over. They are there. But at least we must somehow keep our perspective, our sense that God works through different instruments and not make the personality or appearance the basis for divisive behavior. It's the same with our ordinary acquaintances or people we must deal with on a regular basis. Not all of them will attract us in the same way. Everyone of us has painful and unattractive qualities for someone. We should probably learn to rejoice more in the variety of God's gifts in other people (see Eph 4:1-16), priests included, and see God acting in them.

Thursday of the Twenty-Second Week in Ordinary Time—
Our thoughts

Readings: 1 Cor 3:18-23; Luke 5:1-11
Resp. Psalm: Ps 24:1bc-2, 3-4ab, 5-6 (L 434)

Our human reasoning or thinking—we could even call it wisdom—has a real place in human life. So often we say, "Be reasonable." Or we ask each other to explain our actions in terms of reasons: "Why did you do that? What was your reason for doing that?" And we get suspicious of people who seem to leave reason out of everything. We complain that he or she acts on whims and spur of the moment decisions, apparently with no thought. But there are limits to reason! "Reason is really a poor thing if it cannot recognize its own limits," someone has written (Blaise Pascal). Paul tells the Corinthians that the wisdom of human beings has to learn from what seems to be the unreasonableness, "the foolishness of God" (1 Cor 1:25). "The Lord knows the thoughts of the wise, that they are vain" (1 Cor 3:20; see Ps 94:11). Human reason, after all, is just that, human. There is no guarantee that our thinking is a real match for the complex universe we live in. The Cross of Christ is certainly a complete challenge to reason: God will overcome sin and death, it tells us, by allowing the Son to be put to death. It makes no human sense. For Peter to lower his nets back into the water in the morning after an unsuccessful night of fishing makes no sense either; it isn't reasonable. The night was the best time to fish. But Peter is putting his trust in one who is above and beyond simple human reason. The lesson for us is not to let what our reason tells us is possible put limitations on what God can do in response to our faith and trust. Our prayer, especially, presumes correctly that God is not limited by what our thought says is possible.

Friday of the Twenty-Second Week in Ordinary Time—
Forget the judging

Readings: 1 Cor 4:1-5; Luke 5:33-39
Resp. Psalm: Ps 37:3-4, 5-6, 27-28, 39-40 (L 435)

First Corinthians, which we have been reading, shows us that St. Paul is dealing with a pretty contentious, even feisty, bunch of people. They are suspicious of each other and testy with Paul. What he urges on them today regarding himself applies to all of us. If you don't like what I'm doing or how I'm doing it, he says, at least suspend your judgment; let God do my evaluation. God knows what's in our hearts, what our intentions are (see also Acts 15:8; Rev 2:23). To varying degrees we're inclined to judge everyone we encounter. The Pharisees, as we see them in the Gospels, often represent this judgmental approach. Today they make unfavorable comparisons of the disciples of Jesus with themselves and John's followers. It would be wonderful, a great rest for most of us, if we could suspend all the judging and realize how useless it is. Why do I have to judge other people around me when their actions, their way of smiling or talking, their way of dress, their hair, their voice, etc., has really nothing to do with me personally? When we're tempted to judge others, especially to condemn them in our minds for something they do—or more often, what we imagine they do—why not turn the question on ourselves? I think so-and-so is so aggressive. Why not ask myself: do I, perhaps, come across as aggressive? Am I too bold and thoughtless about others' feelings? Every judgment we're tempted to make can become an occasion for a good examination of our own conscience. "[God] will bring to light what is hidden in darkness / and will manifest the motives of our hearts, / and then everyone will receive praise from God" (1 Cor 4:5).

Saturday of the Twenty-Second Week in Ordinary Time—
The tough ideals

Readings: 1 Cor 4:6b-15; Luke 6:1-5
Resp. Psalm: Ps 145:17-18, 19-20, 21 (L 436)

Though Paul shows a willingness to suffer, go hungry and thirsty, and be poorly treated—all for Christ's sake (see 1 Cor 4:11), he does not give us a picture of one who embraces this condition eagerly, without struggle. The sarcasm in his words is an indication of the difficulty he has in being treated this way: "We are fools on Christ's account, but you are wise in Christ" (4:10). None of us should expect it to be easy either. What Jesus asks of us in the way of turning the other cheek (see Luke 6:29) is nothing natural and easy, something we can routinely nod our heads to in agreement. Our own experience should tell us that such virtue is only learned slowly and haltingly. Reading or hearing some of the psychological approaches to character, one would think the human spirit to be a machine which could be juggled or oiled into smooth running. But Christian belief is based on the notion that our spirit is something much more complex, much deeper. We pray for and work for the realization in ourselves of Christ's demanding ideals. And, possibly even more importantly, we need to put before God our inability to be so forgiving and humble, and trust in the forgiveness which is, after all, God's specialty, something God does better than we do.

Monday of the Twenty-Third Week in Ordinary Time—
Beginning again with God's help

Readings: 1 Cor 5:1-8; Luke 6:6-11
Resp. Psalm: Ps 5:5-6, 7, 12 (L 437)

The beginning of school, no matter at what time of the year, affects many, maybe most of us. We tend to look back on it, as we see the young going to their education, with either relief or with warm nostalgia. The Gospel opens today speaking of Jesus teaching in the synagogue. Teaching and learning are two facets of the lives of many of us. The latter should really never be lacking while teaching is something nearly all of us do in some way or other: either formally in a classroom or by our manner, our words, our life. In today's first reading, which is used during the Easter season also, all of us are urged to make a fresh, new beginning. "Clear out the old yeast, so that you may become a fresh batch of dough, . . . let us celebrate . . . with the unleavened bread of sincerity and truth" (1 Cor 5:7-8). Whether we're at the beginning of a new school year or continuing in our "old job," as we may call it, a fresh, invigorated new beginning is always in order. It will help us and those with whom we work. We can determine to give all we do more of ourselves, more generosity, care, thoroughness, maybe gentleness and good spirit. What would be a better way of doing the old job or beginning a new school year? All we do is done in the strength the Lord gives us (see Phil 4:13). As we ask ourselves the question, it's appropriate "Trust in the LORD" (Ps 37:3) to second our efforts, even to prime them.

Tuesday of the Twenty-Third Week in Ordinary Time—
Our healing potential

Readings: 1 Cor 6:1-11; Luke 6:12-19
Resp. Psalm: Ps 149:1b-2, 3-4, 5-6a and 9b (L 438)

The unused potential of Christians is a fact of Christian life and has given rise to famous lines like the one that says Christianity has been found wanting because it hasn't been tried (Ghandi). Paul deals with a difficulty among his Corinthian converts in today's first reading. He thinks that they have the potential within them that would help solve disputes without recourse to the civil authorities. Some of the wise and good people among them, he argues, could help settle issues and reconcile Christians. And as far as the healing and concern which the crowds sought from Jesus, isn't some of that at least to be found in us who have become the Lord's members by baptism? Our potential to help each other and our world is probably never fully realized in most of us. We can at least be a voice of reconciliation in our society and among our friends. The power which "came forth from [Jesus]" (Luke 6:19) and "cured all" (6:19; NAB, 1st ed.) is ours to some degree. We exercise it often, of course: when we visit the sick (see Matt 25:35), keep vigil with a dying or suffering friend or family member, even when we do more impersonal things like contributing to some good cause. We can volunteer to help in the grade school or with coaching; we can encourage others and recognize their achievements. Some of us may blessedly be unaware of the good we do because it has become so natural (see Matt 25:37). That's wonderful. But we may need to ask more of the potential we have through our union with the power and compassion of Jesus, a union strengthened at this table.

Wednesday of the Twenty-Third Week in Ordinary Time—
Perspective

Readings: 1 Cor 7:25-31; Luke 6:20-26
Resp. Psalm: Ps 45:11-12, 14-15, 16-17 (L 439)

The terrorism and war that mark human life (maybe not just now but always), such violence and viciousness underline themes in today's readings. Paul tells his unmarried readers not to be too concerned about getting married because "the time is running out" (1 Cor 7:29). Many persons of Paul's time expected the end of all things very quickly. Our conception of the universe and human life is different: we are aware of the millions of years our universe has existed and its vast distances; human longevity in our time leads us to expect people to live to eighty or ninety. Yet, terror, war, and disaster, and more daily things like death from cancer and auto accidents all remind us of the shortness of our days. (The title of Psalm 89, that is, Psalm 90 in the old Douay-Rheims translation is "A prayer for the mercy of God: recounting the shortness and miseries of the days of man.") Paul's words and those of our Lord, the Beatitudes of Luke's Gospel, ask us to balance the value we put on this life with its quickly passing character. We should, Paul says, be "using the world as not using it fully. / For the world in its present form is passing away" (1 Cor 7:31). Our grief and joys, our plans and ambitions, our pleasures and our building, we cannot simply despise or ignore them. But our faith tells us to look beyond them. Does any one of us ever find the perfect balance of the present and eternity? Probably not; we go from one emphasis to the other. But still the final word has to be that of Jesus: even though we are poor, hungry, hated, and insulted, even though we weep for those taken from us and the heroes who sought to help them, we are blessed in God's eyes. We are citizens of a world that cannot be bought, collected, or touched, but which lasts forever.

Thursday of the Twenty-Third Week in Ordinary Time—
"Give and gifts will be given to you" (Luke 6:38)

Readings: 1 Cor 8:1b-7, 11-13; Luke 6:27-38
Resp. Psalm: Ps 139:1b-3, 13-14ab, 23-24 (L 440)

No matter what book of the New Testament we open we're faced with a basically consistent teaching. Yesterday we heard St. Paul speak of the detachment a Christian must bring to the serious concerns of ordinary life. Today the words of Jesus stress, without pulling any punches, how unlike the spirit of our world should be the spirit of Christians. Most facets of everyday life involve some pretty serious competition, require that we have successfully completed our assertiveness training, and that we are not pushovers for others. We see it in the headlines on the financial page and the seriousness of commercial sports. Turn the other cheek? Give more clothing than what was already stolen? Do not demand back what someone has taken? Lend without the current rate of interest? The world certainly doesn't run that way. Should we save the "nice guy" approach for personal relations or within the family and be a tiger with the rest of them in the business or professional world? That doesn't seem consistent with the teaching of Jesus. What high and never-to-be-fulfilled ideals he gives us! As with the command to love our neighbor (Luke 10:27), there is never going to be a moment when we can sit back and say, "Well, I've satisfied that obligation completely. Next, please." At the very least this tough teaching of Jesus is meant to prod us continually. We'll never reach an intellectually satisfying solution. Only in practice, in daily life, can we learn the truth of such words as, "Give and gifts will be given to you" (Luke 6:38).

Friday of the Twenty-Third Week in Ordinary Time—
It must begin at home

Readings: 1 Cor 9:16-19, 22b-27; Luke 6:39-42
Resp. Psalm: Ps 84:3, 4, 5-6, 12 (L 441)

We're constantly bombarded in our readings at Mass by realism; there's not much place for sweet dreaming and so-called pie-in-the-sky. Paul's own self-analysis and the words of Jesus speak to any of us who lead others or even hope to offer others support and encouragement. Jesus warns that the blind cannot lead the blind. Paul is concerned that his own life and example be such that while he seems to do good for others, he himself does not end up rejected by God. Beyond this, Jesus warns that efforts to judge and correct others may mask an unwillingness to face our own failings (see also Luke 6:37). Tough stuff, a hard message! This is most obviously a problem for a priest or others who minister. He or she—but all of us to some degree—must by prayer and closeness to God be sure that what we say does not become a taped message detached from our own way of living. The time demands of ministry can make us all shortchange our own lives as followers of Christ. We feel there is no time for prayer and reflection, for meditation or reading. We become busybodies, ultimately becoming empty of what we should be giving. The discipline Paul speaks of can be translated to mean the necessity we are under of setting aside time for personal prayer, for silence, for being alone. And it means not asking of others what we do not ask of ourselves (Luke 6:31): "I drive my body and train it, / for fear that, after having preached to others, / I myself should be disqualified" (1 Cor 9:27). And, "Why do you see the speck in your neighbor's eye, but do not notice the log in your own eye?" (Luke 6:41; NRSV).

Saturday of the Twenty-Third Week in Ordinary Time—
The one Body of Christ (see 1 Cor 10:16-17)

Readings: 1 Cor 10:14-22; Luke 6:43-49
Resp. Psalm: Ps 116:12-13, 17-18 (*L* 442)

In dissuading the Corinthians from any participation in the offerings made to idols, Paul makes a point relevant to us today. From our Western background we have inherited a high degree of individualism which is foreign to the spirit of Paul's time. Taking part in gifts offered to idols, Paul says, makes the person one with the idol. Similarly in sharing the Body and Blood of Christ we become one with him and all who share it: "Because the loaf of bread is one, / we, though many, are one Body, / for we all partake of the one loaf" (1 Cor 10:17). Several centuries of exclusive emphasis on how we become one with the Lord in communion have left many of us strangers to the notion that we become one with *all* who share the same bread. This other emphasis which we have in St. Paul today was strong in early Christianity. To recall and hold more firmly the balancing truth about our union with each other might help us see more the implications for love of others. Restraining our tongues from backbiting and judging (see also Gal 5:15), seeing more clearly our solidarity with the poor and powerless, forgiving the failures of others—all these, among many other actions, are strengthened once we realize we are "one Body" because we share the Body of Christ" (see 1 Cor 10:17, 16).

Monday of the Twenty-Third Week in Ordinary Time—
United with Christ and each other

Readings: 1 Cor 11:17-26, 33; Luke 7:1-10
Resp. Psalm: Ps 40:7-8a, 8b-9, 10, 17 (*L* 443)

Since the custom was changed so early among Christians many of us may be surprised to hear that the people Paul was writing to celebrated the Eucharist in the midst of one of their daily meals. The Lord's Last

Supper had been celebrated in the midst of a festive meal. The early Christians continued the custom. Paul shows us one of the reasons they eventually separated the two: some came with the kind of food that probably embarrassed poorer members; others drank too much. All of this demonstrated the disunity of the Corinthians which so disturbed Paul. Coming together at the altar should strengthen our unity, bring us into union not only with God through Christ, but with each other in "the Body of Christ" (1 Cor 10:17; *Lectionary*). All our tendencies to judge others harshly, to envy them, even to wish them failure, to consider them for whatever reason inferior to ourselves, all of these that we may bring to the Eucharist are opposed to its meaning (see Gal 5:15). Hence, we begin the Eucharist asking forgiveness for our sins. In a sense, every time we come, even if it's daily, we are beginning again in the constant struggle we have to live up to the unifying love of a genuine Christian. The unity of the Eucharist is, of course, not some lockstep uniformity but a willingness to respect and honor others who may differ with us on many smaller matters but agree with us in finding the meaning of life in Christ. Before we come together for Communion we again remind ourselves that our unity with God has to be accompanied by good will towards others by exchanging a sign of that peace. And immediately before we receive communion we take on our own lips the words similar to those of the centurion in today's Gospel: "Lord . . . I am not worthy to have you enter under my roof . . . but say the word and let [your] servant be healed" (Luke 7:6-7).

Tuesday of the Twenty-Fourth Week in Ordinary Time—
What each brings to our common life

Readings: 1 Cor 12:12-14, 27-31a; Luke 7:11-17
Resp. Psalm: Ps 100:1b-a, 3, 4, 5 (L 444)

Paul compares the unity of Christians to the way the parts of the human body must work together in order to function as a unit. The comparison stresses both unity and the fact that not all the members of the body are the same or serve the same function. If we lack the use of one of our limbs or faculties for any length of time, we learn how important each is for the good operation of the body. A brilliant tongue may get more attention but for almost all of us a healthy foot or good functioning organs are pretty basic. Tomorrow, St. Paul will discuss the greatest gift of all; without it all the others are of only relative importance. That gift is love (see 1 Cor 13). But today Paul emphasizes that the "body is one" (1 Cor 12:12) but composed of many different members. All depend on each other for the good functioning of the body. The mind has little impact without a mouth to speak its bright ideas. The imagination remains pretty airy if there are no practical hands to execute its dreams, no feet to move us. If we knew well the interlocking relations of all parts of the body we would be less likely to judge any one part as superior to another. Comparing them is like comparing apples and oranges. Rather than letting ourselves fall into rash judgments about the worth of others, we'd do so much more by attempting to see the gifts and valuable functions that others serve. When we feel like saying to others or just thinking to ourselves that so-and-so is certainly a loudmouth, we might more positively see what genuine service he or she renders that we cannot. United to the Lord in the Eucharist, may we expend more energy in appreciating what others bring to our common life in Christ.

Wednesday of the Twenty-Fourth Week in Ordinary Time—
Love adds the luster

Readings: 1 Cor 12:31–13:13; Luke 7:31-35
Resp. Psalm: Ps 33:2-3, 4-5, 12 and 22 (L 445)

We've heard today's reading from Corinthians many a Saturday in June and at other times of weddings. When the reader began we probably heard the wedding march and looked for the bride. It probably doesn't receive adequate attention at a wedding, when everyone is preoccupied. Yet it deserves better. The text tells us that whatever great gifts we may have that serve vital functions in "the Body of Christ" (1 Cor 10:16; *Lectionary*), they are all pretty shabby if we lack love. We know from our own daily experience how disappointing even great skill is if it isn't accompanied by a generous, kind spirit. No matter how well the bus driver takes the turns and gets through traffic, it disappoints us when he or she barks at people asking information. An efficient pastor who has taken the parish out of the red still lacks luster if we can't discern a genuine interest in the suffering poor. We're likewise unimpressed if the teacher or professor shows incredible knowledge of the field but doesn't bother to know any names or return a greeting. "Love is patient, love is kind. / It is not jealous, love is not pompous, / it is not inflated" (1 Cor 13:4), Paul writes. The much acclaimed athlete who takes time for the little kids who idolize her or him models this love better than one who sees the kids only as nuisances. Our gifts in the sense of talents and abilities are, after all, basically gifts; we may have developed them but we did not create them. To really sparkle they need to be touched with, accompanied by, generous love and readiness to serve others, not merely self (see ch. 12). "If I speak in human and angelic tongues / but do not have love, / I am a resounding gong or a clashing cymbal" (13:1).

Thursday of the Twenty-Fourth Week in Ordinary Time—
God's grace in us

Readings: 1 Cor 15:1-11; Luke 7:36-50
Resp. Psalm: Ps 118:1b-2, 16ab-17, 28 (*L* 446)

"[B]y the grace of God," Paul says, "I am what I am, / and [God's] grace to me has not been ineffective" (1 Cor 15:10). That God should choose this one-time persecutor of Christians to become the great missionary to the Gentiles is truly a mystery. And those Christians who find his writing baffling and his personality prickly see how profound that mystery is. Along with the choice of Judas as disciple and of Peter as head of the apostles, Paul's choice tells us that God is definitely not predictable; we don't have God in our pocket. "God's favor" (1 Cor 15:10; NAB, 1st ed.) took Paul and drastically turned him around. Some of us have likewise had our beliefs changed by God's grace; others of us are more like the woman in the Gospel who has her sins forgiven and a new life begun by grace in the form of forgiveness (see John 7:53–8:11). In any case we should be able to say with Paul, "[B]y the grace of God I am what I am, / and [God's] grace to me has not been ineffective" (1 Cor 15:10). As believers, as anyone is who has been opened to God's influence, we have been showered with God's favor in two major ways: First, in our birth we received an array of gifts, talents, and specific abilities. Second, by baptism and faith we have received more help, more strength, a new life, and a hope which overcomes the world (see Titus 1:2, 3:7). Aware of how short life is and of our tendency to inertia, we need to make prayer for the fruitfulness of our gifts a regular matter. It is so easy to let day after day slip by aimlessly and dreamily, never getting on with the business of living and loving. The Lord has ideas about what we can become by grace; may they be fruitful in us.

Friday of the Twenty-Fourth Week in Ordinary Time—
This good body

Readings: 1 Cor 15:12-20; Luke 8:1-3
Resp. Psalm: Ps 17:1bcd, 6-7, 8b and 15 (*L* 447)

One wonders what idea of the following of Christ, of Christian belief, those Corinthians must have had who did not believe in the resurrection of the dead. They may have shared with their fellow and non-Christian Greeks the idea that eternal life had to be more spiritual than that. In no way could this gross human body have a part in life with God. For many thinkers the world over it has always been—and still is—difficult to imagine that somehow this heavy and recalcitrant body will have any share in eternal life. They would rather conceive of eternity as a liberation from material things including the body. Yet the goodness of matter and of the body is a central belief of Christianity, one founded in the book of Genesis and in the resurrection of Jesus. The body, matter, is the good partner of the spirit in all that it does of good here on earth; it deserves to share the reward of eternal life. The body, matter, this whole earthly environment of ours deserves respect and care as partners and coheirs with the spirit (see Rom 8:17). Lord, help us not to discount the value of anything you have made, including our bodies.

Saturday of the Twenty-Fourth Week in Ordinary Time—
The Spirit's partner

Readings: 1 Cor 15:35-37, 42-49; Luke 8:4-15
Resp. Psalm: Ps 56:10c-12, 13-14 (*L* 448)

St. Paul is stretching for analogies that might help us understand how we will be able to rise again, to have a body in the world of God which we may tend to look on as so spiritual, so lacking in bodies of any kind. He says that what we sow when putting seeds into the ground is nothing like what we find in the harvest, but there is continuity. Our bodies in the resurrection similarly will be different from what is buried but somehow continuous with this body we have now. We would benefit from this difficult time if we came away with a strong conviction that this body which we see as the center of weakness, pain, disease, and temptation is destined for a glorious, new existence. The body, in Christianity, is not something to be despised or something to be gotten rid of so that we can live a better life. As with Christ in his resurrection appearances, our life to come will involve a transformation but one still giving the body an honored place. The body is the partner of the spirit, not, as we so often think or hear its competitor or enemy (the study of "flesh" and "Spirit"—in Romans 8:5-6, for example—invites the interpretation of skilled interpreters and anthropologists). Let's hear this Word of God about our bodies and pray to appreciate more their place in all we do or hope to be. Christians have good reasons for taking care of their bodies and respecting them, reasons that are not simply egocentric or bounded by this world.

Monday of the Twenty-Fifth Week in Ordinary Time—
Truly to listen

Readings: Prov 3:27-34; Luke 8:16-18
Resp. Psalm: Ps 15:2-3a, 3bc-4ab, 5 (*L* 449)

Among the mixture of sayings in today's Gospel is one very odd one. It concerns listening, hearing the Word of God. Paradoxically, those of us who are at Mass most often may have the most difficulty in really hearing the Word of God. Those who hear it rarely may more easily be surprised and even shaken by some phrase or parable. We who are here more often easily feel we've heard all this before and, probably without saying it, "that there is nothing more here to be said to me." True listening is always difficult. In class, as students we drifted off; at Mass on Sunday we worry about brunch or the weather. Jesus says, "Take care, then, how you hear" (Luke 8:18). The truly strange saying which might make us wake up and think is this: "To anyone who has, more will be given, / and from the one who has not, / even what he [or she] seems to have will be taken away" (8:18). The point seems to be that if we do listen well and fruitfully, if we take in the words and apply them honestly to ourselves, our life in Christ will become richer. Life has, in fact, a capacity for indefinite expansion and deepening. If we do not listen well, if we do not make the effort to apply the words and see their implications in our life, whatever genuine life of the Spirit we do have will tend to diminish or wither. We will lose even the little we think we have. It's the idea that, paradoxically, we preserve interior matters the more we give them away. Lord, as a preparation for our communion with you and each other, help us to allow your Word to work in our "hearts and minds" (Phil 4:7; NIV).

Tuesday of the Twenty-Fifth Week in Ordinary Time—
"[T]he cry of the poor" (Prov 21:13)

Readings: Prov 21:1-6, 10-13; Luke 8:19-21
Resp. Psalm: Ps 119:1, 27, 30, 34, 35, 44 (*L* 450)

The Book of Proverbs is a collection of sayings or, in fact, collections of sayings from various sources and times. They vary too in depth of insight and in their religious character. Some seem quite simply worldly and practical, for example, "The plans of the diligent are sure of profit, / but all rash haste leads certainly to poverty" (21:5). Some seem designed to assure our self-interest; others call us further. In today's reading at least two of these proverbs call us to compassion and concern for the poor. One does it indirectly by telling us that "the wicked [person] desires evil; / [a] neighbor finds no pity in his [or her] eyes" (21:10). And the last proverb today is strong on how urgent it is for our salvation that we hear the voice of the needy: "If you close your ear to the cry of the poor, / you will cry out and not be heard" (21:13; NSRV). With the seeming growth of homelessness and poverty rather than their elimination, it is easy to take it all for granted, to become hardened. Yet the proverb tells us, as Jesus does in Matthew 25 (vv. 31-46), that our relation to God can be measured by our response to the poor, the suffering, the deprived. No matter how little or much we can do about poverty, we do need to decide what is possible and practical in our position and do it rather than simply wring our hands in helplessness.

Wednesday of the Twenty-Fifth Week in Ordinary Time—
Using what we have

Readings: Prov 30:5-9; Luke 9:1-6
Resp. Psalm: Ps 119:29, 72, 89, 101, 104, 163 (*L* 451)

The writer of Proverbs says, "give me neither poverty nor riches" (30:8). Undoubtedly most of us are more frightened of poverty than we are of riches. In fact, superficially, riches don't seem to be too frightening at all. We could use a little more leeway in our income; we would enjoy not having to scrimp; we'd like to be able to plan a vacation in Bermuda or put down a payment on that house. As we continue hearing from Luke we'll hear more strictures from Jesus about the dangers of wealth. The author of Proverbs has an even-handed approach. He seems to say: "If I have too much I am liable to ignore God and say to myself, I guess I'm in charge; I don't need anyone else. I may not even need God, since I am able to provide for my own security" (see Prov 30:9a). On the other hand, he says: "If I have too little, there is real danger that I shall at least pant after what I do not have or, further, give in to less than honest means to get more" (see Prov 30:9b). Almost daily our newspapers and media show us the perils of poverty and wealth. Overall the dangers related to having or not having material things come from our attitude, our desires, not from the things themselves. Nothing God has made is evil (see Gen 1:31).

Elsewhere in the Gospel Jesus tells us to have the right priorities, to set our thoughts on the kingdom of God, and all the things we really need will come our way (see Matt 6:33). Not to be swept up in the enjoyment of wealth and what it brings, nor to be saddened by the fact that we do not have these things, this is the ideal. Lord, help us to use your world well for your glory, the necessities of family, and for the good of the less fortunate.

Thursday of the Twenty-Fifth Week in Ordinary Time— *Understanding low spirits*

Readings: Eccl 1:2-11; Luke 9:7-9
Resp. Psalm: Ps 90:3-4, 5-6, 12-13, 14 and 17bc (*L* 452)

Ecclesiastes very likely resonates with our mood at some moment or other, though we'd be in tough shape if we felt like that writer all the time! Sure, there are moments when we feel overwhelmed with the way everything seems to repeat itself. One day seems indistinguishable from another; life seems to be in a rut. Our activities, life itself, may seem empty—that's what "vanity" means in the opening words of Ecclesiastes (1:2). "What's it all for?" we ask. Every line in this melancholy reading echoes in me at some moment or other. There are times when the most pleasant experiences leave us asking, "Is that all there is?" But it is to be hoped that most of us do not feel this way continuously. This book, so unusual in the Bible, has its place. First, it tells us that our desolate moods are understandable; others have felt them. Second, in its own way, it reassures those who are bothered with doubts and much questioning that God understands that. It is not sinful. Finally, it reminds those of us who are more constantly sunny that there are others who are much troubled about life, the world, even about God. We don't have to obscure the joy we have in our faith and trust in Jesus. But while we do our best to share our joy and confidence with others, we are also reminded by this reading to be sensitive and patient with those who find it harder to see the sunshine. Have we experienced their pain? Do we know their isolation? We do not slap them on the back and say, "Cheer up." We don't know the burdens that afflict others. Good cheer, prayer, and genuinely practical help are all good approaches to the misery of others. The Lord reinforces our ability to share in his healing help in this Eucharist.

Friday of the Twenty-Fifth Week in Ordinary Time—
A time to work and a time to accept

Readings: Eccl 3:1-11; Luke 9:18-22
Resp. Psalm: Ps 144:1b and 2abc, 3-4 (*L* 453)

"A time to kill, and a time to heal; / a time to tear down, and a time to build" (Eccl 3:3). The words of today's first reading have become famous through adaptation in a song some years back. It suggests a certain amount of resignation, acceptance of what is. "There is an appointed time for everything" (3:1): For birth and death, war and peace, laughing and weeping. More often in Scripture we meet the idea that the more negative things should be changed, gotten rid of. Peter typifies this attitude in Matthew's Gospel when he reacts to the prediction of Christ's suffering by saying that he will never allow that. As that suffering drew near, Jesus himself prayed that if possible he could forego it (see Luke 22:42). Suffering, death, pain are not normally greeted in the Bible as something inevitable but something to be overcome. The Savior came to save us from all these things, to bring us ultimately into a new and better world (see John 3:16). We honor so many saints for what they did to change the conditions of the poor, prisoners, the suffering and sick, the weak and despised. But granting all that, there are moments in human life when the words of Ecclesiastes may offer some comfort and even strength. For example, we and others have struggled, exhausted every conceivable measure to better a situation, to overcome a difficulty; there may come a moment when we do best to accept what is. There may be, finally, "a time to be silent" or "a time to speak," "a time to mourn, and a time to dance" (Eccl 3:7, 4). The famous Serenity Prayer asks that we may know when that time has come. The Lord himself finally prayed, "Father, into your hands I commend my spirit" (Luke 23:46; see Ps 31:6).

Saturday of the Twenty-Fifth Week in Ordinary Time—
Melancholy and compassion

Readings: Eccl 11:9–12:8; Luke 9:43b-45
Resp. Psalm: Ps 90:3-4, 5-6, 12-13, 14 and 17 (*L* 454)

The sorrowful feelings Ecclesiastes has about old age and some of the bitterness he has about injustice in the world are more understandable when we realize that he and his fellow Jews had no clear idea of reward and punishment in an afterlife. It took the Jews some centuries to arrive at that belief. While poets have spoken of how "the best is yet to come" in one's later years, many an aging person has felt more like Ecclesiastes. He speaks of the evil days to come, the years when one will say, "I have no pleasure in them" (12:1). A great part of today's selection speaks of the failing health and infirmities of old age in figurative language (see the notes in the NAB). It speaks of failing eyesight: "They who look through the windows grow blind" (12:3), of loss of hearing: "the doors to the street are shut, / and the sound of the mill is low" (12:4), of the shaky gait of the elderly: "one fears heights / and perils in the street" (12:5)—those kids racing by on skateboards, the too-quickly changing traffic lights. Ecclesiastes, by its appearance in the Bible, gives permission for our melancholy about aging and our nostalgia for youth. Today's Gospel speaks of the amazement of the disciples at all that Jesus was doing. We followers of Christ have reason to be amazed at what good God can draw out of the pains and worries of old age or of any age, what generosity and kindness it can bring forth in the younger and more healthy, what compassion and gentleness in the elderly. As we are united once again to the Lord and each other at this altar and in his sacrifice, we know we are in contact with the power that can transform suffering into joy, death into everlasting life.

Monday of the Twenty-Sixth Week in Ordinary Time—
Finding meaning

Readings: Job 1:6–22; Luke 9:46–50
Resp. Psalm: Ps 17:1bcd, 2–3, 6–7 (L 455)

The book of Job, from which we read this week, deals with the most wrenching religious question of all: why do the innocent suffer? Why does famine strike the people of one part of the world while others are overstuffed? Why do the poor have to suffer atrocities? Why are children abused by the people who should take care of them? Why does a seventy-five-year-old mother, after decades of giving to others, have to suffer cancer alone? We look for justice, for some rhyme or reason to suffering. Often we think that bad behavior and suffering should be connected, and likewise, good behavior and blessings. Satan speaks in those terms today. God has just pointed out Job as an exemplary man, "blameless and upright" (1:8). Satan says: "Is it for nothing that Job is God-fearing?" (1:9). Why shouldn't Job be upright? You've given him everything: a good family, prosperity, and health. Satan then says that if Job were to lose all this, really face misery and catastrophe, he would soon get over his uprightness. Alongside all this, the concerns of the disciples in today's Gospel about prestige and credit seem so small. We should think about it a bit. Should we expect virtue to be rewarded? Should we expect vice to be punished? What about Jesus? He was a model of obedience and faithfulness to his Father, and what happened to him in this life?—death by crucifixion in his thirties. The answer to our questions, however we phrase them, will be found in the life, suffering, death, and resurrection of Jesus. Truly, there is no other hope for us (see Acts 4:12). Sharing in his offering here at the Eucharist and reflecting on it in relation to our life is the only way we find some meaning for our lives.

Tuesday of the Twenty-Sixth Week in Ordinary Time—
The cross in daily life

Readings: Job 3:1-3, 11-17, 20-23; Luke 9:51-56
Resp. Psalm: Ps 88:2-3, 4-5, 6, 7-8 (L 456)

Occasionally one gets the impression that we select a Cross in our life a bit like a rock star might choose one at a jeweler to hang from her or his ear. But the genuine Cross in our life does not have to be sought out; it will come as an inevitable part of life. Sometime or other we all come close to feeling like Job. Why was I born? Why should I live? Our happiness, our hopes, are dashed to the ground by an accident that harms a family member, by a killing disease that hits us, or by desertion by a spouse. These things make us cry out like the Lord, "My God, my God, why have you forsaken me?" (Mark 15:34; Matt 27:46; see Ps 22:2). These are the true Crosses; nothing we choose could ever equal the ones given to us by life and our situation. The suffering and death of Jesus came about not because he wanted them but because his life and teaching had aroused hatred and ill will in others. Even without our example or words, we can be hated or persecuted irrationally, as is the case in today's Gospel. The Samaritans simply hated any Jew, Jesus included. We all face people and circumstances beyond our control which can harm us. Not to look for extraordinary things to do but to accept what obedience, the circumstances of life bring us, that is probably the most heroic thing we can do. What Cross is more free of egotism than that which comes to us from the unchangeable conditions and people of our life, than what faithfulness to our responsibilities asks from us. Perhaps in this category lie the inconveniences and boredom of everyday life. We find the Lord in these places, above all.

Wednesday of the Twenty-Sixth Week in Ordinary Time—
The awesome universe

Readings: Job 9:1-12, 14-16; Luke 9:57-62
Resp. Psalm: Ps 88:10bc-11, 12-13, 14-15 (*L* 457)

Science definitely tells us more than Job or his contemporaries knew about how earthquakes happen, why the sun and stars are sometimes clouded over, even how the constellations came to be. Yet we can still be awed or terrified by the force of an earthquake, impressed by the scurrying of the clouds and their formations. Even figures and statistics about the skies and the constellations leave us still gaping; they are so outside our ordinary experience—even in times of inflation! To be on Job's level of knowledge about our universe or to have the very sophisticated knowledge available to us today, both leave us with reasons for awe and a sense of mystery, for different reasons. Not to know how far the constellations are away is awesome; to know how far they are away in terms of light years is still awesome. Even though we work to expand our knowledge, we should also be willing and happy to live with all the mystery and grandeur of our universe. Job's sense of God's greatness and how beyond our scale God is, that is something worth imitating, something timeless. Rabbi Abraham Heschel says of this awe, "Standing between earth and sky, we are silenced by the sight."

Thursday of the Twenty-Sixth Week in Ordinary Time—
"[M]y Vindicator lives" (*Job 19:25*)

Readings: Job 19:21-27; Luke 10:1-12
Resp. Psalm: Ps 27:7-8a, 8b-9abc, 13-14 (*L* 458)

Trust in God, another word for faith in much of the Scriptures, is based on what we know of the life and message of Jesus and, above all, that "God raised him from the dead" (Acts 3:15). God's love for us and the consequent hope and faith, therefore, are justified. In Jesus we see how total is God's care and love. We don't have all kinds of information about God, but we know in Jesus that this love of God for us about which we hear so much is genuine and powerful. It rescued him from death. God intends to do the same for us: rescue us from suffering, disappointment, and death. In the midst of his terrible suffering, the loss of his family, and everything else, Job retains the same trust in God. He says: "I know that my Vindicator lives, / and that he will at last stand forth upon the dust; / Whom I myself shall see" (19:25, 27).

The words in an older translation are set to moving music by Handel in his *Messiah:* "I know that my Redeemer liveth." Living before Jesus, Job had no such vivid picture as we have in Jesus of God's love but still, on the basis of what God had done for his people over the centuries, he is able to say that he trusts God will deliver him. At this altar we experience the closeness of God's love and mercy in the presence of Jesus in bread and wine, in God's word and in each other. "I know that my Vindicator," my Redeemer, "lives" (see Job 19:25).

Friday of the Twenty-Sixth Week in Ordinary Time—
Reasons for praise

Readings: Job 38:1, 12–21; 40:3–5; Luke 10:13-16
Resp. Psalm: Ps 139:1-3, 7-8, 9-10, 13-14ab (*L* 459)

Our readings from Job have skipped through this long book with just a few key passages. The argument about why Job has suffered goes back and forth. Today, at the end of the book, God brings the discussion to an end by pointing out to Job that the issue, while we're allowed to discuss and talk about it, ultimately is beyond our understanding. With a number of unanswerable questions God seems to be saying: Maybe we've heard enough on this. After all, what do you know about where light comes from? Have you ever commanded dawn? Job gets the point and says: I've said enough. Reason, we cannot forget, has its place and is well honored in the Catholic tradition, but it should lead to what we celebrate in such saints as Francis of Assisi and others. That is, it leads to awe, reverence, simple appreciation for what is, above all, praise. All those pictures and statues of Francis with birds sitting on his hands or with his hands raised to God show us something of his spirit, the spirit of praise and joy in God's creation. Francis' appreciation of and praise of God's creation shows up beautifully in his Canticle of the Sun. Part of it goes like this: "May Thou be praised, my Lord, with all Thy creatures (cf. Tob. 8:7), / especially mister brother sun, /of whom is the day, and Thou enlightens us through him. / . . . May Thou be praised, my Lord, for sister moon . . . / . . . May Thou be praised, my Lord, for our sister, mother earth" (cf. Dan 3:74) / who sustains us and governs, / and produces various fruits with colored flowers and green plants (cf. Ps 104:13-14). After hearing a few lines from this poem-prayer, each of us could come up with our own additions. For instance: Be praised, Lord, for the people who serve in hospices. Be praised for good neighbors.

Saturday of the Twenty-Sixth Week in Ordinary Time—
We never comprehend God

Readings: Job 42:1-3, 5-6, 12-17; Luke 10:17-24
Resp. Psalm: Ps 119:66, 71, 75, 91, 125, 130 (*L* 460)

The words of Jesus in the Gospel could very easily be put on Job's tongue: "I give you praise, Father, Lord of heaven and earth, / for although you have hidden these things / from the wise and the learned / you have revealed them to the childlike" (Luke 10:21). In yesterday's passage from Job (38:1, 12-21; 40:3-5), God had spoken to Job and pointed out that both he and his friends were out of their depth in trying to understand God's ways. God had more or less said: if you know so much, tell me the answer to all these mysteries of the universe and human life. Today we heard Job saying to God: "I have dealt with great things that I do not understand; / things too wonderful for me, which I cannot know. / . . . / Therefore I disown what I have said, / and repent in dust and ashes" (42:3, 6). Before the true God, our thought, stratagems—explanations for why there is suffering and pain particularly—all these are seen as frail stuff, about as substantial as cobwebs. God, we often need to be reminded, cannot be captured in our words, terms, theology, prayers. We must do our best with them, but God is always more than we can imagine or say. Cardinal Suenens said well: "I could not believe in a God whom I could comprehend." Neither should we.

Monday of the Twenty-Seventh Week in Ordinary Time—
What Paul preached

Readings: Gal 1:6-12; Luke 10:25-37
Resp. Psalm: Ps 111:1b-2, 7-8, 9 and 10c (*L* 461)

To put it mildly, Paul is pretty testy as he begins this letter to the Galatians. He omits the usual thanksgiving and more ingratiating remarks. For us who live in a time when truth seems to so many to be entirely subjective, when religious belief especially seems to be so often simply a matter of how I feel, his approach must seem intolerant and cranky. His obviously intense concern about the Gospel he preached might suggest to us the respect we owe to what we call tradition. What has been handed down to us (see 1 Cor 11) over the centuries in Scripture, beliefs, and practices, may be restated in many different ways to a new world, but there is a central core we need to handle very carefully. What we hear in the Apostles' Creed, for instance, is obviously more basic and central than some trend that just hit us recently, that comes from our culture. The Second Vatican Council pointed out that there is a rank or truths in our faith; that some are more central than others. If we find that some favorite devotion of ours does not seem central in our parish or given enough place in the church itself, it may be that it is some option open to us but not one to be put up there with the Eucharist. The Word of God, Scripture, and the sacraments are where we are assured of meeting God.

Tuesday of the Twenty-Seventh Week in Ordinary Time—
The pace of change

Readings: Gal 1:13-24; Luke 10:38-42
Resp. Psalm: Ps 139:1b-3, 13-14ab, 14c-15 (*L* 462)

Thanks to art, we often picture Paul's conversion to be a scene where he is thrown from his horse and blinded by shafts of light. We don't really have that much physical detail, but such a picture does certainly suggest an unusual experience that changed Paul from persecutor to apostle. He says, "You heard of my former way of life in Judaism, / how I persecuted the church of God beyond measure / and tried to destroy it, / . . . / But when he, who from my mother's womb had set me apart / and called me through his grace, / was pleased to reveal his Son to me, / so that I might proclaim him to the Gentiles / . . . / I went into Arabia . . ." (Gal 1:13-17). Undoubtedly, as Paul's sojourn in Arabia indicates, he had to solidify his belief before beginning his preaching. Ordinarily among all of us, no matter how our turning to Christ takes place, there is always room for change, conversion, new depth in our following of Christ. A very popular preacher stressed recently that there is never a change in "slow motion," that change is always quick and sudden. That really seems mistaken. Don't we all notice more gradual changes, transformations within ourselves or among our friends over long periods? We've probably seen situations where a dramatic change is announced only to find a few weeks later that not much if anything has changed. Given human nature, change is not only from above, change has to be a gradual—even slow—matter accomplished by little steps, new starts, and a lot of plodding effort. Evidence in Paul's letters shows that he had his dark moments later on. We who participate frequently in the Eucharist can easily experience discouragement over the seeming lack of dramatic change in ourselves. Change may be going on, very likely is going on, if we are daily open to the influence and power of God in Christ, in the Word, and the Eucharist.

Wednesday of the Twenty-Seventh Week in Ordinary Time—*Pray, now*

Readings: Gal 2:1-2, 7-14; Luke 11:1-4
Resp. Psalm: Ps 117:1bc, 2 (*L* 463)

By now we Catholics should be in the *Guinness Book of Records* for the speed with which we recite the Our Father in public. And we use it often. In Luke today we have, obviously, a shorter version of that prayer. The one we use at Mass and otherwise is based on the words in Matthew's Gospel. It is a good question whether Jesus meant to give us a prayer to be memorized and used on every conceivable occasion or if he was simply indicating to us the right priorities in prayer. The words came from Jesus in response to a request from the disciples. One wonders sometimes if the continual stream of such requests through- out history for help in praying—"Lord, teach us to pray just as John taught his disciples" (Luke 11:1)—is not rooted in our unwillingness to start praying or in genuine problems with prayer. Are we perhaps looking for another way to actually put off beginning to pray? You know how good we all are at discussing something endlessly rather than getting down to doing what needs to be done. Jesus' response takes the request at face value and gives the disciples some idea of what are the most important matters to pray about. First, the praise of God, then the success of the kingdom; only then do we get to our more self-centered needs like support for our daily existence and forgiveness. What seems presumed—and what many of us need to be encouraged to do—is just speaking directly to God. While Jesus stresses the priori- ties, he says nothing about the language, whether we should use Thee or Thou, be grammatical, etc. Most of us need more encouragement to simply speak to God in our own words, of our own needs, and of those dear to us.

Thursday of the Twenty-Seventh Week in Ordinary Time— *Prayer as trust*

Readings: Gal 3:1-5; Luke 11:5-13
Resp. Psalm: Ps 1:69-70, 71-72, 73-75 (*L* 464)

Recent readings have urged on us that our transformation into Christ is gradual, even slow, and that the whole matter is inseparable from prayer. There is no genuine willingness to receive what God can do without the quiet practice of prayer. A willingness to speak to God in our own terms and language and so develop a unique relationship between God and ourselves is an essential element of practical religion. If we allow God to come close to us through the practice of regular, personal prayer, the conditions are ripe for God to do something in us. Today we hear more encouragement directed to our prayer. Jesus tells the story about a fellow who has the unenviable need of disturbing a neighbor's sleep in order to ask for help with hospitality. The ruffled neighbor finally responds as if to get rid of the pest. Jesus makes clear the point of this funny little story in what follows. He says that persistent prayer inevitably is answered. God who is total goodness will eventually give us what is best. Obviously, he is not saying that our prayer for a mansion on the hill overlooking the lake or for a new Lexus will be answered. It is much more profound than that. Those who pray regularly and directly to God are going to be praying that God work what is best in them, that they become the kind of people God wants. People who pray genuinely soon get over the business of specifying to God that they must have two million dollars or the restoration of their hair. Prayer, as the remarks of Jesus make clear, is not separable from our trust and faith in God. We know God loves us and is out for the best for all of creation. When we pray, we are expressing that trust.

Friday of the Twenty-Seventh Week in Ordinary Time—
Responding to God's love

Readings: Gal 3:7-14; Luke 11:15-26
Resp. Psalm: Ps 111:1b-2, 3-4, 5-6 (*L* 465)

Paul is forceful in his stress on faith and, on the other hand, his rejection of the legal requirements laid down in the Hebrew Scriptures. It's pretty difficult for most of us to share Paul's vehemence about the topic. It seems remote and irrelevant to us. But we read Scripture with the assumption that there is something of value in it for us. Is it possible to translate Paul's concern into something of meaning for us? Though we've undoubtedly had Christianity presented at times as a list of demands or a system of laws, that is not very close to the way Jesus presents it. He gives us steep ideals, assurances of God's love, and encouragement to imitate his love for God. The danger with understanding our faith as a bunch of regulations and rules is, for one, that we imagine we must really wow God in order to get his favor. But Scripture and, in a particularly strong way, Paul, stress that God has "first loved us" (1 John 4:19), independently of what we have done or are. We call it unconditional love, and most of us have also experienced it from our parents or are in the process of giving it to children or others. What Paul insists on is that the best thing we can do is to open ourselves to God's love and receive it with trust and confidence. We speak of receiving Communion, not getting Communion, and receiving is a very appropriate term for how we relate to God. God gives and our part, first of all, is to accept that gift and then to use it in compassion and love. Our deeds of love are the natural response to having received God's love ourselves; we don't have to pile up accomplishments to have God's love. It was given to us long before we were able to do that, usually in our baptism or in the gift of faith.

Saturday of the Twenty-Seventh Week in Ordinary Time—
God's compassionate offspring

Readings: Gal 3:22-29; Luke 11:27-28
Resp. Psalm: Ps 105:2-3, 4-5, 6-7 (L 466)

The woman in the Gospel gives Jesus indirect praise by saying how blessed is his mother for having such a son. The words of Jesus in reply seem to downplay that relationship: "Rather, blessed are those / who hear the word of God and observe it" (Luke 11:28). Yet, if we look at that carefully and recall earlier parts of this same Gospel, we find an emphasis on Mary's essential greatness. After the angel announced her motherhood, she said: "Behold, I am the handmaid of the Lord. May it be done to me according to your word" (1:38). Like every other recipient of God's favor, Mary too is blessed for keeping the word of God; her greatness lies in her receptivity to God's action and word. Mary is depicted in Luke's Gospel as the first and model disciple; she too received "the Word" (John 1:14) into herself and allowed it to be fruitful (see Luke 8:4-8; 11-15). Each of us, Paul tells us, is a son or daughter of God because of our faith in Christ Jesus, because of baptism. We expect that sons and daughters honor their parents not simply by bearing their name but by the way they live (see Exod 20:12). People in our secular world are probably not greatly impressed to hear us say we're sons and daughters of God. They've heard other "religious nuts" make all sorts of outrageous claims. It's much more helpful and impressive if we Christians demonstrate that we are God's sons and daughters not ostentatiously but consistently, by being in the forefront of compassion and involvement for the good of those around us.

Monday of the Twenty-Eighth Week in Ordinary Time—
The signs are all around us

Readings: Gal 4:22-24, 26-27, 31–5:1; Luke 11:29-32
Resp. Psalm: Ps 113:1b-2, 3-4, 5a and 6-7 (*L* 467)

Pretty stern words of Jesus today about unresponsive people, hardened people. The Queen of Sheba came a long distance to hear Solomon, and Jonah by his preaching brought the city of Nineveh to its knees. Yet "there is something greater than Jonah here" (Luke 11:32), Jesus says to his hearers. Apparently our interior life is similar to our physical life. Some of our internal organs seem to harden with age, become less flexible. That's a danger for all of us. Like the people Jesus criticizes in today's Gospel, we also have our tendency to want the big sign. Someone sees the face of Jesus on a refrigerator door in Hoboken and crowds line up to see it. Others expect a message from Mary to clarify the Gospels on when the end of things will happen. Though such signs—and the certainty people hope to get from them—are very rare, we still would prefer the easy way of signs. Jesus just doesn't give us such. But there are signs and messages addressed to us daily, in every life, to which we have become hardened or insensitive. If we walk down the sidewalks of a large city we are sure to see persons asking for money and other sad cases dotting the way. To survive we eventually become hardened to all this. Our television brings us news stories of war, thousands of starving refugees, and terrible crimes—and we don't cry. Our so-called entertainment is often built around macho heroes "blowing away" their enemies. We become immune to the impact of poverty, crime, and violence. We're better off in our relation to God if we can retain some sensitivity and receptivity to what goes on around us and to hear God's message in it.

Tuesday of the Twenty-Eighth Week in Ordinary Time—
Faith in nothing less than the Lord

Readings: Gal 5:1-6; Luke 11:37-41
Resp. Psalm: Ps 119:41, 43, 44, 45, 47, 48 (*L* 468)

At times, people's disappointment with religion or even severe disillusionment, leads some to neglect religious practice or even to fall away. Often, though, the problem is not really with God but with the people, from pope to priest, or with some decision or practice of the church. Do we perhaps put too much faith in them or expect too much from them? All the practices, regulations, and the ministers of religion are to some degree necessary but always, as St. Paul says elsewhere, weak vessels for the grace they bring (see 2 Cor 4:7). They are at the service of our relation to God and are not that relation itself. St. Paul's strong emphasis on faith, faith in God, should help us to make an important distinction. He berates those he writes to for seeking their salvation in the practices of the Law; in doing so, he says, they sever themselves from Christ. "For through the Spirit, by faith, we await the hope of righteousness. For in Christ Jesus, / neither circumcision nor uncir-cumcision counts for anything, / but only faith working through love" (Gal 5:5-6). The external difficulties caused for us by those who minister in the church are not so important that they should discour-age us; our faith is not in them. They may be the contemporary equiv-alent of the practices that St. Paul says are not the true objects of our faith and confidence (see 1 Cor 1 and 3). Our faith is, must be, in Jesus Christ, in his promises and grace, not in his instruments. They are often closely related but never identical.

Wednesday of the Twenty-Eighth Week in Ordinary Time— *Living by the Spirit*

Readings: Gal 5:18-25; Luke 11:42-46
Resp. Psalm: Ps 1:1-2, 3, 4 and 6 (*L* 469)

Flesh and spirit seem so obvious to us. Flesh is the body, especially the sexual powers, and this is something which is, if not bad, at least al-ways drawing us to evil. Spirit refers to the soul, the immaterial part of the human being, and this is where all the good qualities of a person are found, what we call the really spiritual things. But such an under-standing does not match St. Paul's use of the terms or that of Scripture in general. In our text from Galatians "flesh" refers more accurately to the human being who is under the domination of worldly, merely hu-man considerations. While "Spirit" refers to the human being insofar as he or she is being led by the Holy Spirit. St. Paul's list of the fruits of the flesh makes clear that by it he means more than sexuality. Un-derstanding more clearly Scripture's use of these terms should teach more respect for the body and sexuality which are not really singled out in Scripture for censure. After all, as Genesis tells us, they were created good by God (see Gen 1:31). This understanding should also make clear to us that to be "spiritual" according to Scripture means to be open to and receptive to the influence of the Spirit. It is not some denial of or hatred of the body. "If we live in the Spirit, let us also fol-low the Spirit" (Gal 5:25).

Thursday of the Twenty-Eighth Week in Ordinary Time—
A preview of the new human being

Readings: Eph 1:1-10; Luke 11:47-54
Resp. Psalm: Ps 98:1, 2-3ab, 3cd-4, 5-6 (L 470)

God has predestined us through Christ to be his adopted sons and daughters. Ephesians speaks loftily of God's goodness and the great results for us humans who gain this new relation to God by his gift (see also Rom 8:29–30). Ephesians speaks also of how this was accomplished: it is through the blood of Christ that we have been redeemed, forgiven, and raised to this status. But for the nitty-gritty details of our redemption—the hardness, hostility, and blindness of Jesus' opponents—we must go to the Gospel. Rather than dwell on these basically negative matters or even on our moral problems and duties, Ephesians seems intent on inspiring us to a generous following of Christ by reminding us of our dignity as the "children of God" (Rom 8:16). We have been called to and blessed by God with the exalted position of being God's children. Pride in that status and gratitude to God should inspire us to live "holy and without blemish before him" (1:4) and with our fellow human beings. Christians are in a sense the vanguard of a new humanity, bound to present to the world as the picture of people caught up in a better world than that of plotting and persecution, hostility and hatred (the Gospel). In our God-centeredness and our willingness to live in peace and forgiveness the world should see a preview of God's plans and hopes for humanity.

Friday of the Twenty-Eighth Week in Ordinary Time—
God's offspring and God's friends

Readings: Eph 1:11-14; Luke 12:1-7
Resp. Psalm: Ps 33:1-2, 4-5, 12-13 (L 471)

Over the centuries people have often enough gained the impression that Christianity was repression of all good human qualities, a way of casting a shadow on our joy. The spirit of Ephesians certainly gives no support to such a view. Besides what we heard yesterday about our being God's sons and daughters, we have more in today's reading. We were chosen in Christ; we were predestined; we were endowed with the Holy Spirit. To add to the affirmative spirit, Jesus in today's Gospel calls us "friends" (Luke 12:4). This is certainly not a religion of oppression or one which belittles the human being. Ephesians is full of other words of an expansive, generous nature. It speaks of hope (see 1:12), glad tidings, the Holy Spirit given us here and now as an assurance of "our inheritance" (1:14) (a down payment on it), and it speaks twice of praising God's "glory" (1:14). We all need to center our faith, our religion more around such positive realities. Christian life is meant to be a life of joy and hope and praise because God has already, this side of heaven, shown us such good will, such love. To experience the full impact of all this, we need to feed our faith with these truths by recalling them often.

Saturday of the Twenty-Eighth Week in Ordinary Time— *Living by Ephesians*

Readings: Eph 1:15-23; Luke 12:8-12
Resp. Psalm: Ps 8:2-3ab, 4-5, 6-7 (L 472)

The early martyrs of the church exemplify in their lives the Christ-centered and joyous faith of Ephesians. The hopes for Christians expressed in that first reading describe well the eager and love-filled faith of martyrs like Ignatius, Sebastian, Agnes, and Lawrence. The Gospel too describes them: "When they take you before synagogues and before rulers and authorities, / do not worry about how or what your defense will be / or about what you are to say. / For the Holy Spirit will teach you at that moment what you should say" (Luke 12:11-12). By a life of closeness to the Lord and prayer, the martyrs knew the great hope of their calling, the gifts distributed among Christians and the power of God working in us. May our participation at the table of the Lord and our efforts to deepen our faith by reflection on God's Word bring us to share the exuberant confidence and joy of the martyrs in our so much smaller trials. What is bad weather, a case of the flu, a defeat for our sports team, a tiff with our teenager, a grouch at the office, compared to the trials of a martyr thrown to wild beasts?

Monday of the Twenty-Ninth Week in Ordinary Time— *Nourished for service by the Eucharist*

Readings: Eph 2:1-10; Luke 12:13-21
Resp. Psalm: Ps 100:1b-2, 3, 4ab, 4c-5 (L 473)

A lot of blood and ink were spilled among Christians, a few centuries ago, over the place of faith and good deeds. One group of Christians emphasized that we are saved by God's gift and that, as Ephesians says of our salvation, is "by grace you have been saved through faith, / and this is not from you; it is the gift of God; / it is not from works, so no one may boast" (Eph 2:8-9). These were the Protestants. They believed that the others, the Catholics, were saying that our good works saved us; that we could impress God so much that God had to love us. Ephesians tells us that the two go together. Without God's grace, the writer says, we would be slaves of merely earthly values. But God has brought us into new life in Christ out of unmerited love for us. So we are saved by God's gift, not because we're so wonderful. We are God's "handiwork, created in Christ Jesus for good works / that God has prepared in advance" (Eph 2:10). God's idea in giving us new life in Christ by our baptism and faith, is that this life show itself in good deeds. We're meant to act and live like the son or daughter who, often belatedly, recognizes all the good that has come from parents and determines to be worthy of that example. Some will aim more at doing what will change society or bring justice to the marketplace or daily life. Others will show gratitude by daily acts of "generosity," "kindness," "patience," etc. (Gal 5:22)—taking the initiative in doing something about others' needs. Each sharing in this Eucharist reminds us of God's love shown for us in Jesus and strengthens us to show it to our world in turn.

Tuesday of the Twenty-Ninth Week in Ordinary Time—
Living with hope

Readings: Eph 2:12-22; Luke 12:35-38
Resp. Psalm: Ps 85:9ab-10, 11-12, 13-14 (L 474)

Many a poet or thinker has argued that we humans are all alone in a hostile and unfeeling universe. They make it even darker by saying that we are just accidents in the universe's development and there is no sense to our lives. Even without the help of these pessimists we feel that way at times, especially when events in our lives render us lost, forgotten, crushed. Serious illness in the family, in ourselves, in a friend or some tragic accident or failure—any of these can make us believe that no one or nothing cares about us. The coming to earth of Jesus, his life, death, and resurrection are all for the purpose of telling us who were "without hope and without God in the world" (Eph 2:12) that God is near and always cares. The death of God's Son which we have put before us on this altar tells us that God is closest to us in sorrow and death. We "have become near by the Blood of Christ" (Eph 2:14). "Without hope and without God in the world" (2:12) describes, unfortunately, the existence of many people. So Ephesians speaks of our state before we have opened ourselves to God's grace.

To appreciate that we "are no longer strangers and sojourners" (2:19) requires, besides our basic receptivity to God's grace, a daily life of prayer and contact with God. Hope and waiting, the constant preparedness of which the Lord speaks in the Gospel, picture well the state that assures a growth of our life in Christ.

Wednesday of the Twenty-Ninth Week in Ordinary Time—
To give what we have received (see Matt 10:8)

Readings: Eph 3:2-12; Luke 12:39-48
Resp. Psalm: Isa 12:2-3, 4bcd, 5-6 (L 475)

Many think that believers today face an exceptionally large and difficult task. So many of our contemporaries, very good people, see no need for God, for Christ, for all that means so much to the writer of Ephesians. Their excitement is not about the fact that Jews and Gentiles have both been called to be sharers in God's promises. Their excitement is about a new car, a trip to the Azores, Peter's graduation from college, Sally's new job, plans for skiing in Utah. Undoubtedly, many of us may feel a bit guilty about what really thrills us too. Two tasks face us: one is how to be sure that we ourselves are sufficiently convinced about the meaning of Christ for our lives, and the other is what we can do to bring others to share our appreciation and love. And the order of these tasks is important too. Can we expect to be really active in bringing Christ to our world if Christ does not sufficiently inspire our own lives? Ephesians says that through the church all this is "made known" (3:5); we, of course, are that church. We can't just drop the job at the office of the bishop or the priest. The need to pass on our love and faith follows once they become genuine for us. The hope and encouragement that believing in Christ brings us is not a gift to be hugged to our breast but one to be shared. Our Lord, speaking of our stewardship of God's gifts, says that when much has been given to people, much will be required of them. More will be asked of those to whom more has been entrusted (Luke 12:48). Help us, Lord, to be filled with faith in what you have brought to our world and help us be willing to generously share that with those around us.

Thursday of the Twenty-Ninth Week in Ordinary Time—
Love always

Readings: Eph 3:14-21; Luke 12:49-53
Resp. Psalm: Ps 33:1-2, 4-5, 11-12, 18-19 (L 476)

It is interesting to find these words of Jesus about division in Luke's Gospel. We've undoubtedly noticed that Luke is full of the gentleness of Jesus toward the lowly and outcasts. Today's message from him seems out of character. Is it a matter of Jesus having to balance the message of peace and love with this because of the way some have taken his usual message? Do they need a reminder that love and compassion are not the same as weakness and indifference? Parents and teachers may have noticed a similar need at times. But, there's more. In the atmosphere of the life of Jesus where various groups opposed his message, today's Gospel could be literally true. Some of those who followed Jesus undoubtedly met with strong opposition from parents and family members who were following the scribes and Pharisees. In our own time we see how difficult it may be for a family when a member opts for some other religious choice. "I never want to see you here again" and "Get out" are some of the responses. Understandable as such reactions are, and painful as the defections are, we should realize that in the long run trying to show the defectors God's love is still most effective. Ephesians exhorts us: "that Christ may dwell in your hearts through faith; / . . . rooted and grounded in love" (3:17). We pray at this Eucharist for the love and calm that can only come from our faith and "[t]rust in the LORD" (Ps 37:3).

Friday of the Twenty-Ninth Week in Ordinary Time—
Our common faith in Jesus Christ

Readings: Eph 4:1-6; Luke 12:54-59
Resp. Psalm: Ps 24:1-2, 3-4ab, 5-6 (L 477)

Ephesians may be helpful in reminding us that no matter how much some look back at the "good old days" with longing, in general we are lucky they're gone: Days when people who disagreed with your religious beliefs could have you beheaded, days when any questioning of religious authorities was likely to lead to burning at the stake. And many other cruel things marked the "good old days." Unity is important as Ephesians stresses but we all have a right and the need to follow our consciences. Today's first reading speaks of "one Lord, one faith, one baptism, / one God and Father" (Eph 4:5-6), a good reminder to us that Christians of many different stripes often share most of these with us. Practically, the church recognizes this by not rebaptizing converts who were previously baptized. Maybe two practical conclusions can be drawn from the reading. First, that we share a "lot" with our fellow Christians (see Col 1:12; NAB, 1st ed.) and should emphasize that more often. When our Presbyterian neighbor is crushed by sorrow we can speak of the same faith we share in the healing power and presence of Christ. Why not stress that more than the less significant differences we may have? Secondly, with our fellow Catholics we need also to realize we have a deep-down unity despite the fact that we must at times disagree on the implementation of Christ's teaching or about the style of the Mass music. Just as married couples do better to concentrate on what originally drew them together than on minor irritations, we could profitably, with other Christians and fellow Catholics, underline how much we have in common, above all our conviction that through the Lord Jesus we will be finally victorious over sin and suffering.

Saturday of the Twenty-Ninth Week in Ordinary Time—
Thank God for difference

Readings: Eph 4:7-16; Luke 13:1-9
Resp. Psalm: Ps 122:1-2, 3-4ab, 4cd-5 (*L* 478)

Elsewhere St. Paul speaks of how different parts of the body, the eye or ear or foot, cannot wish to replace another or be another (1 Cor 12). The body's functioning depends on each of us having an assemblage of all these working parts; each is indispensable and contributes to the health of the whole. In an age when there are so many calls for appreciation of diversity, we do well to value the gifts we all bring to our life in the Body of Christ. The first reading continues the emphasis on the unity of the Body of Christ by stressing that we have differing gifts, different roles of service to perform. Someone has written that it would be a very dull and flat world if there weren't other people who had abilities we don't have, gifts that can dazzle or impress us, gifts that we can be happy about. We see this at work in one form in the way our society often idolizes a singer, an actor, an athlete, or a successful person. What our Christian belief asks of us is that we see in much more ordinary people, like our neighbors or fellow parishioners, what a variety of gifts are present. We ourselves may not be capable of the patient care someone gives a chronically sick person; we may not be able to lobby and fight local government for traffic lights, but we have some other gifts and should not begrudge others theirs. We should be thankful for them, look for signs of them, realize that we all have some gifts which can be used "for building up the Body of Christ" (Eph 4:12) "until we all attain to the unity of faith / and knowledge of the Son of God, to mature [humanness] / to the extent of the full stature of Christ" (4:13).

Monday of the Thirtieth Week in Ordinary Time—
Always right to give thanks (*see prefaces in* The Roman Missal: The Sacramentary)

Readings: Eph 4:32–5:8; Luke 13:10-17
Resp. Psalm: Ps 1:1-2, 3, 4 and 6 (L 479)

In the Gospel Jesus gives us an example of the service of others of which Ephesians speaks when he cures the stooped woman. Curing her takes precedence over legalistic views of the Sabbath. Ephesians today gets more specific about how we live up to our dignity as members of the body of Christ and how we practice love. Ephesians bases the required morality of Christians on the example of God in Christ. We are to be kind, compassionate, and forgiving as God has been toward us (see 4:32). We are to imitate God in the self-giving of Christ. Our closeness to God should make any trivial use of sexuality out of the question. Instead of the vices mentioned we are to give thanks. Let's conclude with that: thanksgiving. The service we are at is called Eucharist, thanksgiving. Much of the Pauline teaching suggests that thanksgiving would be the umbrella under which all other talk about moral behavior should come. If we live in thanksgiving, grateful for life, redemption, love, our adoption into God's family—make your own individual list of things to be thankful for—everything else should flow from that. How it would cut down on whining, complaining, self-pity, greed, aggression, small-minded self-seeking, if we could begin each day and carry it through filled with thanks.

Tuesday of the Thirtieth Week in Ordinary Time—
Working on the world where we are

Readings: Eph 5:21-33; Luke 13:18-21
Resp. Psalm: Ps 128:1-2, 3, 4-5 (L 480)

We are prevented at times from doing good by thinking that what we can do is so small, so insignificant, why bother? It will change nothing. We too readily give all the credit for accomplishment to the shakers and movers, the top dog, the big tycoon or leader. Even in our religion this is reinforced possibly by the attention or position we give to the great saints, the religious figures who stand out as so extraordinary. The largeness of their accomplishments certainly helps spotlight how we should respond to God. But the two parables Jesus puts before us today ask us to have faith that even the small things we can do to forward the kingdom of God are worth doing; they will have an impact. The lives of most of us ordinary human beings are of value even if we never make the canonization list, the front page of *People* magazine, or the evening television news. The two parables of Jesus today remind us that small beginnings can lead to large, important results. Instead of regretting that we can't help all the homeless in New York, why not do something practical, no matter how small, to better the situation where we live? Instead of regretting that we can't have the impact of some television preacher or famous writer, why not make our own environment, the home, the office, the job, a more hopeful place for others by our comments or attitude? Instead of admiring those who suffer terrible things for goodness and God, why not exhibit patience with the little irritations of our own lives? All of us together, trying to live by the example of the Lord and his grace, are a leaven which gradually transforms our world.

Wednesday of the Thirtieth Week in Ordinary Time—
Practice over theory

Readings: Eph 6:1-9; Luke 13:22-30
Resp. Psalm: Ps 145:10-11, 12-13ab, 13cd-14 (L 481)

The Buddha told a story about a man seriously injured by a poisoned arrow that was stuck in his flesh. The victim's first question is, he says, not "Where did this come from?" or "Why did this happen to me?" but something more like: "Can someone get this out?" The Buddha was saying that practical solutions to suffering and pain are more important than theoretical discussions about why something happened or who did it. Those questions can wait when someone is in danger. In Luke's Gospel Jesus is pictured as following a similar procedure. When his opponents come around with nettling and difficult questions of a theoretical nature, he tends to turn the discussion to something practical which affects the questioner more directly. The questioner today asks about how many will be saved. Jesus doesn't answer the question but urges the questioner to be sure he's in that number. We can avoid the real work of Christian life at times by multiplying difficulties in our minds and really refusing to get on with the work of living well, living in love. The Mass, while it highlights words of Jesus, is above all an action, a call to us to enter into the sacrificial love of our Lord for the world we live in and where we work.

Thursday of the Thirtieth Week in Ordinary Time—
Well-equipped for the battle

Readings: Eph 6:10-20; Luke 13:31-35
Resp. Psalm: Ps 144:1b, 2, 9-10 (L 482)

Nothing light about the words we've heard today. The author of Ephesians speaks in military terms of the battle that still faces us despite
Christ's victory. In the Gospel we hear of plots against the life of Jesus
and, in his own words, of his awareness that like the prophets he will
face lethal opposition in Jerusalem. In very serious terms the readings
stress how weighty is all we do. By the Cross and Resurrection Christ
has conquered the powers of evil (see John 16:33). They know and
we should know that they are doomed. But here and now they retain
enough strength to test us. Paul faced a battle "to make known with
boldness the mystery of the Gospel" (Eph 6:19) and prayed for "the
courage to speak as I must" (6:20). That may be a battle for all of us,
in some sense: to courageously let the world around us know that we
believe in the God of love and love's victory. There are, as we all know,
many other skirmishes we must face in daily life: to control our anger,
our tongues (see Jas 1 and 3), our desires; battles against our laziness
or indifference, against discouragement and hopelessness, and many
others. We are well armed, though, and we need to bring this to mind
again and again. Ephesians describes the armor we all have by our life
in Christ: truth, justice, zeal, faith. We are ready for the tests of daily
life, and each sharing at this altar encourages us to leave this church
conscious of new hope and courage. The strength of our faith in Christ
serves to "quench all the flaming arrows of the Evil One" (Eph 6:16).

Friday of the Thirtieth Week in Ordinary Time—
Promoting and learning

Readings: Phil 1:1-11; Luke 14:1-6
Resp. Psalm: Ps 111:1-2, 3-4, 5-6 (L 483)

The only way to hear or read Scripture for our own profit and growth
is to take the message as of some pertinence to us. Otherwise we turn
it into historical study which may have little effect on our lives. Can
we take Paul's words today as referring to us? "I give thanks to my
God . . . / praying always with joy . . . / because of your partner-
ship for the Gospel / from the first day until now" (Phil 1:3-5). If not
by formal preaching—which is a specific vocation—at least by our
hope, joy, faith, confidence, we are able to and should be promoting the

Gospel. That supposes, of course, a basic grounding in Christian faith, the product of continual practice and some regular reflection. After all, we are not going to do much promotion of something about which we have no strong feelings. On the other hand, we do not have to wait till some impossible time when we have a total and firm grasp of faith before offering others its strength and encouragement. Paul recognizes that the Philippians are still on the way. He prays that their love and understanding grow and that they learn "to discern what is of value" (1:10). Promoting the Gospel in our life and words always does go along with our own struggle to more and more deeply assimilate it ourselves. Promotion and assimilation should go together all our life.

Saturday of the Thirtieth Week in Ordinary Time—
Self-giving, not self-promotion

Readings: Phil 1:18b-26; Luke 14:1, 7-11
Resp. Psalm: Ps 42:2, 3, 5cdef (L 484)

We easily think that scandals involving religious leaders and sordid power struggles are something thought up by our century. But the opening lines in today's first reading seem to refer to some rivalry for power that was going on among the Philippians while Paul was imprisoned. In the Gospel, Jesus comments on the same phenomenon, the fight for position, among his contemporaries. He counsels the opposite. While undoubtedly not happy about his kind of self-seeking, Paul says that what counts is: "Christ is being proclaimed" (Phil 1:18). All of this highlights what is possibly the deepest problem any of us faces in living out the Christian life: trying to forget self, to eliminate selfish considerations from our actions. Religion and religious thinkers the world over have noted this. The most popular Hindu scripture urges repeatedly: Do your work, your deeds, without thought of reward; act without selfish desire. The Mass and the Scriptures we hear here are in many ways a school of selflessness. In them is put before us the self-sacrifice and self-forgetting of the Lord. More than that, in God's word and the Eucharist we are strengthened to share this most demanding virtue. For Paul "life is Christ" (1:21). For us too, genuine life comes about insofar as we become one with his self-giving.

Monday of the Thirty-First Week in Ordinary Time—
Something outrageously generous

Readings: Phil 2:1-4; Luke 14:12-14
Resp. Psalm: Ps 131:1bcde, 2, 3 (L 485)

We'd probably not write to our friends from prison and ask them to "complete [our] joy" (Phil 2:2). "What joy?" would be our question. But that's the high state in which Paul writes his flock in the northern Greek city of Philippi. Paul is concerned about reports of Christian preachers who seem to be disturbing them with a contradictory message. Paul is a pastor, justifiably worried about the consequent factions and bickering in the community. The same problems have afflicted Christian communities over the ages and still do. Despite legitimate differences we can hope for and aim to possess "the same love, / united in heart, thinking one thing" (2:2). We do best if we can rise above or even ignore the bickering and pettiness that can enter into the life of the Christian community. Rather, we might be more intent on making use of our precious days and years to practice and spread that love Paul speaks of, "united in spirit and ideals" (2:2; NAB, 1st ed.). Otherwise we'll be left wondering: where have all the hours gone? What have we been doing with our lives? The lives of Paul and many others, of course, tell us to seize the initiative now (see 2 Cor 6:2), to do outrageously generous things like what our Lord commends in the Gospel. Do something in imitation of the self-emptying of our Lord (see Phil 2:5-11) which we celebrate here, do something like going out of our way for the poor, the lame, the crippled, the blind, beggars.

Tuesday of the Thirty-First Week in Ordinary Time—
Living up to our commitment

Readings: Phil 2:5-11; Luke 14:15-24
Resp. Psalm: Ps 22:26b-27, 28-30ab, 30e, 31-32 (L 486)

We often think of it as a sad commentary on our times that people seem to take commitments so lightly. It is often hard to pin us down; if we say yes to a request or invitation, we may under our breath say something like "unless something better comes along." Self-interest often limits our willingness to commit. Yet today's Gospel shows us three examples from two thousand years ago of similar reneging on commitments. The three offering excuses for not coming to the dinner had all been invited and presumably accepted. Now one has to inspect some new real estate, another can't wait to see how his new oxen perform, and the third has discovered great urgency about his life as one newly married. None of these excuses refers to a real emergency; the only emergency is the self-interest, the self-concern of the three invitees. So often the dominant influence in our lives and behavior is that passion for dear old me and my concerns. Yesterday's reading from Philippians, in which Paul tells his flock to look to other's interests rather than their own (2:4) leads into today's words. Paul puts before us the ultimate model of that emptying of self for others, Jesus Christ the Lord. "Who, Though he was in the form of God, / did not regard equality with God / something to be grasped. / Rather, he emptied himself" (2:6–7). Turning from self-interest to the interests and needs of others is often, even always, hard for us. May the Lord in this Eucharist pour into us some of his generous willingness to give of himself.

Wednesday of the Thirty-First Week in Ordinary Time—
Living Christian life with some forethought

Readings: Phil 2:12–18; Luke 14:25–33
Resp. Psalm: Ps 27:1, 4, 13–14 (L 487)

Possibly we can cut through the somewhat confusing mix of parables and admonitions in today's Gospel. We'll try. The first speaks of a man building a tower. Before going ahead with the project he should figure out how much of the various materials he will need, how much money to finance it, and so forth. Otherwise he'll start this ambitious undertaking and end up with a half-finished building which people will inevitably point out as "Fred's Folly" or something else as uncomplimentary. In the second story it is a king about to go into battle. The reminder here is that before deciding to march on another king and his army, the first king must calculate whether he is able, with an army the size of his, to meet the other king with any chance to victory. If he miscalculates, many lives will be lost and the king will earn some title like "Windbag" or "Bluster Bob." In their setting these parables remind us who hear them that if we are serious about being followers of Christ we must not rush in like empty-headed fools but be aware of the demands and requirements of that following. The requirements are four in this talk by the Lord. First, we must turn our backs on family, that is, the Lord must be our first priority. Second, we must turn our backs on our own selves; self and self-interest cannot be the determining factors in the way we live. We must, in the third place, take up the cross after Jesus, be willing to accept our share in the suffering of his way. Finally, we must renounce our possessions: neither wealth nor things can be our security. As we meet the Lord at this altar, we can trust him to strengthen us for his way.

Thursday of the Thirty-First Week in Ordinary Time—
Sharing a meal

Readings: Phil 3:3-8a; Luke 15:1-10
Resp. Psalm: Ps 105:2-3, 4-5, 6-7 (L 488)

We are all pulled along by the rapid changes that technology imposes on our lives. Whether we want them or not, often we have no choice. Credit cards, access numbers and codes, packaged items of all sorts: often we must simply accept them. Television, frozen food, and hectic schedules (made possible by the ease with which we can get around) all work together to prevent family meals or meals with the people with whom we live. For centuries, eating together has most signified and reinforced spiritual ties and closeness. Should we allow this to disappear? Possibly this is one place where more of us should be cranky rebels against our society. In today's Gospel "the Pharisees and scribes" are shocked because by eating with "tax collectors and sinners" (Luke 15:2, 1) Jesus is saying that he and they are one. Meals play a large role in Luke's Gospel, always with the meaning of a union of those eating together. Eating with these sinners signifies the solidarity of Jesus with all human beings, not only with those who think themselves to be good people. One lesson for us from this is to recall that all of us are sinners, in some sense; we have no reason to feel so separate from those who easily appear to us to be unsavory or lost. There are or will be people in our lives or families who seem not only lost but resistant to any well-meaning overtures. Mildly and persistently we need to keep up our contact with them, maybe by a lunch or a coffee break, all the while hoping to stay close to God's action through prayer.

Friday of the Thirty-First Week in Ordinary Time—
Trivial pursuits

Readings: Phil 3:17–4:1; Luke 16:1-8
Resp. Psalm: Ps 122:1-2, 3-4ab, 4cd-5 (L 489)

We think of those whose "God is their stomach" (Phil 3:19) mentioned in today's first reading as gluttons or people intent only on their sensual satisfaction. And that makes it fairly easy to understand how Paul contrasts that attitude with a less worldly one: "our citizenship is in heaven" (3:20). But in the context, Paul is referring to some of his disciples who are still making much of the dietary laws of their Jewish upbringing. In fact, Paul thinks they are making too much of these regulations. We are saved, he stresses, by the suffering and death of the Lord on the cross. To put our trust in external practices—so many repetitions of this prayer, not eating this or that, or the wearing of some religious article—can be a form of competition with the Lord's salvation. Worldliness, in other words, comes in several forms. Obviously, putting too much importance on food, clothing, shelter, all the comforts of life, can be a too worldly emphasis. But Paul reminds us here of another type of worldliness: putting excessive trust in the performance of certain actions and the carrying out of regulations. Above all our faithfulness to some particular prayer or novena, to the rosary or so many First Fridays, to the necessity of wearing a particular medal, all this should point to and reinforce our trust in the Lord and not limit our help to the needy and sorrowing. We shift the emphasis from Christ's sacrifice not simply by being preoccupied with our comfort but also by turning our religious life into time-consuming concern about externals, how or how often something is done. Daily, at this altar, the central action of our life in Christ is celebrated.

Saturday of the Thirty-First Week in Ordinary Time—
To lighten our burden, simplify our life

Readings: Phil 4:10-19; Luke 16:9-15
Resp. Psalm: Ps 112:1b-2, 5-6, 8a and 9 (L 490)

No matter how other-worldly we think our faith is, it is unavoidably bound up with, of course, this world of matter but also with money and finances. Concern for the poor itself dictates involvement with money. And there are many other points of contact. Both readings today touch the issue in several ways. We can afford to spend some time thinking of how money, possessions, and things affect us. For most of us who live in the fairly affluent hemispheres it is vital that we learn to simplify, to reduce our dependence on so many unnecessary things, and to live with less. Today, in the first reading, Paul speaks of being able to live both "in abundance and . . . in need" (Phil 4:12). Living in either one offers challenges to the Christian. Most of us, perhaps, need to reflect on how much of our energy and time is taken up with things, many of them unnecessary and simply encumbrances. They take energy and time that could be spent on people, family, friends, the good of the world around us. "You cannot serve God and mammon" (Luke 16:13), we hear in the Gospel. The term mammon refers to property and possessions in the sense of perils to our Christian life. In other words, things, money, possessions are not simply innocent trinkets but rivals to God. In a consumerist society like ours—where shopping can become an end in itself, not just a means to getting things that are needed—this is an important issue. Shouldn't we think about the need to simplify our lives and our way of living? Possessions and our desire for the means to get them can eventually destroy our peace and fill us with self-inflicted worry. Then, truly we discover that we cannot serve both God and possessions.

Monday of the Thirty-Second Week in Ordinary Time—
Our impact

Readings: Titus 1:1-9; Luke 17:1-6
Resp. Psalm: Ps 24:1b-2, 3-4ab, 5-6 (L 491)

In a society like ours it is almost a daily occurrence to hear how some popular or influential figure has been exposed as a thief or adulterer or an abuser of children or other powerless persons. An example, whether in church or government, of genuine integrity is much to be valued. While we cannot easily do a lot about the examples that bishops, priests, presidents, senators, and tycoons give us, we can expect high standards from ourselves, knowing that we are certainly an example for someone. Parents must, somewhere along the line, see clearly how their good or bad traits are reflected in their youngest. Their little ones are watching everything from the way they act in the supermarket to the way they respond in difficult traffic. They're listening to what they say about anyone or anything. The concern in Titus about the qualities of bishops indicates that our society was not the first to produce unworthy or scandalous public figures. Jesus says: "Things that cause sin will inevitably occur, / but woe to the one through whom they occur" (Luke 17:1). Despite a lot of loose talk about how each of us has only himself or herself to consult in regard to what we do, we all do affect others. We are often very important to others' faith, hope, and their perseverance in good. That is not a burden but an honor, an opportunity to be valued for what we are. At Mass we have a few moments each day to let God's light illuminate our interior and strengthen us to ask forgiveness, to begin anew living a life that contributes to the tone and character of all human life.

Tuesday of the Thirty-Second Week in Ordinary Time—
A life of thanksgiving

Readings: Titus 2:1-8, 11-14; Luke 17:7-10
Resp. Psalm: Ps 37:3-4, 18 and 23, 27 and 29 (*L* 492)

The Letter to Titus speaks of how we have been cleansed in order that we be "eager to do what is good" (2:14). Any eagerness that we have "to do what is right" (2:8; NAB, 1st ed.) is spoiled when we make a big deal about how good we are or insist on calling attention to our good works (see Matt 6:5-8). Both readings today suggest some deflating of our tendency to become too self-important, too aware of what a service we are doing for God and others. The first reading seems to say that once we have been blessed with the grace of God, accepted Christ's sacrifice for us and the cleansing it brings, we should spontaneously, out of gratitude, be "eager to do what is good" (2:14). In the Gospel our Lord says something similar when he tells us that we should be less concerned about commendation and praise than about doing what life and our relationships demand of us. "When you have done all you have been commanded, say, / 'We are unprofitable servants; / we have done what we were obliged to do'" (Luke 17:10). What makes possible such lack of concern for recognition and reward is a strong sense that life and all we have is a gift (see Eph 2:8), that our waking thought and governing attitude should be praise, thanksgiving. The time we spend here in the church, around this altar, is termed Eucharist from the Greek word for thanksgiving. If we're not convinced of the power and dynamism of thanksgiving, why not make an effort to live one day, this day, in thanksgiving, an effort to turn all our feelings and thoughts to thanks? Instead of complaining or feeling sorry for ourselves or wanting more of everything, why not try to live and feel and think and act out of thanksgiving? The proof is in the doing.

Wednesday of the Thirty-Second Week in Ordinary Time—
Thankful for so many gifts

Readings: Titus 3:1-7; Luke 17:11-19
Resp. Psalm: Ps 23:1b-3a, 3bc-4, 5, 6 (*L* 493)

Yesterday it was suggested that we only learn the power and effects of a life lived in constant thanksgiving by at least giving it a try. Take one day and try to turn every thought and feeling into thankfulness. We have nothing to lose by it and we and all around us stand to gain a lot. The first reading today again reminds us that "the kindness and generous love / of God our savior" (Titus 3:4) has not only, of course, created us but saved us from the evil of our world. And the Gospel story tells us about the ten lepers cured by Jesus and of the one, a despised Samaritan, who was the only one to return and give thanks. Even when the benefits to us or the good done for us is extremely obvious, we have a tendency at times to take that all for granted. We seem to think: why should not the whole world want to do good things for me? Turning around our expectation that it is only appropriate that we receive all kinds of good things is not easy. Trying thankfulness all through one day would be a beginning and would show us how hard it is for us. Maybe we should try it for another day, with the help of Jesus, our model and pioneer in thankfulness. It may also help if we attempt more frequent inventories of all the good that has come to us, all the good that is given to us day after day, moment by moment. Think of all the people who have given us time, energy, surprising and generous care and concern, who have made our life happy, even comfortable, who go beyond the call of duty to thank and praise us. Each of us can make his or her own customized list of reasons to be thankful.

Thursday of the Thirty-Second Week in Ordinary Time—
Paul's manner of persuasion

Readings: Phlm 7-20; Luke 17:20-25
Resp. Psalm: Ps 146:7, 8-9a, 9bc-10 (L 494)

Today's selection from Philemon is the only one in our daily readings from this very short letter of Paul to one of his converts, Philemon, about another, Onesimus. The big difference is that Onesimus was a slave who ran away from his master, Philemon. It is very hard for us to set aside our concern about the very idea of slavery but the fact is that concern about the issue of slavery had not yet arisen. Good people like Paul saw slavery as one of the realities of daily life but did not as yet see its incompatibility with Christian morality. Paul is concerned, in sending Onesimus back to Philemon, that the latter treat him as the fellow Christian he now is and not inflict punishment on him for having run away. Paul addresses the letter to the whole community where Philemon lives, probably to put additional pressure on Philemon. While Paul says he has the right to command Philemon (v. 8), he prefers to lead Philemon into seeing the rightness of what he asks, that he welcome Onesimus "no longer as a slave but more than a slave, a brother / . . . / as a man and in the Lord" (v. 16). Paul's manner here

211

tells us all something about how we should, when that's appropriate, urge others to the good without trying to force them or throw around our own weight. Concern about getting things done and not wasting time will tempt us at times to a more dictatorial manner. In the long run it will often lose not only time but trust and respect. Jesus did not assert his position as Son of God but took on our form in order to draw us to God (see Phil 2).

Friday of the Thirty-Second Week in Ordinary Time— *Time out*

Readings: 2 John 4-9; Luke 17:26-37
Resp. Psalm: Ps 119:1, 2, 10, 11, 17, 18 (*L* 495)

Throughout the Gospel today we hear references to what absorbs most of our time: eating and drinking, sleeping, planting, taking husbands and wives, building, buying and selling. They not only absorb our time, they easily absorb our interest and energy and dominate every moment. The tone of Jesus' words today says that we are in danger of being too bound to all these activities and pursuits. It seems obvious and tragic to us well-off Westerners that the wretchedly poor we see on our television screens or read about must spend every available moment scratching out an existence. We are hardly in a position to fault them for their earthly absorption. But what about us who have so much and still push ourselves so that we are more and more absorbed in these this-worldly activities? Jesus' teaching tells us to take all this with a little less grim seriousness and leave some space in our lives for attention to the end of all this and to the world to come. The end, whether of our world or our lives, will come in the midst of the ordinary pursuits of daily life. They are not wrong or bad in themselves; it's only that we need to keep them in perspective, not allow ourselves to be totally absorbed in them. There should be time in our lives for each other, for God, for prayer and reflection, for worship, for silence and quiet, even for so-called "useless things" like poetry and music. Possibly those of us who do take time for these things have an obligation to insert some witness to this into our public lives.

Saturday of the Thirty-Second Week in Ordinary Time— *Persistence*

Readings: 3 John 5-8; Luke 18:1-8
Resp. Psalm: Ps 112:1-2, 3-4, 5-6 (*L* 496)

212

The star of today's Gospel is a woman. Stories abound in our time of women who have persisted in fighting and working for the freedom or whereabouts of their husbands and children who have been unjustly imprisoned, whisked away, or crushed by totalitarian governments. Many married men attest to the support that their steady and persistent wives give to them and the whole family. The woman in today's Gospel story is persistent and vigorous in a way that has marked many extraordinary women throughout history. Additionally, today's story may be one of the few examples that we can detect, from our perspective, of humor in the Gospels. We can easily picture the widow swinging a handbag or brandishing an umbrella at the unjust and indifferent judge and him cowering and, finally, surrendering. The point for us, Luke tells us explicitly, is "the necessity . . . to pray always without becoming weary" (18:1). Persistent prayer proves the faith and trust we have in the God we pray to. To continue in prayer in a society which requires that everything be instant is possible only through the strength that comes from the offering of Jesus himself. Joined to him in persistence we can hope to give an affirmative answer to the question at the end of the Gospel: "when the Son of Man comes, will he find faith on earth?" (18:8).

Monday of the Thirty-Third Week in Ordinary Time—
Knowing our blindness

Readings: Rev 1:1-4; 2:1-5; Luke 18:35-43
Resp. Psalm: Ps 1:1-2, 3, 4 and 6 (L 497)

The episode about the blind man reads like a miniature picture of the Christian life, at least in its beginnings. The man knows he is blind and would like to see: "let me see" (Luke 18:41). The beginning of the Christian life in anyone of us requires this recognition that the life and world we face is—to put it mildly—confusing, hard to figure out. We need vision and a vision. The man's trust, a basic ingredient of faith, opens him to the power of Jesus. "Have sight; your faith has saved you" (18:42). Trust opens us to Jesus, to his power and vision. That, in turn, improves our vision, our ability to make sense of this world and life. We make that vision our own, we benefit from our faith in the Lord, to the extent that we aim to follow him: "He immediately received his sight / and followed him" (18:43). The logic of this scene underlines the fact that the power of what Jesus has to say only becomes clear to the extent that we try to practice it, to follow him. It is not a matter of endless study—though there's nothing wrong with some study—but more of daily following. The blind man, Luke tells us, got his sight, began to follow Jesus, and gave God the glory (see 18:43). Most of us have some familiarity with the fervor of first beginnings, "the heights" of which the first reading speaks. That reading also repeats the old, old lesson that the essence of our following is love. The Lord's complaint there is that "you have lost the love you had at first" (Rev 2:4). Our loving following of Jesus is strengthened as we join at this altar in his sacrifice.

Tuesday of the Thirty-Third Week in Ordinary Time—
Hospitality to the Lord

Readings: Rev 3:1-6, 14–22; Luke 19:1-10
Resp. Psalm: Ps 15:2-3a, 3bc-4ab, 5 (*L* 498)

Hospitality to the Lord can bind together our two readings today. "Listen! I am standing at the door, knocking; if you hear my voice and open the door, I will come in to you and eat with you, and you with me" (Rev 3:20; NRSV). As if to concretely illustrate the point we see the wealthy tax collector, Zacchaeus, welcoming Jesus "with joy" (Luke 19:6). The richly symbolic pictures from the Book of Revelation tell us that the Lord is always standing at the door, knocking, calling. "Jesus is calling" goes the old evangelical hymn ("Softly and Tenderly" by Will L. Thompson, 1880). Our part is to hear and to open up, to be sufficiently free of absorption in our own interests to hear and then to allow entry into our hearts and lives. Once we allow him entry we will eat together, a powerful sign especially in Jesus' culture of friendship, good will, even intimacy. The effectiveness of our sharing at this altar, in the Lord's Supper, depends on the depth of our hospitality. Zacchaeus exemplifies what being open to the Lord means: he is willing to turn around his life, the shady one of a tax collector, make restitution, and give to the poor. We who sit down, possibly daily, at the table of the Lord need to be reminded of how important is our hospitality, our recognition that we need this nourishment and our willingness to be changed. Lord, we hear you calling, we hear your words in the readings; let them prepare our hearts and minds so that we may be transformed by sharing your food at this Eucharist.

Wednesday of the Thirty-Third Week in Ordinary Time—
Adoration and praise

Readings: Rev 4:1-11; Luke 19:11-28
Resp. Psalm: Ps 150:1b-2, 3-4, 5-6 (*L* 499)

With two lengthy readings and one of them, the Gospel, containing a number of problems for the modern reader, one can only speak to one or the other theme. The praise and adoration of God which fill the first reading can afford to be stressed in our world and time when our tendency is to put, at least theoretically, all the emphasis on serving God through other human beings. There is a place for and a great value in the adoration and worship of God. Science has long since removed the earth from any central position in our universe but in so many ways our thinking is still centered not only on this earth but on ourselves. Turning to God in worship and thanksgiving is a way of expanding our souls and horizons, at least for a while. We think of and praise the One from whom all this amazing and inexhaustible visible universe comes. Adoration and worship are just the appropriate response to such a creation which is in many ways one huge gift to us human creatures. We can enjoy it, try to understand it and, as is all too obvious, use it even unwisely. Taking the spotlight off ourselves occasionally, even daily, is not a bad idea. It is in fact a liberating and expansive one. "Worthy are you, Lord our God, / to receive glory and honor and power, / for you created all things; / because of your will they came to be and were created" (Rev 4:11).

Thursday of the Thirty-Third Week in Ordinary Time—
To remember the Resurrection

Readings: Rev 5:1-10; Luke 19:41-44
Resp. Psalm: Ps 149:1b-2, 3-4, 5-6a and 9b (*L* 500)

One sees in today's vision from Revelation just one of many examples of the extraordinary visions which fill this book. They led one preacher to speak of the book as a "technicolor account of a nightmare." The praise we heard yesterday in this same book is today made more specific and centered on the Redeemer, on Christ who has won the victory over sin and death. He is pictured alternately and even simultaneously as a lion and a lamb. The standing "Lamb" (Rev 5:6) is the risen Christ while he also appears as one who had been slain. The mystery by which we are saved is the death and resurrection of the Lord. Death and resurrection, suffering and victory, are both intrinsic to who Christ is. And after Christ the two are always partners in human life. At times the suffering and death aspect of human life can be so oppressively real that it is hard even to remember the Resurrection, let alone hope for that phase. With Christ, many of his followers, many of our fellow human beings, must go through a feeling of abandonment such as is on the lips of Jesus in the Gospel: "My God, my God, why have you forsaken me?" (Mark 15:34; Matt 27:46; see Ps 22:2). Aching, crushing suffering does not easily yield to thoughts of Resurrection. Pain and near despair must at times be allowed space. When we cannot see the Resurrection or a better state for ourselves or others, we still need to, out of some rock-bottom trust, pray that God will raise us up from our desolation. That, after all, is one of the great lessons of the passion of the Lord, that God has shared our suffering—and overcome it.

Friday of the Thirty-Third Week in Ordinary Time—
Rescue from inertia

Readings: Rev 10:8-11; Luke 19:45-48
Resp. Psalm: Ps 119:14, 24, 72, 103, 111, 131 (L 501)

The episode about the little scroll in today's reading from Revelation describes in symbol the prophet's vocation and, of course, that of Jesus. To be singled out by God to deliver the divine message may be an honor, even "sweet" to taste (Rev 10:9). But the message itself is often demanding and unwelcome to the hearers, making the "stomach sour" (10:9). Even the Son of God in his human nature must have found the prophet's task frightening at times. The agony in the garden, among other things, shows us that Jesus could fear and tremble before the implications of his vocation (Luke 22:39-44). Luke's picture of Jesus cleansing the Temple is without the details found in the other Gospels and shows less of the confrontation it involved. But the fact that the leaders of the people found him so threatening that they "were seeking to put him to death" (19:47) shows us the real impact of his teachings and actions. But there was a roadblock to their intentions: "they could find no way to accomplish their purpose / because all the people were hanging on his words" (19:48). Like the chief priests and scribes, our resistance to anything new, including the teaching of our Lord, is often related to our perception that this threatens our status or the comfort of our present state. Inertia is a law of the spiritual life as of the physical. Genuine prayer, being open to what God may suggest to us in silence can allow the words and actions of Jesus to really make a difference in our lives. Here at Mass we need to be present with an open, willing spirit.

Saturday of the Thirty-Third Week in Ordinary Time—
Salvation for all the suffering

Readings: Rev 11:4-12; Luke 20:27-40
Resp. Psalm: Ps 144:1, 2, 9–10 (*L* 502)

The two mysterious witnesses or prophets in the first reading are vindicated and raised to heaven. Resurrection, which is such an irreplaceable element in Christian belief, was not accepted by the Jewish group called Sadducees though it was accepted by the Pharisees and other Jews of Christ's time. In our day too many think that the Resurrection sounds so much like a fairy tale that they share the Sadducees' concentration on this life and regard the Resurrection as wishful thinking. Others seem to think it detracts from the energy and dedication we should give to this present life. But no matter how much we try to live well in the present, the sad fact remains that many elements of this present life are not simply unsatisfactory but downright horrible for many people. Are we to preach to them some nobility in living this present, we who often have a pretty safe and comfortable present? There are many in our world and around us who do not and will not have satisfying or what we would call full lives. The triumph of Christ over the horror of the crucifixion assures us that fulfillment and happiness are not just for healthy—and, probably, wealthy—suburbanites but for the starving, persecuted, mentally and physically challenged, the long-suffering victims of disease, and many others. We trust in the Lord not only for our own Resurrection but for all these suffering people.

Monday of the Thirty-Fourth Week in Ordinary Time—
Virtue is a gift

Readings: Rev 14:1-3, 4b-5; Luke 21:1-4
Resp. Psalm: Ps 24:1bc-2, 3-4ab, 5-6 (*L* 503)

The Lamb standing on the mount and receiving the adoration of the redeemed is the Christ we celebrate at the end of the church year as king. His followers, the hundred and forty-four thousand, seem almost too good to be true in the picture we get today. They don't sound like you or me, do they? They are described as "unblemished," and "[o]n their lips no deceit has been found" (Rev 14:5). In fact, the destitute widow in the Gospel sounds way out of reach for us in her virtue. She "offered her whole livelihood" (Luke 21:4). We usually make sure that our contributions don't leave us shortchanged or lacking. But the point is that any kind of virtue of the quality mentioned here has to be God's gift

to us (see Eph 2:8), a result of our receiving the salvation, the help offered us by the Savior. The qualities described in Revelation are not proclaimed to make us despair or become scrupulous. We don't, we can't,
just grit our teeth and come up with flawless lives, absolute purity, total generosity. They are God's gift available only to those recognizing
their need and willing to receive help. These awesome pictures of total
virtue should not so much arouse worry and concern in us as trust
and confidence in the Lord from whom alone can come such holiness.
The Lord is present here to forgive, renew, and strengthen.

Tuesday of the Thirty-Fourth Week in Ordinary Time— *Urgency*

Readings: Rev 14:14-19; Luke 21:5-11
Resp. Psalm: Ps 96:10, 11-12, 13 (*L* 504)

How appropriate the words of Jesus in Luke for any time! We have
seen in our own time at least one religious leader claiming he is the new
messiah. One could fill a good-sized room with paperbacks announcing that the Persian Gulf War or some Israeli-Arab conflict was to be
the final battle. As we neared the year 2000 even more such books ap-
peared, announcing that December 31, 1999, was the end or January
1, 2000, or something similar. "The time is at hand" (Luke 21:8; NAB,
1st ed.) they do and will tell us. Our time too certainly hasn't lacked
for wars and insurrections, earthquakes, plagues, and famines. Both
phony prophets and world-wide disasters are never lacking. The words
of Jesus in Luke are always true, always being fulfilled. The message is
reinforced by the brilliant images in the first reading. One called "a son
of man" (Rev 14:14) will cut down the harvest. "The growing season
is over" is an angel's message. Urgency about our own growth plus
vigilance and readiness are always appropriate. These reminders could
force us to think fruitfully about how we use our time and energy,
about what stupid and useless ways we waste them both at times.
This doesn't mean we should take no time for recreation, for friends
and fun, but it does mean we should take a look at the quality of all
that. Why expend our so short and precious moments on activities
and entertainment, for example, which debase humanity or cheapen
human existence and persons? The urgency in the air of these readings
means that all time can be "quality time."

Wednesday of the Thirty-Fourth Week in Ordinary Time—
The witness of our speech

Readings: Rev 15:1-4; Luke 21:12-19
Resp. Psalm: Ps 98:1, 2-3ab, 7-8, 9 (*L* 505)

"[B]ecause of my name," the Lord says, the disciples will be "giving testimony" (Luke 21:12-13). Testimony, of course, comes when something has happened, when witnesses can confirm the truth of an occurrence, character, or belief. Some Christian churches set aside a particular time or service for members to give witness to and for each other. People are asked to stand up and encourage others by telling how God has been at work in their lives, what God has done for them (see Luke 8:39). The hymn sung by God's worshipers in the reading from Revelation expresses the hope that the world will come to worship God because of God's "righteous acts" or "mighty deeds" (15:4; *Lectionary* and NAB, 1st ed.). Our belief that God has spoken in the words and life of Jesus prompts us to share the comfort and strength that come from knowing we are all the objects of God's love. Many of our fellow human beings, often for very understandable reasons, feel they are alone in a hostile world. Buttonholing them or pushing pamphlets on them may not be the best way to give witness, but the tone and spirit of our lives, the confidence and joy with which we live them, could tell others that we know something of significance, something encouraging. We can counter the spirit of a world where conversation is peppered with four-letter words. By our language, manner, and reverence for life, we convey the value of every human we meet, many of whom indicate the emptiness and worthlessness they feel in life by their language and manner. At this altar we celebrate how graphically God has shown the deep value of human life. God's Son died and rose to save it from all destructive forces.

Thursday of the Thirty-Fourth Week in Ordinary Time—
"[R]aise your heads" (Luke 21:28)

Readings: Rev 18:1-2, 21-23; 19:1-3, 9a; Luke 21:20-28
Resp. Psalm: Ps 100:1b-2, 3, 4, 5 (*L* 506)

We have come to expect the strong, even frightening words of Scripture during these closing days of the church year. We hear in the first reading in colorful, concrete language the promise that God will ultimately be triumphant over the competing powers, the corrupt and oppressive forces of this world. Here they are symbolized in Babylon, itself a symbol for the Roman Empire, which so often oppressed the early Christians. But whatever the name, our world is full of strong powers hostile, at least in spirit, to the teachings of the Savior, of one who showed power by dying on a cross. The opposing force considers money and power to be its salvation, not a suffering messiah. The Gospel echoes the first reading in its seriousness about the end of things. But wonderfully—and so typical of Luke—the most encouraging and positive words come concerning how we should respond: "when these signs begin to happen, / stand erect and raise your heads, / because your redemption is at hand" (21:28). Unlike fear-mongering preachers of the past and of our time, the words of Jesus in Luke urge us to see in " the Son of Man / coming in a cloud with power and great glory" (21:27) the definitive sign of our redemption, the arrival of true, lasting happiness and union with God. The message of Jesus must always fill those who live in trust in him with confidence and joy. Christians have no right to live in fear and worry because of their faith. Other things may certainly drive us in that direction but not our faith. "[S]tand erect and raise your heads, / because your redemption is at hand" (21:28).

Friday of the Thirty-Fourth Week in Ordinary Time—
The new world

Readings: Rev 20:1-4, 11–21:2; Luke 21:29-33
Resp. Psalm: Ps 84:3, 4, 5-6a and 8a (*L* 507)

The fantastic and hard to decipher descriptions in Revelation should at least make us think about the end of things. Our world or universe, according to science is, over a very long time, running down; the amount of usable energy is becoming less and less as the ages roll by. We don't have to picture the new Jerusalem, the site of God's final triumph over evil, pain, and sorrow as some place near Mars or west of Oregon. But what is necessary is our belief and trust that God will achieve the divine goal for the universe and us. We rightly avoid any truck with those who try to situate the period of a thousand years somewhere specific in our history. The symbolism of Revelation is concerned with demonstrating that God will triumph; we are to trust and be faithful. Everything good in our universe, from the first pages of Genesis till now, is God's gift and despite human resistance and the power of evil, the gracious and giving character of God will win out. Our times and our culture are so centered on this world that thought about the final state of things comes to us only with difficulty. Here and now, today, this morning or afternoon, this vision of God's re-placement for the corrupt and harsh kingdom of this world should reinvigorate our hope in the face of present sorrows and difficulties. These will pass, Revelation tells us. The bitterness and weariness that family difficulties, ill health, and tragedy can cause will not be allowed to endure, says our God. In our communion at this altar we have now the promise and pledge of the triumph of God and the power to assist it ourselves.

Saturday of the Thirty-Fourth Week in Ordinary Time—
With heads lifted up we stand hopeful and attentive

Readings: Rev 22:1-7; Luke 21:34-36
Resp. Psalm: Ps 95:1-2, 3-5, 6-7ab (L 508)

Hearing these reminders about the "the Son of Man coming" (Luke 21:27) and the end of time tends to make us nervous and fearful. When we are healthy and successful, in the prime of life, enjoying life's little pleasures, we don't welcome the prospect of leaving this world, nor do we welcome any big change in our circumstances. Luke, in his presentation on the coming of the Son of Man, tries to make us see it more positively. But Luke faces an uphill battle with many of us, it seems. Earlier in this discourse we heard Luke encourage us to lift up our heads and eagerly await the coming of the Son of Man (see 21:20-28). There's more of the same in today's reading. Here the Lord tells us, "Be vigilant" (21:36), be awake. That itself is an encouragement to living fully. To be awake means to be eager, alert, attentive, even expect-ant of good things and of opportunities. Too often we take vigilance or attentiveness to mean that we should be on the lookout for some dire happening or some catastrophe. Luke, on the contrary, encourages us, as baptized members of Christ, as people who believe and trust in the Lord, to be confident and hopeful. We have received so many gifts from God and so many signs of God's love, why should we expect that God is going to cut that off now? We are invited to prayer, vigilance, and strength "to stand before the Son of Man" (21:36) when he comes.